WOMEN WORKERS IN THE SOVIET INTERWAR
ECONOMY

STUDIES IN RUSSIAN AND EAST EUROPEAN HISTORY AND SOCIETY

General Editors: R. W. Davies, Emeritus Professor of Soviet Economic Studies, and E. A. Rees, Senior Lecturer in Soviet History, both at the Centre for Russian and East European Studies, University of Birmingham

Recent titles include:

Arup Banerji
MERCHANTS AND MARKETS IN REVOLUTIONARY RUSSIA, 1917–30

Vincent Barnett
KONDRATIEV AND THE DYNAMICS OF ECONOMIC DEVELOPMENT

R. W. Davies
SOVIET HISTORY IN THE YELTSIN ERA

John Dunstan
SOVIET SCHOOLING IN THE SECOND WORLD WAR

Stephen Fortescue
POLICY-MAKING FOR RUSSIAN INDUSTRY

James Hughes
STALINISM IN A RUSSIAN PROVINCE

Peter Kirkow
RUSSIA'S PROVINCES

Taras Kuzio
UKRAINE UNDER KUCHMA

E. A. Rees (*editor*)
DECISION-MAKING IN THE STALINIST COMMAND ECONOMY

Vera Tolz
RUSSIAN ACADEMICIANS AND THE REVOLUTION

Matthew Wyman
PUBLIC OPINION IN POSTCOMMUNIST RUSSIA

Studies in Russian and East European History and Society
Series Standing Order ISBN 0–333–71239–0
(*outside North America only*)

You can receive future titles in this series as they are published by placing a standing order. Please contact your bookseller or, in case of difficulty, write to us at the address below with your name and address, the title of the series and the ISBN quoted above.

Customer Services Department, Macmillan Distribution Ltd
Houndmills, Basingstoke, Hampshire RG21 6XS, England

Women Workers in the Soviet Interwar Economy

From 'Protection' to 'Equality'

Melanie Ilič
Senior Lecturer in History and Women's Studies
Cheltenham and Gloucester College of Higher Education
Gloucestershire, and
Research Fellow
CREES, University of Birmingham

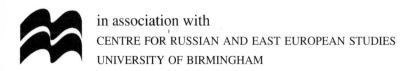

in association with
CENTRE FOR RUSSIAN AND EAST EUROPEAN STUDIES
UNIVERSITY OF BIRMINGHAM

First published in Great Britain 1999 by
MACMILLAN PRESS LTD
Houndmills, Basingstoke, Hampshire RG21 6XS and London
Companies and representatives throughout the world

A catalogue record for this book is available from the British Library.

ISBN 0–333–67419–7

331.40947
I28w

First published in the United States of America 1999 by
ST. MARTIN'S PRESS, INC.,
Scholarly and Reference Division,
175 Fifth Avenue, New York, N.Y. 10010

ISBN 0–312–21780–3

WD Library of Congress Cataloging-in-Publication Data
Ilič, Melanie, 1962–
Women workers in the Soviet interwar economy : from 'protection'
to 'equality' / Melanie Ilič.
p.   cm. — (Studies in Russian and East European history and
society)
Includes bibliographical references (p.   ) and index.
ISBN 0–312–21780–3 (alk. paper)
1. Women—Employment—Soviet Union—History.   2. Soviet Union–
–Economic conditions—1917–1945.   I. University of Birmingham.
Centre for Russian and East European Studies.   II. Series.
HD6166.I44   1998
331.4'0947—dc21   98–19155
                                                           CIP

This book is printed on paper suitable for recycling and made from fully managed and
sustained forest sources.

10   9   8   7   6   5   4   3   2   1
08   07   06   05   04   03   02   01   00   99

Printed and bound in Great Britain by
Antony Rowe Ltd, Chippenham, Wiltshire

Contents

List of Tables

Acknowledgements

This book is the result largely of research conducted at archives and libraries in Moscow. I would like to thank the many archivists and librarians who have assisted in my research. I would also like to thank the librarians at the Baykov Library (Centre for Russian and East European Studies, University of Birmingham), London School of Economics and Political Science and the British Library (London), Library of Congress (Washington, DC), Russian and Law Libraries (University of Illinois) and the Slavic Library (Helsinki).

This book has grown out of my doctoral thesis, supervised by Professor Bob Davies and Dr Arfon Rees (CREES). My warmest thanks to them both for their helpful comments, invaluable recommendations and judicious editing of this final script, through which we all managed to retain a sense of proportion and humour. Many others have contributed in a variety of ways, particularly the discussants and participants at the seminars and conferences where preliminary research findings and earlier drafts of chapters were presented for debate. Chapters 7 and 10 have developed from papers contributed to *Europe-Asia Studies* and I am grateful to the journal for the opportunity to reproduce the research here in its final form.

I am grateful for financial assistance especially to the Research Committee of the Faculty of Arts and Education, Cheltenham and Gloucester College of Higher Education, which has sponsored a number of research trips to Russia and the United States. I am grateful also to colleagues in the fields of history and women's studies, as well as other colleagues and friends in Cheltenham, who have supported my research, commented on drafts and provided much-appreciated hospitality. My family, friends in Birmingham and my travel companions to Russia have been equally supportive.

Needless to say, any outstanding errors and shortcomings in the book remain my own responsibility.

MI

Glossary of Russian Terms and Abbreviations

artel'	workers' cooperative
CPSU	Communist Party of the Soviet Union
FZU	Fabrichno-zavodskoe uchilishchie Factory training school
ITR	inzhenerno-tekhnicheskie rabotniki engineering and technical personnel
kustar'	artisan
KZoT	Kodeks Zakonov o Trude Code of Laws concerning Labour
makhorka	cheap tobacco
Narkompit	Narodnyi komissariat pocht i telegraf People's Commissariat of Post and Telegraph
Narkomsnab	Narodnyi komissariat snabzheniya People's Commissariat of Supply
Narkomsobes	Narodnyi komissariat sotsial'nogo obespecheniya People's Commissariat of Social Security
Narkomtrud	Narodnyi komissariat truda People's Commissariat of Labour (1917–33)
Narkomzdrav	Narodnyi komissariat zdravookhraneniya People's Commissariat of Health
NEP	New Economic Policy
NKVD	Narodnyi komissariat vnutrennikh del People's Commissariat of Internal Affairs
RKK	Rastsenochno-konfliktnaya komissiya Wage Rates and Conflicts Commission
RSDLP	Russian Social Democratic Labour Party
RSFSR	Rossiiskaya Sovetskaya Federativnaya Sotsialisticheskaya Respulika Russian Soviet Federative Socialist Republic

Sovnarkom	Sovet Narodnykh Komissarov Council of People's Commissars
SSSR	Soyuz Sovetskikh Sotsialisticheskikh Respublik Union of Soviet Socialist Republics
stradnaya pora	harvest time
TsIK	Tsental'nyi Ispolnitel'nyi Komitet Central Executive Committee
TsSU	Tsentral'noe statisticheskoe upravlenie Central Statistical Administration
TsUSStrakh	Tsentral'noe upravlenie sotsial'nogo strakhovaniya Central Administration of Social Insurance
VSNKh	Vysshii Sovet Narodnogo Khozyaistva Supreme Council of National Economy
VTsIK	Vserossiiskii Tsentral'nyi Ispolnitel'nyi Komitet All-Russian Central Executive Committee
VTsSPS	Vsesoyuznoi Tsentral'nyi Sovet Professional'nykh Soyuzov All-Union Central Council of Trade Unions
Zhenotdel	Zhenskii otdel Women's Department (of the CPSU)

1 Introduction

Zakon dlya togo i pishetsya, chtoby ego ne vypolnyat'.
The law is indeed written in order not to fulfil it.

THE INTERNATIONAL CONTEXT

The achievement of women's rights to vote at the beginning of the twentieth century, including in Russia in 1917, by no means marked the end of the women's movement or feminist political campaigns in Europe and the USA. The continuing debates surrounding the existence and extension of protective labour legislation for women proved no less divisive to the women's and feminist movements in the 1920s and 1930s than had the use of violent tactics in the suffrage campaigns and women's differing attitudes to the outbreak of war in 1914.[1]

Those concerned with the existing conditions of women's industrial employment were anxious to advance the labour, social and welfare reforms which had already secured some improvement in factory conditions and benefits for female employees. Such progressive reformers were often closely identified with left-wing politics and were greatly influenced by socialist thinking. In contrast, women's opposition to the further extension, and indeed the very existence, of protective labour laws for female labour was identified with the bourgeois feminist movement. From this perspective, women argued that the system of protective labour legislation operated in such a way as to restrict women's opportunities to gain employment.[2]

The historic roots of protective labour legislation for women lay in the humanitarian, paternalistic and social reform traditions of the nineteenth century. Many countries in western Europe and the United States adopted a range of laws which regulated the conditions of women's employment.[3] In general, the most important protective labour laws covered such issues as the hours of women's employment, the identification of jobs in which the employment of female labour was to be

1

prohibited, the introduction of maternity benefits and family allowance schemes and, to some extent also, consideration of minimum wage regulations. Occasionally, regulations were also introduced which established maximum weights of loads to be carried by women and obliged employers to provide specific sanitary and health facilities for their female labour force. In contrast to improvements in the conditions of work for the majority of men, which had mostly been secured via organised trade union activity and direct negotiation with employers, the laws regulating the employment of women were more often the result of government initiatives. For much of this period women were excluded from, or remained marginal to, the male-dominated trade union movement.

Support for progressive labour protection laws was an important cornerstone of nineteenth-century socialism.[4] For most socialists, the operation of a system of protective labour legislation acted as a vital restriction on the ability of capitalist industrialists to exploit the working class. In contrast to the more essentialist assumptions of Marx and Engels, August Bebel's *Woman and Socialism* (1879) was significant for its recognition of sexual divisions in capitalist societies as social rather than natural constructs. Bebel depicted a socialist future without inequalities between the sexes. He was a keen advocate of the introduction of legislative measures to protect the employment of working-class women.[5]

The theoretical writings of the nineteenth-century socialists revealed an important Catch-22 for women. Involvement in the processes of social production via paid employment was identified as progressive and an important element in women's liberation. Yet, at the same time, the employment of women for wages left them particularly vulnerable to exploitation under capitalism. This situation, the socialists argued, required specific legislative regulation. In the light of the historical evidence concerning the realities of industrial employment, factory environments and the high levels of mortality and ill-health arising from inadequate industrial safety regulations, the importance of the claims of socialists for improvements in day-to-day working conditions for all workers, and especially for women, would be difficult to deny.

The underlying principle of nineteenth- and early twentieth-century protective labour legislation was that women's different biological and physiological constitution, along with their specific social role in connection with their reproductive functions, required special treatment in the law. Not only could protective laws bring about improvements in women's working conditions, they could also help to alleviate women's double burden, which consisted of a combination of paid employment and unpaid domestic labour. Whilst the bourgeois feminists can be criticised for ignoring the realities of everyday life for the majority of working-class women, there appear to have been no suggestions in any of the contemporary debates on women's double burden that there should be a review of traditional sexual divisions of domestic labour so that men would take on more responsibility for household tasks.

The advocates of protective labour legislation were openly critical of the class bias of those women who objected to an extension of the factory regulations. Beatrice Webb, a Fabian socialist, wrote on this issue at the end of the nineteenth century. For Webb, middle-class women's opposition to the extension of protective labour legislation revealed their ignorance of the realities of the conditions of employment for working-class women and their scepticism about the benefits of factory regulation, not only for women but for all workers. She had seen little evidence of feminist support for protective labour laws which were not based on sex. Webb asserted that whereas equal rights campaigners perceived women's subordination in terms of inequalities between the sexes, and, therefore, that the removal of legal obstructions would allow middle-class women entry into the professions, for working-class women subordination did not result so much from their competition with male colleagues as from the subordination of the entire labour force to capitalist industrialists. Webb noted that 'unfortunately, working women have less power to obtain legislation than middle-class women have to obstruct it'.[6]

The factory system, Webb argued, offered great potential for the extension of female employment. However, she saw little evidence of women and men competing directly against each other for jobs in industry. She believed that sex segregation in the workplace had developed in parallel with the growth of the factory system. Women's subordinate position in the workforce, she argued, resulted from their lack of industrial training and technical skills, their own 'amateur-ism', rather than from competition with men or prejudices on the part of the employers arising from the constraints of the protective labour laws which regulated women's employment. Webb also maintained that many aspects of factory employ-ment, such as sanitary and environmental conditions, were better suited to state regulation than collective bargaining via the trade unions.[7]

The proposal by the American National Women's Party of the Equal Rights Amendment (ERA) in 1923 forced debates on the utility of protective labour legislation for women workers into a prominent position. The proposal identified a clean-sweep approach in the opposition to all sex-based legislation. It urged the removal of all inequalities between women and men in legislative enactments, which were identi-fied as discriminatory towards women. This overtly feminist approach to women's liberation was underpinned by the belief that women would never be able to achieve equal status if they were treated differently from men. Sex-based laws were criticised for the fact that they identified women as the weaker and inferior sex, whilst the radical advocates of the equal rights approach regarded women as robust, energetic and eager to work. In addition, it was argued that women should not be classified alongside minors in legislative enact-ments because this practice promoted their exclusion from the democratic process. The ERA proposal caused controver-sies and dissension in the international women's movement.

Advocates of the extension of the laws, however, argued that an 'equal rights' approach in the regulation of labour did not match women's needs.[8] From the standpoint of pro-gressive reformers, women workers were overburdened and vulnerable elements in the labour force. The protective laws could, and sometimes did, bring about substantial improve-ments in the conditions of work in industries in which women workers formed the bulk of the labour force, and in this respect the legislative initiatives had been effective.

Yet the laws could also prove detrimental to women's inter-ests by excluding them from employment. The most com-monly articulated opposition to the specialist protection of women in labour regulations was that the legal enactments placed restrictions on women's access to jobs. Equal rights campaigners argued that women could not be protected without being handicapped. By its imposition of strict regulations and costs on employers, protective labour legislation reduced women's competitiveness in the labour market.

It was also suggested that the restrictive practices acted as a brake on women's advancement in work and helped to confirm their secondary status in the labour force by confining them to lesser skilled and lower paid jobs. Women themselves raised objections to their enforced exclusion from areas of employment where protective labour laws were strictly adhered to. Moreover, the operation of the system of protective labour legislation served the interests of male employees, articulated via their relatively influential trade union organisations, rather than women workers. Working men were able to secure for themselves the better paid jobs, and eventually improved conditions of work, by refusing women entry into specified areas of employment.

The protective measures were more often imposed, it was claimed, for unjustifiable moral concerns rather than for genuine practical reasons. Arguments were raised against the practice of prohibiting areas of employment to women on the grounds of their perceived physical weakness and supposed relative inferiority. Such restrictive practices, Crystal Eastman argued, resulted from moral objections to women being employed in the specified working environments rather from the fact that women were incapable of successfully fulfilling the task at hand.[9]

Many of the industrial employments prohibited to women involved heavy physical labour, working in unhealthy factory environments or with harmful substances. The prohibition was often imposed on the grounds that such employments severely undermined women's health, their reproductive functions and the well-being of their babies and infant children. However, those who objected to such a practice argued that there was no absolute evidence to suggest that women were any more susceptible to injury or ill-health as a result of many of the restricted occupations than were men. Infections of the blood, for example, could just as easily be passed through husbands and fathers as through women to their children. Supporters of the equal rights approach argued that protective labour legislation should be applied according to occupation, where high levels of industrial injury had been recorded, for example, rather than on the grounds of sex. The well-documented example of British attempts to exclude women from working with lead-based paints illustrates a number of relevant arguments.[10]

The proposal that male employees should be subject to the protective labour laws on the same grounds as women workers was perhaps the strongest argument of the equal rights proponents. They could not deny that certain types of work and specific working environments were potentially harmful to women, but such jobs were most often equally dangerous for men. The only debate that remained was whether to 'level up', in order to bring male workers under the terms of the protective labour laws to which women were already subject, or to 'level down', so that women and men worked under the same unregulated conditions. Many British feminists, and some factory reformers, were moving towards the former policy of bringing all adult workers under the terms of the existing regulations.[11] In this way, early restrictions on women's employment served to bring about improvements for the entire industrial labour force.

It would be difficult to measure the extent to which women's employment was affected, either positively or negatively, by the imposition of protective labour legislation. The protective labour laws were most often designed to regulate factory employment, which accounted for only a small proportion of women's paid labour in these decades. Even in the example of the restricted occupations, it was argued that few women were affected by their legal exclusion because female labour tended not to be found in such areas of employment anyway.[12] The question of the impact and role of protective labour legislation for women in the regulation or restriction of female employment, whether to recognise women's different needs in law or to treat them as equals to men, remained unresolved in the international women's movement before the outbreak of the Second World War.

THE SOVIET CONTEXT

This book examines Soviet official policies towards protective labour legislation for women workers between 1917 and 1941.

The Bolsheviks were aware of the contemporary western debates and divisions on the issue of protective labour legislation. They adopted a route of progressive reform in the 1920s, both in recognition of women's different physiological constitution and in an attempt to bring about immediate improvements in the conditions of work for female labour.

The Bolsheviks' ideological vision of sexual equality originally incorporated the liberation of women from the drudgeries of housework and individualised child care. Instead, alongside their reproductive and maternal duties, women were to take an active part in productive labour, which was to be based on the principle of equal pay for equal work. Soon after the revolution, however, faced with a depleted agricultural sector and collapsing industry, the ideological ambitions of the Bolsheviks gave way to the more pragmatic considerations and competing priorities of restoring the economy. The limited effectiveness of Bolshevik attempts to put their ideological policies on women's liberation into practice is not in question.[13]

During the 1920s, the notion of women's biological and physiological distinctiveness, their reproductive functions and supposed physical inferiority were used as the basis for promoting protective labour laws which would ease women's accommodation into the industrial labour force. A concern for the regeneration of the population after the losses of the First World War and civil war years, as well as for the health of future Bolshevik generations, was also evident in the labour protection debates in this decade. In this respect, legislative enactments focused to a significant degree on women's potential and actual role as mothers.[14]

The trend of progressive reform was reversed after the early 1930s. Few new protective labour laws were enacted and the supervisory agencies responsible for their enforcement were disempowered. Stalin declared women's equality a reality in the Soviet Union. Yet, in many ways the 1930s marked the return to more explicitly conservative values in regard to traditional sex roles and gender demarcations in Soviet society. This was especially the case after the promulgation of the 1936 Constitution, which declared women's equal citizenship. The Constitution was also indicative of the paternalistic and pro-natalist concerns of Stalin's regime.[15] In the 1930s, a number of the legislative enactments related explicitly to women's actual role as mothers. In their capacity as industrial workers, however, women were to be treated, as far as possible, in the same way as men.

A major concern of this book is to identify the changes in official policy and attitudes towards both the formulation and the application of the protective labour laws for women workers. The study also assesses the nature of these changes in relation to the broader economic goals of the Soviet regime in the 1920s and 1930s. The topic is suggested partly by the fact that the economic and social history of women in the Soviet Union in the 1920s and 1930s is as yet underwritten. Much of the western published literature and current research on women in the Soviet Union during the interwar years tends to concentrate on women's changing political, social and family roles.[16] These issues are easily located within the contemporary ideological debates on the 'woman question'. Furthermore, despite the extensive literature on Soviet economic development, the Stalinist industrialisation programme and the formation of the Soviet working class in these decades, very little attention has been paid to the specific contributions and developmental roles of women workers in these processes or to the changes in gender identities which resulted from the mass entry of women into the industrial labour force.[17]

The topic of protective labour legislation also offers a broad range of questions for interrogation. It is important to determine the scope of protective labour legislation as it was applied to female labour in these decades and to identify the areas of women's work encompassed by the terms of the laws. When there were changes in official policy towards the application of these laws, it is interesting to see if these changes correlated with the more fundamental shifts in Soviet economic policies in this period, and most notably during the transition from the New Economic Policy to the planned economy in the late 1920s. It is more difficult to establish, firstly, how far the law effected an improvement in the conditions of female employment and, secondly, what was the impact of the protective labour measures on the structure of the industrial labour force.

Responsibility for the administration, enactment and enforcement of the protective labour laws was assigned to two major institutions: the People's Commissariat of Labour and the All-Union Central Council of Trade Unions. For ease in the text, the People's Commissariat of Labour is referred to by its widely used Russian acronym – Narkomtrud. For the benefit of non-Russian speakers, however, the trade union organisation is referred to by its more easily recognisable anglicised acronym – ACCTU (except in the notes referring to Russian language sources, where the Russian acronym, VTsSPS, is used). This study focuses predominantly on the work of these two organisations at union (USSR) level and on the published findings of the scientific research institutes which were established to aid their work. An analysis is provided of official state policy and debates on the protection of female labour. Illustrations of its practical effect are provided from the sectoral studies commissioned and undertaken by these organisations, which are to be found in the archives and in the published journals.[18]

Other agencies also played a significant role in the formulation and implementation of protective labour legislation for women workers in this period. For example, at republican level, the Russian People's Commissariat of Labour, Narkomtrud RSFSR, and the RSFSR People's Commissariat of Health, Narkomzdrav, were involved in the formulation of the protective labour laws and in the work undertaken by the various scientific research institutes.[19] The agency responsible for the administration of social insurance, TsUSStrakh, was involved particularly with the provision of maternity benefits. It is evident too that the Bolshevik Party women's department, the *Zhenotdel*, until its dissolution in 1930 also played an important role in the consultative process and in the mediation of women workers' disputes with respect to the application of the regulatory measures.[20] The legal and judicial agencies were involved in the original framing of the legislation and in prosecuting those who infringed the terms of the statutes.

The research conducted by contemporary agencies into such issues as the prevention of industrial accidents and the eradication of occupational diseases, questions of technical safety, the elaboration of sanitary-hygienic regulations and the bodies responsible for overseeing the implementation of these measures at enterprise level also contributed to the debates on protective labour legislation for women workers.

In this examination of the administration of the protective labour laws only a limited discussion has been included of the role played by the labour inspectorate in the legislative regulation of the female workforce in this period.

Many of the decrees and instructions introduced by the Bolsheviks from October 1917 in an attempt to improve and regulate conditions of employment for the industrial proletariat applied to female and male workers alike. They included a range of general measures on the protection of labour. Numerous contemporary handbooks outlined such issues as wages and benefits, contractual obligations, collective agreements, vocational training and worker education programmes, etc.[21] Two Labour Codes (*Kodeks Zakonov o Trude* – *KZoT*) were introduced, in December 1918 and then a revised version in November 1922. These codes detailed the rights and obligations of the Soviet labour force, including the entitlements to labour protection. The Labour Code was not fully revised again until 1978.

This study focuses primarily on the protective labour laws introduced specifically for adult women workers. The measures regulating the employment of young female workers up to 18 years of age are discussed in passing. It is important to note also that, like adult workers in other countries, Soviet women themselves sometimes complained that they were treated separately by the laws and that they were classified with young workers rather than adult male workers in the discussions and legislation.[22]

From a range of perspectives the protective labour laws for women workers were limited in their application. Firstly, and most importantly, they applied predominantly to state employees in the industrial labour force. The mass of the female peasantry and agricultural workers, women employed in small-scale artisan, *kustar* and cooperative workshops, in private trade or in domestic service remained largely untouched by the terms of the decrees. Despite the fact that increasing numbers of women were being drawn into the industrial labour force in these years (and this was especially the case after 1930), female industrial workers constituted only a small proportion of the total female population and less than half of the number of women in paid employment, even by the outbreak of the Second World War.[23]

More detailed regional, sectoral and enterprise-based studies may modify and refine the general trends outlined here.
Such studies may help to establish the full scope of the contemporary debates, the variations in the practical application
of the protective labour laws, the extent of their infringement
and their reception and resistance on the part of the female
industrial labour force. Clues to some of these issues are to be
found in the pages of the contemporary newspapers, such as
Trud, the daily publication of the trade union organisation,
the women's magazine, *Rabotnitsa*, and in the observations
and memoirs of both workers themselves and visitors to the
Soviet Union in these decades.

A major restriction in assessing the application of protective labour legislation has been the difficulty in determining
the extent to which the laws were actually ever implemented
and enforced in practice. This fact is noted also as a common
feature of Soviet legal developments in these years, as has
been suggested by Peter Solomon:

> The actual implementation of most laws – even without dis-
> tortions from administrative acts or party resolutions –
> remained problematic. The officials charged with executing
> laws and administrative acts often lacked the resources to
> implement them. In addition, they faced pressures that
> made some laws or directives more important than others.
> No historian of the USSR can afford to take laws at face
> value.[24]

The initiatives to introduce protective labour laws were
taken predominantly at government level and were partly
influenced by the examples of regulations already in existence in other countries. The Bolsheviks introduced relatively
extensive, detailed and original measures in a range of areas
to do with labour policy in general and the protection of
female labour in particular. Individual chapters in the book
each deal with a distinct area of labour protection: maternity,
hours of work, 'menstrual leave', weights of loads, restricted
occupations and underground work.

A number of contemporary published sources discuss
in varying detail the protective labour laws which applied
specifically to women workers.[25] All major government enactments were included in the official collections of laws and

instructions: *Sobranie uzakonenii i rasporyazhenii RSFSR* and *Sobranie zakonov i rasporyazhenii SSSR* (SU and SZ respectively in the notes). The detailed decrees and instructions of the People's Commissariat of Labour were also set out in its own publication – *Izvestiya Narkomtruda* (*Izvestiya NKT* in the notes). The journal of the trade union organisation, *Byulleten' VTsSPS*, continued the publication of the protective labour laws in the later 1930s. In addition to the detailed notes on the Russian language sources to the relevant decrees, a summary in English of the protective labour laws for women workers is provided as Appendix 1.

2 The Protection of Women Workers in Tsarist Russia

The origins of Russia's protective labour regulations for women workers are to be found in nineteenth-century legislative enactments. The actual practice of state intervention in the regulation of conditions of work, however, can be traced back much further. The principal terms of the early regulations, at least on paper, were designed to limit the hours of work of identified categories of employees and to protect those considered to be the most vulnerable social groups from the excesses of industrial employment.

The earliest attempts at regulating conditions of employment were made by Peter the Great. In 1722 the tsar attempted to restrict the hours of employment for workers at the Admiralty to ten hours in the winter and to thirteen hours in the summer. In the following year, Peter sent instructions to one of the mines in the Urals region stating that hours of work should be limited to fourteen hours in the summer, twelve hours in the spring and autumn and ten hours in the winter. It was only after Peter's death, however, that attempts were made in 1741 to extend the regulations on the conditions of labour and that three government commissioners were appointed to oversee conditions of work in the factories. A number of subsequent decrees also aimed to regulate the conditions of industrial employment, but G. M. Price, in his study of Russian labour protection, has noted that these had little real effect in view of the fact that the regulations were rarely either enforced or monitored.[1]

A decree introduced in 1845, during the reign of Nicholas I (1825–55), provided the first major example of tsarist protective labour legislation which was designed to restrict the areas of economic activity of identified groups of industrial workers. By the terms of this decree, children under 12 years of age were prohibited from working at night in factories.

13

The 1845 law, as with earlier legislative enactments, however, was not without its failings. Price has noted that 'this and other provisions of the law were worthless because of the lack of administrative machinery'.[2] The protective measures, therefore, were limited in their efficacy when there were no mechanisms in place to oversee their implementation and enforcement. Nor were the terms of the decrees designed specifically to improve the conditions of employment of the labour force. A second law of 1845 introduced punitive measures to deal with striking workers, who now found themselves liable to arrest.[3]

Despite the appointment of a number of government-sponsored investigations and the establishment also of a number of private commissions to investigate issues of labour reform during the reign of Alexander II (1855–81), no further substantive protective labour legislation was introduced until after his assassination in 1881.[4] At the same time as appointing commissions to investigate the conditions of industrial labour, however, Alexander II also introduced regulations in 1878 which gave the security forces powers to search and make arrests at factories where there was believed to be a threat of industrial disturbance by the workers.

The examples of the 1845 decree, the 1870s' commissions and 1878 supervisory regulations illustrate the differing interpretations of the goals of the legislative regulation of factory conditions. On the one hand, they might be interpreted as sincere attempts on the part of the government to sweep away the excesses of industrial exploitation for the most vulnerable elements of the labour force. This perspective views the autocratic regime as being fundamentally paternalistic in nature. On the other hand, the regulatory powers of the enactments have also been interpreted as attempts to both pacify and control labour unrest, which was regarded as a serious political threat to the autocratic regime. This revisionist perspective emphasises the limitations of the benevolence of the autocracy, which sought to stabilise and preserve its own position of authority throughout the nineteenth century.[5]

A decree introduced on 1 June 1882 extended the provisions of the 1845 law by prohibiting entirely the employment of children under 12 years of age. In exceptional circumstances only, the employment of children over the age of 10 years was permitted. In addition, workers between the ages of 12 and 15 years were prohibited from working at night or in the injurious trades and they were allowed to work for a maximum of eight hours during the day. They were also to be allowed to attend school.

The 1882 decree is significant also because it established a government factory inspectorate within the Ministry of Finance to oversee the regulations. A total of twelve inspectors were appointed to work in nine separate districts of the country. According to Price, the first factory inspectors were recruited from the liberal intelligentsia and tended to be professionals, such as economists, lawyers and physicians. They were devoted to the 'real protection of labour and to the prevention of illegal exploitation of workers'.[6] However, because of the resistance on the part of some factory owners, the establishment of the factory inspectorate did not become properly effective until May 1884. The rights and responsibilities of the factory inspectorate were defined in two sets of instructions issued by the Ministry of Finance in 1884.[7]

Under the terms of the 1882 decree, each district was provided with a staff of junior inspectors. The inspectors were commissioned to enumerate the employment of children and to enforce the terms of the protective labour laws in this regard. They were also to begin examining the conditions of employment for women workers. To some extent, it was argued, the limitations placed on the employment of children and young workers would increase the scope and scale of employment for female labour. Indeed, the findings of an extensive survey of the Moscow district by one of the newly appointed factory inspectors, I. I. Yanzhul, had shown this to be the case by 1885. By this date child labour had been reduced to less than one-third of its 1882 level, whilst the proportion of the labour force constituted by women in certain sectors of the textile industries had risen from around 35 per cent to nearer 40 per cent. Yanzhul also reported that women had almost entirely replaced child labour in the tobacco industry.[8]

Initially, the work of the factory inspectorate was restricted to the most industrialised and economically advanced regions of the country. The scope of factory inspection was only extended to cover the whole of the empire in 1898.

Pospielovsky has noted a further limitation of the regulatory body in that, very often, subsequent rules and regulations created loopholes which enabled employers to avoid the protective labour laws.[9] Pospielovsky has also noted that 'there was no such leeway to be noticed in those sections of the laws which dealt with the workers' obligations towards their employers' and, in view of the close connection between the Ministry of Finance and the interests of the industrialists, 'by the end of the century the Russian Factory Inspectorate had to a great extent become the protecting body for the employers'.[10]

The extent of resistance to any kind of factory regulation by some factory owners and, to a greater degree, the level of antagonism between different groups of industrialists are illustrated by the debates surrounding the introduction of the first major protective labour laws with respect to women workers in the mid-1880s. The debates on the regulation of female labour also illustrate the point that the proponents of protective measures in this period did not always consider the improvement in the conditions of employment for the women as their primary concern.[11] Giffin's study of the introduction of the prohibition on night work by women in the cotton textiles industries in 1885 highlights the antagonism which developed between St Petersburg industrialists, who initially proposed the regulation, and factory owners in the Moscow and Central Industrial Regions, who, on the whole, opposed the night work restrictions in the hope of maintaining their competitive economic edge.[12]

The industrial slump of the early 1880s proved especially severe in St Petersburg, where many factories were forced to lay off some of their workers. In 1884 the St Petersburg industrialists presented a petition to the government in which they identified the widespread use of night shift employment in Moscow and the surrounding regions for over-production in the manufacturing industries. The relatively advanced nature of the production process in St Petersburg, including the broader use of more technologically advanced machinery and the fostering of higher levels of skill within the industrial labour force, had already resulted in the introduction of shorter hours of work and the virtual absence of night shift employment. The St Petersburg industrialists also put forward an argument on humanitarian grounds that night work was physically and morally harmful to women.

The industrialists of the Moscow and Central Industrial Regions argued that night work was an essential feature of Moscow factory life and that the St Petersburg industrialists' motivation for private gain was insufficient grounds to justify the introduction of the restrictive measures. The representatives of the Central Industrial Region industrialists at the Manufacturing Council in Moscow argued that production in this area was greatly dependent on the employment of women workers, who comprised around one-third of the total labour force. They argued that manufacturing output would decline significantly if the hours of women's work were restricted. They suggested further that night work by women was no more harmful than some of its alternatives and that it was regarded as an essential part of family integrity in manufacturing districts, where often both wife and husband were employed at night.

The divisions which emerged during the course of the negotiations amongst the factory owners of the Central Industrial Region themselves, however, were finally to settle the dispute. The high prices of fuel had raised the costs of production to such an extent that night work had already been abandoned in some areas. In practice, those factories which operated only daytime shifts had not suffered in relation to those still employing night workers. On the basis of such arguments, the Manufacturing Council eventually conceded to the introduction of a night work prohibition for women workers. The potentially damaging impact on levels of industrial competition and on industrial production, therefore, seem to have been the major concerns informing the introduction of the first night work regulations for female labour in Russia, rather than concern for the impact of such employment on the women workers themselves.

On 3 June 1885 Bunge, the Minister of Finance, introduced regulations, applicable from 1 October 1885, which banned the employment of women, and of young workers up to the age of 17 years, on night shifts initially in cotton-spinning factories, and then also in other textile factories. The hours of night work were not set out in the decree but, on the basis of the 1882 regulations, were generally agreed to fall between nine o'clock in the evening and five o'clock in the morning.[13]

Provision was made in the decree for the Ministry of Finance to extend the night shift prohibitions to other sectors of industry. Under the terms of the 1885 provisions the Ministry of Finance and the Ministry of the Interior were charged with investigating further the regulation of night work and were to submit a report on this issue within the next three years. It would be safe to assume that the law prohibiting night work by women was not widely implemented. Factory legislation was widely ignored. It did little to protect the workers and it annoyed industrialists. It took some time before the protective regulations were effectively enforced.

Glickman, in her study of Russian female factory workers, has pointed out that the decree failed to establish any sanctions to be used against factory owners who did not comply with its terms, nor did it ascribe supervision of the decree to any specific administrative body. Responsibility for determining punishments, therefore, fell to the factory inspectorate, which imposed only limited fines on errant employers.[14] Proper sanctions for failure to observe the terms of the night work regulations were not introduced in law until 1890.

The factory inspectorate was expanded and reorganised in June 1886 and again in the 1890s, but by this time it had taken on an entirely different role and character. The 1886 and 1892 regulations allowed for the establishment of provincial bureaux on factory and mining affairs under the authority of local governors. The regional offices were responsible for overseeing health provision, medical conditions and safety regulations in factories.[15] Glickman argues that by the early 1890s the offices proved very responsive to the needs of women workers and special provision was being made particularly for pregnant women.[16] A further reorganisation of the factory inspectorate in 1894, however, displaced the specialists who had constituted the factory inspectorate's first personnel. The inspectorate now took on a more bureaucratic and technocratic character and was concerned more with the avoidance of industrial conflict than with improving the conditions of work.[17] The close connection of the factory inspectorate with the police department by the mid-1890s,

Price has argued, made its staff 'oppressors instead of protectors of labour'.[18]

Subsequent amendments to the 1885 night work regulations introduced specific provisions for the imposition of fines and punishment by imprisonment for violations of the terms of the decree. The amendments also recognised the potentially damaging impact of the night work prohibition on family life. Many people felt that it was unreasonable to require family members to work on different shifts and so revisions to the regulations allowed women and young workers to be employed at night when husbands and parents were available to supervise them.[19] Factory owners were also permitted to employ married women without the permission of their husband, thereby overriding a provision of 1835 which had made such a practice illegal. Despite the amendments, Glickman has argued that the primary concern of the protective labour laws in the 1880s and 1890s was 'to promote the health of Russian industry' rather than to protect the health of workers. The revision of the 1835 decree, for example, was designed to meet the demand for labour rather than offering married women a greater degree of freedom and independence.[20]

The next major enactment of government legislation on the protection of labour was issued under Witte. The 2 June 1897 regulations established a maximum working day of eleven and a half hours for all adult workers and limited work on night shifts, on Saturdays and on the eve of holidays to ten hours. Overtime working, however, was subsequently permitted by mutual agreement of the employer and employee. In practice, however, overtime was sometimes made obligatory.[21] In the following year night work was banned in the phosphorous matches industry, where large numbers of women and young workers were employed.[22] Night work by women was also prohibited in the mining industry.[23] A maximum eight-hour day was established in 1901 for workers in a range of specifically identified dangerous occupations where female labour was commonly employed.[24]

As with other protective measures, the effectiveness of the 1897 regulations and subsequent decrees is difficult to gauge.[25] The new regulations again proved difficult to enforce and were easily evaded.[26] Moreover, some of the more modern factories, in St Petersburg, for example, already operated

a shorter working day than that set out in the 1897 regulations.[27] The shortcomings of the new regulations have again
given rise to criticism that 'the protection of labour by the
Tsarist government was always backward in its provisions and
half-hearted in its administration and enforcement'.[28]

As with other statements on the purpose of nineteenth-
century factory laws, the Bolshevik reformer Sergei Kaplun
argued after the revolution in 1917 that 'it is obvious that
under tsarism the protection of labour was actually turned
into the protection of capital against labour'.[29] Although his
claims may seem somewhat exaggerated, he pointed out in
addition that:

> With regard to the protection of women's labour nothing at
> all was undertaken. No care whatsoever was taken of the
> sanitary and hygienic state of factories or workshops. In the
> sphere of technical safety and safeguard from dangerous
> machines the government acted very timidly, almost refrain-
> ing from establishing any important rules or obligatory
> regulations.[30]

The limitations of the protective labour provisions can be
seen also by the fact that they applied only to factory and
industrial employment. As Bonnell has pointed out, no provision was made for the thousands of workers employed in artisan workshops or as sales personnel and clerical staff.[31]
Despite this, the coverage of health and medical care provisions for industrial employees was expanding. According to
Seton-Watson, two-thirds of the industrial labour force were
employed in the large-scale factories subject to inspection
by the beginning of the twentieth century.[32] Crisp has also
pointed out that 'the number of women employed in manufacturing firms subject to inspection rose at a much higher
rate than the labour force as a whole'.[33]

Industrial workers, however, were often ignorant of the laws
and benefits which could have helped to alleviate their working lives. The absence of effective trade union organisations
in this period also meant that they lacked the means by which
to promote their demands and enforce their entitlements.
The factory inspectorate lacked the staff and level of compe-
tence necessary to monitor and enforce the regulations, if
indeed they were enforceable in practice. The effectiveness of

labour policy in this period, McDaniel has suggested, was further undermined by its own administrative rather than political basis. Factory inspectors were more concerned with enforcing labour policies determined by the government than negotiating their scope and intent.[34]

Yet even within the industrial sector, it has been argued, although the factory regulations to some extent imposed a form of homogeneity in the conditions of work, the over-whelming quality of Russian industry in this period remained its heterogeneity.[35] Women's interests were often significantly different from men's, such as in the demand for improved maternity provision. This division of interests aroused antag-onism, very often situating women in opposition to men. One recent study of popular misogyny in nineteenth-century Russia has pointed out that:

> taunts of 'class traitors' [were] thrown by Russian male workers at their female co-workers when they argued that shorter hours were more valuable than higher pay, and ... male workers [held the view] that their female colleagues were retrograde, 'creatures of a lower order', 'backward and uncultured'.[36]

In the early years of the twentieth century the Russian gov-ernment introduced laws which made provision for the social insurance of industrial workers. These measures were largely concerned with welfare issues rather than the regulation of working practices. They made employers responsible for the payment of compensation to workers who had sustained injuries at the workplace, for financial support for both tem-porarily and permanently incapacitated workers and for con-tributions towards funeral expenses for workers who died as a result of industrial injuries. It has been suggested though that the welfare provisions were far from extensive. Price, for example, has argued that the measures were 'not primarily enacted for the protection of workers but to reduce to owners the cost of medical assistance, as it compelled the workers themselves to bear the cost of sickness'.[37]

Women workers articulated their own demands for improved maternity provision. Glickman cites an early and unusual example from 1880 of women striking in the demand for an extension by three months of the established six-month period allowed for breast feeding at one factory. On the whole, however, Glickman argues that women protested against special treatment under the law because they feared this would result in a loss of earnings.[38] Maternity issues were evident in the demands put forward by women during the strike movements of the 1890s and were voiced again in 1905. The safeguarding of the employment rights and the provision of maternity leave for pregnant women and new mothers were an important part of the Russian Social Democrat's party programme as early as 1903. By 1905 the Social Democrat's programme had taken up the demands for paid maternity leave and the provision of child care facilities at factories. The absence of paid maternity leave and the lack of both time and space to feed nursing babies had a very detrimental impact on levels of infant mortality. Glickman notes the results of a 1912 survey which revealed 'that almost 75 per cent of women workers worked up to the onset of labour, 18 per cent left work two weeks before labour, and 7 per cent stopped work two to four weeks before labour'.[39] Barbara Engel has suggested that 'as many as two thirds of the infants of factory workers died in the first year of life'.[40]

The question of maternity provision was debated at the First All-Russian Congress of Women, convened in St Petersburg in 1908. The congress was dominated by wealthy and middle-class women who mostly had no direct experience of physical or industrial labour themselves. A small group of working women attended the congress, organised by Alexandra Kollontai, but the mass of peasant women remained virtually unrepresented. The grim conditions of employment for pregnant working women were a particular topic of concern raised during the session on 'women in the economy'.

In her study of the congress, Edmondson has noted that 'maternity insurance and leave were almost unknown, and consequently women sometimes gave birth on the factory floor'.[41] Special provision was demanded for pregnancy and maternity in particular, as well as the protection of women workers in general. Edmondson argues that 'there was remarkable unanimity on the need to protect female labour, through restrictions on working hours, the safeguarding of machinery, the prohibition of women's work in certain industries, medical facilities and factory inspection'.[42] There were calls also for the scope of inspection to be extended to the as yet unregulated workshops and craft industries, where many women were employed.[43]

The 23 June 1912 Insurance Law proved to be the last major enactment of the tsarist regime which dealt with the protection of industrial workers and it was this law which first introduced significant maternity benefits. Women were prohibited from working in the final four weeks of pregnancy and provision was made for maternity leave.[44] McKean has pointed out that 'pregnant women for the first time were to be paid a maternity allowance for six weeks'.[45] The law also established a system of employee and employer contributions to a sickness fund in private enterprises with over 100 workers. It should be noted, however, that more advanced welfare provision was already being offered by state-run enterprises.[46] Pregnant women could, therefore, be compensated during the prescribed period of maternity leave by payments from these funds if they worked in factories where such a system was in operation. Women were also encouraged to sit on the committees which administered the funds.

The far left political parties in Russia on the whole opposed the introduction of the 1912 social welfare provisions, arguing that the law served only to divert workers' attention away from opposition to the tsarist regime. It has been argued, alternatively, that this 'half-hearted, grudgingly conceded, measure of social reform' was insufficient to heal the rift between the labour movement and the monarchy.[47] The long-standing and wide-ranging debates on the establishment of a separate women's factory inspectorate were resolved before the outbreak of the First World War, but the events of 1914 forestalled the implementation of the agreed provisions.

It is worth reviewing here in brief some of the issues which informed the debates in Russia from the 1880s on the role of protective labour legislation in its specific application to women workers because many of these controversies and concerns were also evident in the debates of the 1920s and 1930s. A commonly articulated concern was the belief that women had a more delicate physiological constitution, which was in need of protection from the harsh conditions of factory life by the introduction of state regulations on their employment. This concern was evident also in many of the contemporary European debates on the need for the protection of female factory workers and in many instances an idealisation of domesticity and motherhood came to dominate these discussions.[48] A number of the early Russian factory inspectors argued that women's participation in industrial labour should be limited in view of their reproductive functions and because of the need to protect the health of the entire nation.[49] Pregnancy, however, was not considered a sufficient cause for dismissing women workers, but it did necessitate specialist provision. In its extreme this set of arguments suggested that women's emancipation required the liberation of women entirely from the demands of hard physical labour.

At the same time, however, there was also some recognition of the fact that the vast majority of women in Russia were peasants and that most women were, therefore, used to hard physical labour and long hours of work.[50] Where women worked in factories they often needed to do so in order to provide for the support of their family. Excluding women from industrial employment or restricting their hours of work, it was argued, would deprive them of wages and force them into less congenial occupations, such as prostitution, for example. From the perspective of the employers, women constituted a significant proportion of the labour force in a number of industries and industrial production was dependent to some extent on their employment. This line of argument, therefore, suggested that industrial labour in itself was not harmful to women and that protective labour legislation should be designed only to mitigate the worst conditions of factory employment.

Finally, the changing position and role of women in Russia's industrial labour force should be outlined. Whilst protective labour legislation may have served to expand female employment by removing children and young workers from the paid labour force, it may also have served to restrict the opportunities of women workers to find jobs in situations of competition with men. Women were, on the whole, less mobile than men and constituted a smaller proportion of the migratory labour force. The lower proportional representation of women, especially in the heavy industrial labour force, was also the result of the growing importance of the male-dominated mining and metallurgical industries at the turn of the century, which offered only a limited range of jobs to women but employed cheap male labour on a mass scale. According to data cited by Mints, in 1900 female employees, including girls, constituted 28.4 per cent of all workers in the twelve selected industries included in his survey. This proportion, however, would be reduced considerably by the inclusion of the male-dominated mining and related industries.[51]

Women workers were employed predominantly in the textile industries. During the first decade of the twentieth century they also came to be employed in a broader range of industrial jobs than ever before. Women's relative position in the paid labour market improved to some extent during the Russo-Japanese war. After the turmoil of 1905 women came to be favoured as more reliable and docile elements in the industrial labour force. Under pressure to improve working conditions after 1905 and to cut production costs, employers more readily hired cheaper and less militant female workers. In a range of manufacturing processes, women workers started to be substituted for men. (See Appendixes 2 and 3.)

In addition to this, women were employed widely in a range of occupations not subject to factory regulations or inspection. Female peasant labour was the mainstay of agriculture and women workers were employed also in a whole range of service and domestic jobs. They were also frequently employed in *kustar*, or artisan, production, where the flexibility of the occupations meant that women could combine employment with domestic responsibilities.[52] It should be noted also that girls and young women formed a higher proportion of the adolescent labour force than women in the adult labour force. Young female workers constituted roughly 40 per cent of the adolescent labour force, whereas adult women constituted roughly 30 per cent of the adult labour force.[53] Girls and young women were widely employed in the textiles and chemical industries.[54]

By 1913 the actual number of women engaged in industrial employments totalled over half a million and women constituted 30.7 per cent of industrial workers.[55] Both the number and proportion of women employed in industry continued to rise until 1917, by which time, according to Mints, women constituted nearer 40 per cent of the industrial labour force. (See Appendixes 2 and 3.)

Tsarist policies on the regulation of women's labour focused mainly on the prohibition of female employment on night shifts and in some of the potentially injurious occupations. Protective measures were also introduced before the outbreak of the First World War to promote the health and welfare of pregnant women workers and their babies. The lack of development of independent trade unions in nineteenth-century Russia, as had been witnessed already in many other European countries and the United States, meant that factory regulations were not introduced as a response to worker initiatives or demands, and that the laws were seldom perceived to operate in the interests of labour. The pre-revolutionary initiatives were extended under the Bolsheviks after the October revolution and the coverage of the protective labour laws was also expanded to encompass previously unregulated aspects of women's work.

It is clear from the debates outlined here that the benefit to the female labour force was not always the prime motivating factor behind the introduction of tsarist protective labour legislation. The extent to which this remained the case in the Soviet period is also open to question. The difficulties experienced in tsarist Russia in enforcing the legal regulations, which resulted from both the inadequacies of the supervisory agencies and the resistance expressed on the part of the female industrial labour force to their application, were difficulties which were experienced also during the 1920s and 1930s.

3 Women Workers and Soviet Industrialisation

In the two decades of the 1920s and 1930s the Soviet regime employed contrasting recruitment and employment strategies in relation to women workers. The move from 'protection' to 'equality' in official policies towards female labour had far-reaching consequences not only for women workers but also for the Soviet labour force as a whole.[1] A brief examination will be made in this chapter of some of the basic indicators of changes in the rates of female employment and unemployment, both in absolute terms and as a proportion of the total industrial labour force constituted by women, the distribution of women workers in different sectors of the economy and by different levels of skill.[2] The very nature of female employment had changed by the end of the 1930s. Women were actively encouraged to work in jobs, and indeed entire sectors of the economy, which had formerly been dominated by men.

Working for wages and industrial labour were not new to Russian women. Many thousands of women had been employed in the tsarist economy as full-time, part-time and seasonal industrial labourers, as white-collar employees and as hired workers in other sectors of the economy. The employment of women had grown rapidly in virtually all of the industrial sectors of the economy during the First World War.[3] According to data compiled by the Soviet statistician, L. Ye. Mints, by 1917 female workers (including girls and young women) constituted around 40 per cent of the industrial labour force.[4] (See Appendixes 2 and 3.) From this time, however, the actual numbers of women in paid employment fell. Women began to lose their jobs as the levels of male unemployment rose and when soldiers returned from the front. During the upheaval of the 1917 revolutions and the civil war, many women undoubtedly also voluntarily gave up paid employment in urban areas in order to seek food and security in the villages.

The Bolshevik Party believed that sexual equality and the liberation of women could be achieved by the full participation of women as paid workers in the production process. In his 'Speech at the Non-Party Conference of Women Workers' in 1919, Lenin argued that:

> As long as women are engaged in housework their position is a restricted one. In order to achieve the complete emancipation of women and to make them really equal with men, we must have social economy, and the participation of women in general productive labour. Then women will occupy the same position as men.

Interestingly for this study Lenin proceeded to argue that:

> This, of course, does not mean that women must be exactly equal with men in productivity of labour, amount of labour, length of the working day, conditions of labour, etc. But it does mean that women shall not be in an oppressed economic position compared with men.[5]

Economic independence, therefore, was identified as an important element in achieving women's liberation and sexual equality. The Bolsheviks attempted to put these policies into practice after October 1917, but during the chaotic years of civil war and war communism it proved difficult for the Bolshevik Party to implement its social welfare programme, which was in part designed to ease the accommodation of women into the industrial labour force. During 1918 some of the trade unions made attempts to prevent the mass dismissal of women workers.[6] The first Soviet Labour Code, issued in December 1918, imposed the duty of productive labour on all Soviet citizens of working age.[7] Overall, except for a slight variation in 1920, the actual numbers of women in industrial employment declined steadily between 1918 and 1921/22 and the proportion of the industrial labour force constituted by women continued to fall until 1923/24.[8] (See Appendix 2.)

After the years of turmoil due to war and revolution, the introduction of the New Economic Policy (NEP) in 1921 saw the partial retraction of many war communist policies. The introduction of the NEP also signalled a period of stabilisation and restoration in the economy and allowed for an expansion in the size of the female industrial labour force. It was in these years in particular that social policy directives, scientific research and actual legislative enactments were aimed at the 'protection' of female labour. The period of economic recovery lasted until 1926, by which time both agriculture and many industrial sectors had been restored to their pre-war levels of output.[9]

By the early 1920s evidence presented by some of the western visitors to Soviet Russia in these years suggested that many workers, especially those with Bolshevik sympathies, had developed a new attitude towards work.[10] Structures had been introduced which allowed industrial employees greater involvement in the day-to-day running of enterprises and which promoted a feeling of ownership in the production process. Despite the fact that many factories and much of the capital equipment and machinery were in a poor state of repair, which resulted in many workers being employed in unsanitary, unhealthy and dangerous environments, efforts were being made to improve working conditions, for example, through better ventilation and lighting, the distribution of protective clothing and the allocation of soap and dietary supplements to those worst affected.

From 1922/23 the growth in female industrial employment was initially steady, but was also much slower than that of male workers.[11] This meant that, as Tsyrlina, the chair of a special commission investigating questions of women's labour, pointed out, the actual proportion of the industrial labour force constituted by women declined rapidly in the early years of the 1920s, from over 40 per cent in 1921 to less than 30 per cent by 1924.[12]

As is illustrated by Table 3.1, according to data published by the State Planning Commission (Gosplan), in large-scale industry in the four-year period from 1 January 1923 to 1 January 1927 the number of female factory shopfloor workers, including trainees (*rabotnitsy* and *ucheniki*), increased from 423 200 to 673 800. 1925 alone saw an increase of almost 170 000 in the total number of women engaged in industrial employment (including engineer-technical workers (*ITR*), and white-collar employees). Over 130 000 of these were shopfloor workers.[13]

Almost two-thirds of the overall increase in female employment in these four years took place in the textiles industries, with the number of women employed in cotton textiles alone more than doubling over this period. According to Rashin's

Table 3.1   Employment of Women in Large-Scale Industry, 1923–27

	Total No. of Women	Index (1923 = 100)	No. Shopfloor Workers	Index (1923 = 100)
1923	462 800	100	423 200	100
1924	454 500	98.2	425 900	100.6
1925	543 100	117.3	513 200	121.3
1926	710 200	153.5	643 600	152.1
1927	743 000	160.5	673 800	159.2

Source: Gosplan SSSR, *Trud v SSSR: statisticheskii spravochnik* (Moscow, 1936) p. 25. Indices are own calculations.

study of women workers in the USSR in the 1920s, by 1 January 1927 over half of all female industrial workers (excluding junior service staff) were employed in cotton, linen and woollen textiles. With the addition of women workers in the food industry and clothing and cosmetics, these five sectors accounted for just over 70 per cent of all female industrial workers.[14] Women workers, therefore, remained concentrated in the traditional areas of female employment: in the light industries (textiles and the garment industries in particular), public catering, health and education and other public services. In contrast, on 1 January 1927 over 50 per cent of male industrial workers were employed in two heavy industrial sectors alone: firstly, mining and mining-related industries and, secondly, metal processing and machine-building.[15]

Despite the growth in the overall number of women employed, the actual proportion of the industrial labour force constituted by women remained quite steady over the four-year period from 1923–27, as can be seen from Table 3.2. It is apparent from these figures that whilst the actual numbers of women engaged in industrial employment were rising over this period, the proportion of the labour force constituted by women remained fairly constant. The absolute increase in the size of the male industrial labour force, therefore, was far greater than the expansion of the female labour force. In fact, by 1927, in comparison with 1923, women workers constituted a smaller proportion of the labour force in many large-scale industries. According to official data on

Table 3.2   Women Shopfloor Workers as a Proportion of the Total Labour Force in Large-Scale Industry, 1 January 1923–1 January 1927

1923	1924	1925	1926	1927
29.5%	27.5%	28.8%	28.5%	28.5%

Source: Gosplan SSSR, *Trud v SSSR: statisticheskii sprav-ochnik* (Moscow, 1936) p. 91. Own calculations.

labour statistics (*Trud v SSSR*, 1936), the exceptions were in the cotton and linen textiles industries (but not wool), shoes and food. Noticeable declines were recorded in the tradition-ally male-dominated heavy industrial sectors of coal mining and the extraction industries, the chemical industry and the metallurgical and machine-building sectors.[16] By the begin-ning of 1927, however, the proportion of the total labour force constituted by women in a whole range of industrial sectors exceeded 1913 levels, but the overall proportion remained significantly lower than the peak years of 1917 and 1918.[17]

Table 3.3 illustrates the fact that women employed in the industrial sectors of the economy remained concentrated in lower skill grades and were predominantly unskilled and semi-skilled workers. This was partly the result of lower levels of vocational and technical training and higher levels of illiteracy amongst the female labour force. A study of the skill grades of adult industrial workers (182 100 women and 455 900 men) was conducted on 1 March 1927. This survey revealed that 88.7 per cent of female industrial workers were employed in grades three to six and a further 7 per cent were placed in the lowest skill grades, one and two. In comparison, 59.9 per cent of male industrial workers were placed at skill grades three to six and 88.6 per cent of all men worked in the higher skill grades four to nine.[18] Despite this, women could be found in the higher skill grades in some industries. The average grade for women workers in the printing and gar-ment industries, for example, was above six. Women workers in the leather and food industries were also employed at

Table 3.3 Levels of Skill amongst Women Workers, Selected Industries, 1 May 1925 (in percentage terms by sector)

Industry	Skilled	Semi-skilled	Unskilled
Coal mining	0.4	37.0	62.6
Ferrous metallurgy	5.5	33.2	61.3
Machine-building	28.7	37.7	33.6
Printing	26.7	51.1	22.2
Porcelain and china	20.7	44.6	34.7
Glass	5.9	34.8	59.3
Matches	16.1	9.0	74.9
Tobacco	2.2	84.4	13.4

Source: Central Statistical Administration (TsSU) data, cited in A. G. Rashin, *Zhenskii trud v SSSR* (Moscow, 1928) pp. 5–6.

grades which averaged five and above. In the heavy industries, such as metallurgy and mining, women predominated in the lowest grades one to three. The overall average grade for the industrial workers included in the survey was 4.3 for women and 6.0 for men.[19]

Despite the principle of equal pay for equal work, which appears to have been operational by this time, as a result of such discrepancies in levels of skill between female and male workers, women received wages which were considerably lower than their male colleagues. Women, on average, earned less than 68 per cent of their male colleagues' wages in 1928.[20] Even in the cotton textile industry, where wage disparities were far less apparent, women's wages, on average for all ages and levels of skill, were approximately 77 per cent of male earnings in 1929.[21] Gosplan data revealed that in the late 1920s, even in occupations where women and men were employed in identical tasks, women were still paid less than their male colleagues. In occupations where the wage disparity had favoured women in 1928, this had been eradicated by 1929 in two out of three cited examples.[22]

In addition to industrial employment, women also worked in the service industries and as white-collar personnel. According to data cited by Serebrennikov, the proportion of the labour force constituted by women in medical and public health organisations rose from 60.7 per cent in 1923 to 65.4 per cent in 1928.[23] Women remained a high proportion of workers in the service industries and caring professions (public catering, education and health) during the 1930s. (See Appendix 4.) To some extent women were also able to build on advances brought about by the First World War. In the 1920s and 1930s women workers were to be found in increasing numbers and proportions in a whole range of non-industrial employments. For example, in Moscow in 1926 the proportion of women workers rose to 8.6 per cent in the railway and transport sectors, compared to a 1912 level of 1.5 per cent, and to 72 per cent in medicine and nursing, compared to 56.5 per cent in 1912.[24]

Women constituted 27.2 per cent of the total employed labour force (including non-industrial occupations) by 1929.[25] Statistical data, however, do not allow for an assessment of the qualitative changes in the conditions of female employment. In the post-revolutionary period attempts were made, despite severe shortages of funding, to provide improved social and cultural facilities and communal services for women workers and to attract female labour, especially young workers, to training and education programmes. At this time, women were also the subject of a number of labour laws which were introduced partly in recognition of their different physiological constitution and to protect them from the harshest conditions of industrial employment.

The restoration of the economy from 1921, however, was not without its problems. Although the introduction of the NEP allowed for the expansion of the industrial labour force to some extent, it also generated widespread unemployment, especially in the cities. This was the case particularly in the years leading up to 1924, when an official attempt was made to reduce the numbers of unemployed registered at the labour exchanges. Many women were the early victims of the shift to cost accounting policies introduced from 1921. By the end of October 1921 over 13 000 women had lost their jobs and female workers accounted for 60 per cent of the unemployed.[26] In the early 1920s legislation was introduced, which, in theory at least, aimed to protect the employment rights of female labour, especially of pregnant women and nursing mothers, and which introduced equal terms for the dismissal of women and men in conditions of redundancy. Single mothers were given preferential employment rights. (See Chapter 5.)

Yet at the same time and despite these measures, women workers, especially those who were unskilled, were frequently victims of redundancy and unemployment.[27] According to data cited by Goldman the numbers of unemployed women officially registered at the labour exchanges rose from 60 975 in December 1921 to 369 800 in October 1927. In these months women constituted 62 per cent and 45.5 per cent respectively of the total numbers of registered unemployed workers. These figures, however, do not take into account those women who were seeking work for the first time and before 1925, therefore, were unable to register as unemployed. Goldman has also pointed out that under conditions of rising unemployment the trade unions were more interested in securing the rights of workers already in employment than in finding jobs for the unemployed. By 1929 women still accounted for around half of the unemployed, despite the fact that women were less likely to be seeking employment than man.[28] Data included in the documentation for the First Five-Year Plan indicated that the average length of unemployment for women was 12.4 months and that higher proportions of women were to be found amongst the long-term unemployed.[29]

Grunfeld has suggested that the growing levels of female unemployment in these years had little to do with the terms of the protective labour laws and the costs which these imposed on enterprises, but was more often the result of discriminatory practices by those responsible for hiring labour, many of whom still expressed a preference for employing men rather than women.[30] Many male workers themselves were no less receptive to the idea of working alongside women for the same rates of pay in some jobs. Such attitudes persisted into the 1930s when the protective measures were less rigorously enforced.[31] It should be remembered, however, that the protective labour laws did impose hidden costs on employers and made women, in their eyes, potentially and comparatively more expensive employees than men, as Goldman has recently pointed out.[32] Traditional prejudice and discriminatory attitudes combined with the financial burdens imposed by the judicial implementation of the protective labour laws to restrict women's employment in the 1920s.

It was probably also the case, as one contemporary report suggested, that the lower levels of trade union organisation amongst women in the 1920s meant that female workers were less able to defend their own rights to work.[33] Efforts were made throughout the interwar period to raise the levels of skill amongst women workers by expanding their admission to technical training courses and reducing levels of illiteracy. In fact, one representative from the Narkomtrud Department of Labour Protection argued in 1924 that the best way to protect the interests of female labour was through raising the levels of skill amongst women workers.[34]

With Stalin's 'left turn' in 1928 and the formal adoption of the First Five-Year Plan in the following year, new demands were placed on the Soviet Union's economic resources, including the country's labour reserves. Great emphasis was placed on the development of large-scale, heavy industrial sectors of the economy. The successful fulfilment of the Stalinist industrialisation programme during the first three Five-Year Plans (1928–41) required the overall expansion of the Soviet labour force and, in particular, an increase in the number of workers employed in the industrial sectors of the economy. The success of the Five-Year Plans rested partly on the recruitment of women to industrial employment. An active campaign which aimed at the mass recruitment of women to the industrial labour force was launched in 1930. The social dislocation caused as a result of the collectivisation of agriculture and by the purges also undoubtedly had consequences for the levels and rates of growth of female employment. The economic imperatives of Stalin's industrialisation programme and the growing threat of war by the late 1930s had even more far-reaching and longer-lasting consequences for the employment of women.

During the 1930s the total number of women employed in the Soviet economy and the proportion of the labour force constituted by female labour both increased dramatically. In this decade, however, far less emphasis was placed on the introduction, implementation and enforcement of the specialist protective labour measures for women workers. The status of women in the Soviet economy now came to be judged more by their participation in the industrial labour force on equal terms with men.

The extensive participation of women in paid employment in the 1930s was used as a measure of their increasingly equal status in Soviet society. Yet, despite the fact that women constituted well over half of the new recruits to the industrial labour force in a number of years in this decade, very little was done to relieve them of their 'double burden', which consisted of a combination of paid work and almost entire responsibility for unpaid labour in the home and for child care. By the end of the 1930s women constituted around 40 per cent of all paid workers. The very nature of 'women's work' had changed significantly with many thousands of women now employed in jobs which had only previously been undertaken by male workers.

According to the published data, the numbers of women employed in the Soviet economy during the First Five-Year Plan were scheduled to increase by around 30 per cent in the initial variant, and nearer 40 per cent in the optimum variant. By the end of the First Five-Year Plan women were planned to constitute 31.2 per cent of the employed labour force according to the initial variant, and 32.5 per cent according to the optimum variant, which required the recruitment of a greater number of unoccupied urban women to the paid labour force.[35]

On 10 January 1931 the Central Executive Committee (TsIK) debated the question of the mass entry of women into the industrial labour force. Soon afterwards a decree was issued indicating the planned recruitment of 1.6 million women to employment in the Soviet economy.[36] Individual enterprises were required to identify areas of their work where men could be replaced by women. The 1931 annual control figures of the First Five-Year Plan for the first time included figures for the distribution of female labour in the economy. Enterprises were encouraged to take on a minimum fixed percentage of female workers. In reality, by the end of the First Five-Year Plan (nine months ahead of schedule on 31 December 1932) women shopfloor workers (*rabotnitsy*) constituted well over one-third of the total number of shopfloor workers in large-scale industry.[37] The total number of women employed in large-scale industry rose by over one million during the First Five-Year Plan, from 879 900 on 1 January 1929 to 2 206 700 on 1 January 1933.[38] The annual average total number of female workers in the economy as a whole rose from 3.3 million in 1929 to just over 6 million in 1932.[39] (See Appendix 4.)

Specialist organisations were established to encourage women to take up work in heavy industry, putting into practice the findings of the scientific-research institutes of Narkomtrud and the People's Commissariat of Health (Narkomzdrav) in their study of 138 heavy industrial tasks. The results of the study suggested that there were no sanitary-hygienic reasons or concerns related to levels of illness, traumatism or the economic effectiveness of labour why women should not be employed in a whole range of tasks in heavy industry. Developments in technology and mechanisation, it was argued, facilitated an expansion in the range of jobs in which women could be employed.[40]

The early rapid expansion in the numbers of women in paid employment was achieved largely through the recruitment of new groups of workers to industry, particularly urban housewives and school leavers, many of whom had no previous experience of paid employment. Former housewives constituted around 30 per cent of the women entering production at this time.[41] New women workers were also recruited from amongst the peasantry and national minorities, who similarly had little experience of industrial employment. Such women were often very young, had very low levels of professional education, literacy and technical training and little or no previous experience of paid employment. A report on the recruitment of women workers in the Russian republic during 1931 noted that 63 per cent of new female trade union members were under 23 years of age.[42] Women were, therefore, often relegated to unskilled tasks and their labour remained undervalued in relation to men's.[43]

Women undoubtedly also often had to contend with a hostile reception from their male colleagues in the workplace. A 1932 report on the recruitment of women workers to the 'Dinamo' factory in Moscow noted that the factory committee had not taken the plans seriously.[44] A quota system was introduced in an attempt to secure places for female workers, particularly young women, on special technical training pro- grammes, but these quotas were not always adhered to. Enterprise managers were responsible for drawing up lists of women to be specially trained for more highly skilled work, but adherence to this policy was often tokenistic. In a study of shopfloor politics, Goldman has noted that:

> women were passed over for training and promotions and subject to vicious abuse when they entered 'male' shops or apprenticeships. Men frequently refused to work with women, asserting that newcomers did not belong in certain jobs or sections of factories.[45]

Contemporary official reports and writings about women workers often noted the favourable attitude towards work wit- nessed amongst the female labour force.[46] Such an attitude was well encapsulated in a speech by a Ukrainian representa- tive at the All-Union Trade Union Conference on Work Amongst Women in February 1931. Yanovskaya noted that 1.5 million (sic) women were now being recruited to work in industry and that this was nothing to be afraid of: 'we have an appetite, the time has come to eat'![47] Women workers were frequently reported as being more disciplined than men. Generally, lower levels of labour turnover and higher levels of productivity were reported for women workers. Women took less days off work through ill-health, even when taking into account absence due to pregnancy in some cases, and unspeci- fied absenteeism.[48] Women were also often reported to be keen participants in the work campaigns of the early 1930s and were actively engaged in socialist emulation and shock brigades. However, at the same time, it should also be noted, women were also still reported to have lower levels of literacy than their male colleagues.

Table 3.4 provides data for the expansion of female employment, in absolute numbers and proportion of the total labour force constituted by women, including white-collar employees, for the period 1929–37.

The distribution of the female labour force by different sec- tors of the Soviet economy changed significantly during the First and Second Five-Year Plans. Shortfalls in the planned recruitment of women to industrial production in the Russian

Table 3.4   Employment of Women in the
National Economy, 1929–37

	No. (in '000s)	Percentage
1929	3304	27.2
1930	3877	26.7
1931	4197	26.9
1932	6007	27.4
1933	6908	30.5
1934	7204	31.7
1935	7881	33.4
1937	9357	35.4

Source: Gosplan SSSR, *Trud v SSSR: statis-ticheskii spravochnik* (Moscow, 1936) p. 25, for 1929–35. For 1937 see Ye. Orlikova, 'Sovetskaya zhenshchina v obshchestven-nom proizvodstve', *Problemy ekonomiki*, July 1940, no. 7, p. 112, which also offers a detailed sectoral breakdown.

republic during the First Five-Year Plan were recorded in the oil industry and machine-building. Shortfalls were also reported in the planned recruitment of young women to training courses in the factory-based training schools.[49] During the period 1929–35 increases in the proportion of the total female labour force by sector of the economy were witnessed particularly in large-scale industry, construction, transport, trade, public catering, education and health.[50] (See Appendix 4.)

The advances made by women in employment in the large-scale industrial sectors during the first three Five-Year Plans were unprecedented. The increase in the employment of women as shopfloor workers in large-scale industry between 1932 and 1939 is set out in Table 3.5.

The data for the proportion of the total labour force in large-scale industry constituted by women (including, there-fore, non-manual employees) offer slightly lower overall fig-ures, but reflect also the very significant expansion of female employment as engineering-technical workers and white-collar

Table 3.5 Employment of Women Shopfloor Workers, 1932–39

	Number	Percentage of all shopfloor workers
1 July 1932	1 699 000	35.1
1 January 1933	1 663 400	35.6
1 January 1934	1 825 600	36.9
1 July 1935	2 245 900	39.8
1 July 1937		41.6
1 July 1938		42.2
1 November 1939		43.4

Sources: 1932–35: Gosplan SSSR, *Trud v SSSR: statistich-eskii spravochnik* (Moscow, 1936) p. 95. 1937–39: Ye. Orlikova, 'Sovetskaya zhenshchina v obshchestvennom proizvodstve', *Problemy ekonomiki*, July 1940, no. 7, p. 114.

employees. Over half of all white-collar workers in large-scale industry by the end of the 1930s were women.[51]

It is clear from these data that the expansion of the female labour force continued throughout the period of the Second Five-Year Plan (1933–37). The Second Five-Year Plan witnessed a net expansion of approximately 3.36 million in the number of women in paid employment.[52] Adult women were recruited from the families of blue- and white-collar workers already in employment. One western authority on Soviet labour policy in the 1930s, Solomon Schwarz, has noted that in reality 82 per cent of all new workers recruited during the years of the Second Five-Year Plan were women.[53]

It was in these years in particular that women came to be employed more widely in the heavy industrial sectors of the economy, notably metallurgy and machine-building and in mining, where there were higher levels of productivity and wages. It has been estimated that women constituted 25.8 per cent of the workers employed in heavy industry by the beginning of 1934.[54] It is also important to note here, however, that although women were being recruited to non-traditional areas of female employment in increasing numbers, the inadequacies of industrial training schemes, amongst other factors, meant that women workers remained concentrated in unskilled and semi-skilled tasks.

By 1936 the recruitment of women workers to the heavy industrial sectors of machine-building and metallurgy had outstripped the number of women recruited to the more traditional light industrial sectors of the textiles and garment trades. The number of women employed in machine-building and metallurgy had increased by 497 000. Over the same period the number of women employed in the textiles and garment industries increased by 389 000. Comparative figures for employment in large-scale industries indicate that by 1936 a slightly higher proportion of women was being employed in metallurgy and mining than in textiles.[55]

During the Third Five-Year Plan (1938–41) the expansion in both the absolute and relative size of the female labour force continued. Official statistics recorded that just under 13.2 million women were in paid employment by 1940. Women workers constituted around 43 per cent of the labour force in large-scale industries, and 39 per cent of the labour force as a whole, by 1940.[56] In this period, to some extent, the Soviet economy was able to build on developments of earlier years so that mechanisation and automation of the production process expanded the range of tasks in which women could be employed. Changes again were particularly significant in the heavy industrial sectors and women came to constitute increasing proportions of the industrial labour force in a number of key sectors of the economy, including metallurgy, timber and paper, mineral extraction and mining and chemicals.[57]

Despite this, in some of these sectors the proportion of the total labour force constituted by women remained relatively low and these areas of industrial employment remained dominated by men. Even by the end of the 1930s women constituted less than a quarter of all workers employed in electric power and in the extraction industries (except peat). Female labour constituted just over a quarter of those employed in ferrous metallurgy. However, in terms of the distribution of the female labour force alone in large-scale industries, it was during the period of the Third Five-Year Plan that a significantly higher number of women came to be employed in metal processing and machine-building than in textiles.

These years also saw a significant expansion in the numbers of women employed in transport and in construction. At the same time, female labour still predominated in a range of light industrial sectors: matches, printing, textiles and the garment industries, shoes and leather, rubber and asbestos, tobacco and a number of the food industries.[58]

The threat of foreign intervention must also be considered as one of the motives behind the expansion in the levels of female employment in this period. Throughout the 1930s women workers were viewed in part as a reserve army of labour, which could be drawn upon to maintain industrial production in a period of international crisis.[59] The growing threat of war towards the end of the 1930s, therefore, undoubtedly influenced the distribution of female labour in the Soviet economy and encouraged the recruitment of women workers to industries with military significance as preparations were made for women to take over the jobs of male colleagues. Specialist training programmes, in the oil industry for example, were designed to encourage women to take on these new tasks.[60] One commentator has argued that 'the fact that women in Soviet Russia were being feverishly trained in peacetime to speed up war production and to replace men in wartime has certainly contributed much to Russia's resistance of Hitler's onslaught'.[61]

4 The Administration of the Protective Labour Laws

The revolutionary year of 1917 greatly enhanced the priority of labour protection in Russia, and particularly for women. From February 1917 the Provisional Government initiated attempts to investigate and improve the poor conditions of work which existed for millions of workers in factories and mines. The earlier debates on the regulation of night work by women were taken up again in this period. The Provisional Government established its own Ministry of Labour to look into questions of labour protection and the Ministry sought to mitigate some of the harsh conditions of work in factories and mines for women and young workers. A number of the wartime initiatives which had allowed for the unregulated expansion of the industrial labour force were retracted. The Provisional Government also established a number of commissions to investigate a range of labour issues but these were largely ineffective.[1]

The Provisional Government attempted to reorganise the Factory Inspectorate and to redefine its work and functions. A conference was held in Moscow in June 1917 at which factory inspectors debated their future constitution, powers and responsibilities.[2] However, the efforts of the Provisional Government to establish a professionally based organisation for the inspection of factories and the implementation of labour protection measures met with a hostile response and an organised offensive by industrialists and employers. For their part, the soviets objected to Provisional Government plans to appoint factory inspectors from the existing ranks of technical experts and university graduates rather than for them to be elected by the workers themselves.[3]

From October 1917 the Bolsheviks introduced more substantive and far-reaching changes in the content and coverage of the labour protection measures, in the administrative

43

framework for the oversight and implementation of protective labour legislation and in the constitution and terms of reference of the labour inspectorate. As part of the process which determined the legal framework for the protection of labour under the Soviet regime, particular attention was paid to the conditions of work for women in industry and a range of other employments as well as to the regulation of female labour in general. The basic principles which were set out in these early months of Bolshevik rule formed the foundation for Soviet protective labour laws for many decades. The administrative changes which took place with regard to the specific provision of maternity benefits and general maternal welfare issues during the Soviet period were complex and extend beyond the scope of this study.[4]

One of the earliest legislative initiatives of the Bolsheviks was to introduce regulations on working hours and the structure of the working day. The decree introduced a maximum eight-hour day and 48-hour working week for all adult workers. A shorter working day was established for industrial workers in especially difficult jobs, for those employed in unfavourable working environments (in especially high temperatures, for example) and in underground work. The decree also stated that workers should be allowed regular breaks from work for rest and to eat. In respect to female labour, the decree prohibited night work, between the hours of nine o'clock in the evening and five o'clock in the morning, to women and banned their employment in overtime work.[5]

From October 1917 the Bolsheviks assigned the oversight of labour policy to its newly established People's Commissariat of Labour (Narkomtrud RSFSR), which was headed initially by A. Shlyapnikov. The staff also included the prominent women's campaigner Alexandra Kollontai, who, for a short time, was partly responsible for labour protection issues.[6] A separate Department of Labour Protection was set up within Narkomtrud RSFSR in July 1918. By the end of 1918 Narkomtrud had also established a number of local bureaux for labour protection in industrial centres where the numbers of hired workers exceeded 20 000.[7] These local bureaux were to meet regularly, at least once a week, and were given responsibility for overseeing labour regulations in their area. They were to conduct inspections of conditions of work and to make recommendations for the introduction of new protective labour measures, as well as ensuring the implementation of the existing regulations.[8]

During the early Soviet period, the Bolsheviks relied heavily on the trade union organisations to negotiate with the newly elected factory committees and to implement their labour protection measures. This resulted in the formation of the All-Russian Central Council of Trade Unions (ACCTU). The ACCTU held its first conference in January 1918, at which, Carr argues, 'the principle of the subordination of the trade unions to the state' was settled.[9] Each factory committee had its own specialist sub-committee to deal with labour protection issues. The number of representatives serving on the committee, between three and seven, depended on the number of employees at the enterprise. It has been suggested that the work of these committees was not well received in the early years of their existence and that this led to a substantial review of their responsibilities.[10]

The system of factory inspection was reorganised so that priority was now given to improving the conditions of work for the labour force rather than protecting the interests of factory owners as had been the case, it was argued, under the tsarist regime. The old factory inspectorate was officially disbanded and its functions were overhauled. A reorganised Labour Inspectorate was appointed from 18 May 1918. According to a decree issued in the following July, the personnel of the newly established Labour Inspectorate was to be recruited without regard to sex, age or nationality.[11] The portfolio of the inspectorate covered all areas of employment, including factories, mines, agriculture, transport and both the domestic and private sectors. The inspectors were given authority to enter places of work at any time of day or night and were responsible for the enforcement of the protective labour law provisions, the sanitary and hygienic conditions of work and for social welfare issues. It was also responsible for the imposition of fines and prosecution of violations of the protective labour laws. Training courses were soon established for the instruction of the newly appointed inspectors.[12]

In its responsibilities to women workers, the Labour Inspectorate was to enforce the prohibition on the employment of female labour on night shifts, in overtime work and in the restricted occupations, including underground work. The inspectors were also to ensure that maternity provisions were being observed. The administrative provision for the protection of labour was further enhanced in 1920 by the recruitment to the work of the Labour Inspectorate of technical experts, to investigate the causes and ways of preventing industrial accidents, and health specialists, to investigate sanitary and hygienic conditions of work and to provide for medical supervision at enterprises.[13]

The coverage of protective labour legislation was greatly expanded by the Bolsheviks and the laws were codified, initially in 1918 and then subsequently in 1922. On 10 December 1918 the Soviet government issued its first 'Labour Code' (*Kodeks zakonov o trude* – KZoT), which provided an extensive listing of entitlements and obligations at the workplace. The Labour Code reiterated the earlier protective regulations for female labour with regard to hours of work and employment in the restricted occupations. Entitlements to maternity leave and nursing breaks were clearly defined. The 1918 Labour Code also set out, in theory at least, the principle of equal pay for equal work. Responsibility for the oversight of the Labour Code was invested in the Labour Inspectorate. Each inspector or '*inspektris*' was to be nominated by a factory committee and formally appointed by the trade union organisations. Their work was overseen by Narkomtrud.[14] On the whole, however, the 1918 Labour Code remained 'mostly a paper code' as most of its provisions were unenforceable in the chaotic years of civil war and war communism, and the work of the labour inspectors was often frustrated and undermined by the economic circumstances of the period.[15]

As part of the campaigns to restructure the work of the Labour Inspectorate, special attention was paid to the recruitment of women as labour inspectors. It was estimated that there were around 200 properly recruited and fully active labour inspectors in total in 1919,[16] 405 in April 1920 (of whom only 30 were women)[17] and 1000 by 1921.[18] Despite the rapid increase in the total number of labour inspectors, the proportion of female staff remained small and has been estimated at about 5 per cent in this period.[19] However, Soviet

female labour inspectors were responsible for the full portfolio of tasks, in contrast to the many European countries in
which female labour inspectors dealt exclusively with the
protection of women workers and juveniles.

A profile of thirty-five Soviet female labour inspectors published in 1921 revealed them to be relatively young, mostly
falling between the ages of 25 and 29 years. Despite their
positions of responsibility, most of the women had received
only a basic formal education. Many of them had been
actively engaged in the revolution and, as might be expected,
had a strong commitment to Bolshevik policies.[20] Despite the
broad brief given to labour inspectors, it is likely that on a
practical level female inspectors did concern themselves to a
greater extent with the needs of women workers. It was their
responsibility, for example, to ensure that women were transferred from the restricted occupations and to look into ways
of establishing child care facilities in larger enterprises.[21]

The campaigns to recruit more women to the Labour
Inspectorate continued in the 1920s but the numbers
remained small. On 20 February 1923 a circular was issued
which urged the recruitment of more women to the Labour
Inspectorate in industrial centres where female labour constituted over 70 per cent of employees.[22]

On 15 November 1922 the Soviet Labour Code was revised
and reissued.[23] The 1922 Labour Code was to have union-
wide application in the newly created USSR. In theory, it was
designed to offer universal coverage to all hired workers in
industry, agriculture, transport and the military, in permanent, temporary and seasonal employments, and in private as
well as in state enterprises. In effect those not covered by the
terms of the Code included the vast numbers of peasants not
engaged in the hiring and sale of labour and those workers
engaged in individual, home-based production. The Code set
out details of a wide range of labour concerns, including
employment contracts and wage structures as well as protective labour regulations. The 1922 'KZoT' extended the provisions of the 1918 Labour Code and included special sections
on maternity provisions and the protection of female labour,
which provided a detailed listing of regulations for women
workers. In subsequent amendments to the regulations on the
protection of female labour, direct reference was usually made

to the specific clause of the 1922 Labour Code which was being addressed.

During the 1920s the efforts of Narkomtrud and the ACCTU to improve provisions for the protection of labour were supported at both republic and union levels by the establishment of a number of museums, scientific-research institutes and laboratories, and specialist committees. These organisations conducted laboratory investigations into a broad range of labour protection, sanitary-hygiene and technical safety issues. They also conducted field research and surveys of actual conditions of employment for workers in different sectors of the economy. Some of the work of these institutions was designed specifically to look exclusively at questions concerning the protection of female labour. In this period, Narkomtrud worked in conjunction with the People's Commissariat of Health, Narkomzdrav, to investigate ways of improving the environmental conditions of work. The collaboration of these two commissariats provided for the close association of labour protection and health protection measures in the 1920s.

The Central Museum for the Protection of Labour and Social Insurance was established in Moscow in 1923 and on 8 March 1925 it opened a specialist section on 'Women's Labour and its Protection'.[24] The Museum provided displays of different equipment and techniques used in the protection of labour and its exhibits showed different methods which could be used in the prevention of accidents. The Institute for the Study of Occupational Diseases, which became known as the Obukh Institute, was made responsible for investigating questions of labour hygiene in 1923. The Obukh Institute was located in Moscow and provided a scientific basis for research into occupational safety. Its personnel consisted of both research specialists and clinical staff. On this model, similar research institutes were established in other major industrial centres.[25] At this time Narkomtrud began publishing the results of surveys and investigations into labour protection issues in its specialist labour hygiene journal, *Gigiena truda*.

On 11 May 1925 a separate State Institute for the Protection of Labour (with the acronym IOT) was established in Moscow under the authority of Narkomtrud, the People's Commissariat of Health and the Supreme Council of the

National Economy (VSNKh, the administrative body responsible for the management of state industry). This Institute was responsible for conducting wide-ranging research into questions of the protection of labour, including conditions of work, health regulations, safety equipment and environmental matters, such as ventilation, temperature control and lighting. The Institute was headed by S. I. Kaplun, a 28-year-old professor from the Moscow Medical Institute, where he had founded a specialist department on labour hygiene. Kaplun had been a keen advocate of Bolshevik labour policies from 1917, had been actively engaged in promoting labour protection issues and initiating legislative measures since the revolution, and had published a substantial number of important books on this area of work, which included comparisons with European research findings and legislation.

In the mid-1920s a number of specialist committees were established by leading government bodies to deal specifically with issues which concerned women workers. Part of the task of these committees was to investigate the impact of the application of protective labour measures on the level of female unemployment, which was rising disproportionately in this period. One such committee was established by a recommendation of the Central Executive Committee (TsIK) on 9 February 1924. Narkomtrud was charged with the responsibility for organising a commission of leading experts 'on the improvement and study of women's labour in production'. On this basis, Narkomtrud later requested its regional departments to convene regular meetings to discuss women's employment.[26]

Such a commission had been established by June 1924, when it convened its first meeting. The commission was chaired by a representative from the Bolshevik Party women's department (the *Zhenotdel*), Ye. Tsyrlina, and included representatives from, amongst other areas, the Narkomtrud Department of Labour Protection, and from other government bodies, including the administrative body responsible for the provision of social insurance and maternity benefits (TsUSStrakh), the labour exchanges and various local organisations.[27] In a further circular issued on 3 July 1924 Narkomtrud also recommended that similar committees should be established by local labour organisations.[28]

At its first meeting, the Central Commission for the Improvement and Study of Women's Labour in Production confirmed its composition and established its terms of reference. The meeting decided to invite representatives from local and national trade union bodies to their future sessions. The Commission agreed to confine its agenda to the discussion of important issues related to the regulation of female labour. The members of the Commission were all familiar with the contemporary concerns and were assigned the task of providing reports on their own area of expertise over the following four weeks.[29] On the whole, the work of the Commission was directed towards investigating ways of reducing the levels of unemployment amongst women, by improving their skills, for example, and to ensuring the proper application of existing protective labour measures.[30] In the fulfilment of these objectives the Commission was to work closely with the Workers' and Peasants' Inspectorate (Rabkrin).[31]

The report of the representative from the Department of Labour Protection, Vinnikov, outlined the major laws already in existence for the protection of female labour dealing with the restricted occupations, weights of loads and 'menstrual leave'. The numbers of women still employed in hazardous occupations and on night shifts remained important matters of concern, although there was also some discussion of the possibility of reducing the number of jobs prohibited to women workers.[32] There was also obvious concern for the need to reduce the levels of unemployment amongst women, which had provided the topic of the report of the previous week.[33]

Vinnikov's report drew attention to the fact that few women had been recruited to the work of the Labour Inspectorate and stressed the importance of the need to establish an effective female labour inspectorate, especially in the textile districts. The report pointed out that, at this time (1924), of a total of 1210 labour inspectors only 27 were women. The 'inspektris', therefore, constituted only 2.2 per cent of the total number of labour inspectors, despite the fact that, according to Vinnikov's figures, women constituted around 27.6 per cent of the total labour force in production and 38.2 per cent of those employed in the textile industry.[34] Vinnikov's report called on the Bolshevik Party Women's

Department, the *Zhenotdel*, to do more in the active recruitment and training of women for the Labour Inspectorate.
The numbers and proportion of women working in the
Labour Inspectorate do appear to have risen slightly from
this point. In the Russian republic alone, the number of
female labour inspectors increased from 71, or 5.5 per cent
of the total, in December 1926 to 81, or 6.2 per cent, in the
following year.[35]

At republican level, a similar 'Commission for the
Improvement of the Work and Life of Women' was established in the Russian republic on 20 September 1926. This
Commission included representatives from a number of
important commissariats and soviets. Similar organisations
were established in the localities. One of the four main areas
of work set out by the Commission in their overall task
of promoting women's emancipation was identified as an
investigation into legislation and women's rights.[36]

On 26 May 1928 the Central Executive Committee also
established a 'Commission for the Improvement of the Work
and Life of Women of Culturally-backward National Groups',
which was assigned a broad range of responsibilities.[37] By
the later 1920s, however, the central commission on women's
labour and both the RSFSR and USSR commissions appear
to have been far less active in the area of labour protection
issues. During the years of the First Five-Year plan in particular, their work became overshadowed by the discussions
which aimed to establish ways of expanding the numbers of
women in industrial employment, by raising their levels of
training and skill, for example, and expanding the social and
cultural facilities available to women, which would facilitate
this end.[38]

During 1928 specialist appointments were made to the
Labour Inspectorate of officials with particular responsibility
for women workers. A 'Chief Inspector for Women's Labour',
answerable to the director of the Narkomtrud Department of
Labour Protection, was appointed on 7 July 1928. The Chief
Inspector was given responsibility not only for the protection
of female labour, but also for expanding the sphere of
employment for women and overseeing the work of existing
inspectors of women's labour at republican and local levels. The
Chief Inspector was instructed to liaise with the Narkomtrud

scientific-research institutes on questions of women's labour.[39] At the same time Narkomtrud also reviewed the work and responsibilities of labour inspectorate personnel at republican and local levels who had been appointed to oversee female labour issues.[40] A few days later, Narkomtrud issued a circular to the commissions on women's labour in the union republics requesting the appointment of labour inspectors throughout the country with special responsibilities for women workers. This decree was signed by E. S. Serina, as the new Chief Inspector for Women's Labour.[41]

Further steps to improve the effectiveness of the Inspectors for Women's Labour were taken in the following year. On 4 April 1929 a circular 'on the work of the Inspectors of Women's Labour' was issued. This circular set out their responsibilities with regard to labour protection, increasing the number of women in productive employment, the reduction of female unemployment and the further study of female labour. The inspectors were instructed to work closely with the research institutes and scientific laboratories to investigate the impact of various professions of women's physical organisms, particularly with regard to women's reproductive and maternal functions, and the comparative productivity of female labour. The inspectors were also instructed to work in conjunction with the trade union organisations on these issues. Serina signed the circular as the Deputy Director of the Narkomtrud Department of Labour Protection.[42]

A subsequent circular, issued on 20 April 1929, made the Inspectors for Women's Labour responsible for ensuring that pregnant women and nursing mothers were not employed on night shifts in the Russian republic. The inspectors were also instructed to pay particular attention to the work of women in heavy industrial sectors so that the transfer of female labour from the identified restricted occupations should not adversely affect production, nor was it to lead to a reduction in the overall numbers of women in employment.[43]

The central trade union body, ACCTU, in addition to being responsible for the implementation and enforcement of labour protection laws at enterprise level, was also much involved in the legislative debates and research into the protection of female labour in the 1920s. The ACCTU worked closely with Narkomtrud and the scientific-research institutes in overall policy formulation and conducted its own surveys into the conditions of employment for identified groups of women workers, including in the heavy industrial sectors of the economy, such as metallurgy and mining.[44]

By the middle of the 1920s the question of the protection of female labour was a contentious issue both for trade union officials and representatives of women workers. A discussion of the impact and even the utility of the protective labour laws for women workers took place at the VI Trade Union Congress in November 1924. Shmidt, the People's Commissar for Labour, called for a revision of the existing laws on the protection of female labour and one female delegate argued that what was needed to improve women's working lives was less protection and more jobs.[45]

The work of the trade unions on labour protection issues was divided between the social-cultural and tariff-economic sectors of the ACCTU by the end of the 1920s. The social-cultural sector discussed such issues as the supply of specialist protective clothing, which was generally regarded as unsatisfactory, and attempts to reduce the amount of overtime worked by women, which remained too high in their opinion. The tariff-economic sector discussed such issues as funding for maternal welfare and the provision of child care facilities. However, much of the work of these sectors by the beginning of the 1930s seems to have become concerned less with labour protection issues and more with the extension of social and cultural facilities to ease the accommodation of women into the industrial labour force. For example, at a meeting of the ACCTU social-cultural sector held on 13 August 1930, one representative, Uvarova, stressed the close links between improvements in everyday living conditions, productive work and the protection of labour.[46]

The ACCTU also organised a number of important union-wide meetings and conferences to discuss issues relating to women workers, including labour protection. For example, the II All-Union Meeting on Work amongst Women, 25–31 June 1928, discussed the impact of economic rationalisation measures on the protection of female labour and women's employment more generally.[47] Delegates at this meeting called for the trade unions to take action to reduce the number of female redundancies and dismissals. At the same time the meeting also called on the trade unions to ensure the proper enforcement of protective measures with respect to pregnant women and nursing mothers, where they were regarded as most necessary.[48]

In February 1931 the ACCTU organised a major 'All-Union Trade Union Conference on Work Amongst Women'.[49] One of the speeches on the opening day of the conference was given by E. S. Serina, who, whilst advocating the rapid expansion of female employment in industry also cautioned against the engagement of women workers in tasks which were potentially injurious to their health.[50] In addition, the conference also heard reports and speeches from a number of other leading figures in the area of female labour protection, including representatives from the scientific-research institutes and local trade union organisations. A wide range of issues were discussed, including the weights of loads to be transported and carried by women and the employment of women as tractor drivers, in the mining industry and in heavy physical labour more generally.[51] The conference also discussed the reorganisation of the work of the trade unions in respect to labour protection issues.

The Labour Inspectorate was overhauled in 1931. Thousands of voluntary inspectors for the protection of labour (*obshchestvennyi inspektor po okhrane truda*) were appointed at enterprise and local level from 30 June 1931 to supplement the work of the officials appointed by Narkomtrud. It was anticipated that many thousand such inspectors would eventually be appointed. The new voluntary inspectors were given responsibility for labour protection and technical safety in the workplace. They were workers with first-hand knowledge and experience of conditions of work in individual factories and enterprises and were sometimes able to effect real changes in the organisation of production.[52]

For example, the trade union newspaper, *Trud*, reported that at the 'Krasnyi Bogatyr'' factory the labour inspector, Lapshina, introduced a new conveyor system specifically to ease the work of women with children.[53] Elsewhere, however, it was reported that the innovation of a 'maternity conveyor' (a conveyor belt on which only pregnant women and new mothers were employed) at this factory and another enterprise received a less favourable reception. Women were reluctant to work on this type of production line because it could result in a reduction in their wages.[54]

Trud also reported that the task of inspectors was frequently undermined by administrative obstacles. The success of labour protection measures in the later 1930s was restricted further by the fact that the reorganisation of the Labour Inspectorate had unrealistically envisaged the appointment of hundreds of thousands of 'voluntary inspectors', but there were reported to be 'only around 70–80 thousand' in office by the end of 1934.[55]

The research undertaken by the various scientific-research institutes and the debates conducted at the different committees and conferences on women workers culminated in a number of significant revisions and additions to existing laws on the protection of female labour which were introduced in 1931 and 1932. Overall, the decrees introduced in these years reviewed some of the provisions of the 1922 Labour Code and, except for a number of revisions to the protective measures introduced in the later 1930s and in the immediate post-war period, these remained the basis of Soviet protective labour legislation for women workers until the Labour Code was fully revised again in 1978. Included in the legislation introduced in the early 1930s were two decrees which, it could be argued, clearly defined what was considered to be 'women's work' in the Soviet Union by establishing, firstly, a list of jobs to be reserved predominantly for female labour and, secondly, a separate list of tasks in which the employment of women was officially prohibited.

These decrees also proved to be the last major enactments of Narkomtrud with regard to the protection of women workers. The Soviet regime gave overwhelming priority to rapid industrialisation in the 1930s and this resulted in a significant reduction in the amount of time and money spent on research into labour protection issues and in concern for the implementation of protective measures. Narkomtrud was disbanded on 23 June 1933 and many of its functions were absorbed by the ACCTU, including the oversight of technical safety and industrial sanitation measures.[56] Responsibility for the oversight of labour protection and the management of the Labour Inspectorate was also handed over to the trade union organisation.[57]

It has been argued, however, that in the 1930s 'the trade unions insufficiently fulfilled these important functions'.[58] In a recent study, Rossman has pointed to the weaknesses of the trade unions in this period, stating that they were not widely perceived as a vehicle for the defence of working-class interests and that factory committees often sided with the enterprise managers. He argues persuasively that 'most union representatives knew that their function was to keep the labour force passive and productive'.[59] Complaints sometimes appeared in the press of the lack of attention paid to labour protection issues by the trade unions and of the frequent infringements of the protective labour laws by enterprise managers.[60]

The work of the research institutes also came under review. Some of the institutes were criticised for failing to undertake an adequate amount of work, despite having an extensive staff at their disposal. A number of the research institutes for the protection of labour were closed down in the mid-1930s and some of their employees were transferred to the Labour Inspectorate.[61] The work of many of the various laboratories for the protection of labour was rationalised and relocated to regional research institutes, whilst other laboratories were closed down altogether.[62] It is important to note, however, that not all of the research on the protection of labour was terminated. Research continued to be undertaken by at least two of the established institutes, in Moscow and Khar'kov.[63]

As noted earlier, the ACCTU itself appears to have given little attention to the issues of labour protection and inspection by the later 1930s. It has been suggested that such issues had become closely identified with opposition to the goals of the Stalinist regime by this time.[64] The growing threat of war towards the end of the 1930s also undermined any efforts by the trade unions to enforce the labour protection measures and to improve safety standards. Ruble, in an extensive study of Soviet trade unions, noted that 'as the Soviet economy geared up for war, the trade unions grew increasingly powerless against deteriorating working conditions and the widespread use of overtime labour'.[65] The number of complaints in the Soviet press by the later 1930s about the infringement of the protective labour laws for women workers would seem to confirm this claim.

5 Maternity

The provisions for pregnant women, nursing mothers and maternal welfare introduced after 1917 were a major aspect of labour protection. They reflected a concern for the general state of health of female workers, especially those in industry, and of children. At the same time they were imbued with the paternalistic and pro-natalist Bolshevik vision of women's role in the building of socialism. The extensive provisions for maternity protection undoubtedly contributed greatly not only to the accommodation of women into the industrial labour force but also to combatting the high levels of infant, and possibly maternal, mortality that Russia had been experiencing for many decades. The level of infant mortality declined steadily over the period covered by this study. By 1926, infant mortality (that is, the number of babies who died before reaching one year of age per 1000 live births) had already fallen to 174, as compared to 273 in 1913. By 1938 the infant mortality rate was 161 according to official data.[1] The level of maternal mortality declined steadily in the 1920s.[2]

Paid maternity leave and 'nursing breaks' at work offered new mothers time to care for their babies and some degree of financial security. One contemporary commentator noted that 'leave without payment would simply make her position more difficult by forcing her to seek temporary casual work, frequently more burdensome than her own, in order to obtain the necessary means of subsistence'.[3] By the end of the 1920s, Artyukhina, the head of the Bolshevik Party Women's Department (the *Zhenotdel*), speaking at the IV All-Union Congress on the Protection of Maternity and Childhood, argued that 'work on the protection of maternity and childhood is the fundamental basis of all measures of the party in the liberation of women workers and peasants'.[4]

The 1918 Labour Code outlined the provisions, first introduced in December 1917, for paid maternity leave calculated on the basis of the average earnings in the previous three months.[5] Most white-collar workers were entitled to fully paid maternity leave of six weeks before plus six weeks after the birth (allowing a total of twelve weeks, or eighty-four days).

Industrial employees, and from 1920 specific categories of white-collar workers with more taxing jobs, were entitled to leave of eight weeks before plus eight weeks after the birth (allowing a total of sixteen weeks, or 112 days). Maternity leave was additional to ordinary holiday entitlements. The period of leave could be extended if necessary on the production of a medical certificate if the mother had not recovered sufficiently from the birth.[6]

Social welfare payments were extended to women who breast fed their babies and who, as a result, had to reduce their hours of work. A decree of 31 October 1918 established that payments should be made to nursing mothers employed in physical labour for seven months and all other categories of workers for seven and a half months.[7] Provision was also made in the 1918 Labour Code for a nursing mother to be allowed to take a 30-minute break to feed her baby at least every three hours. It was the employer's responsibility to provide hygienic conditions for nursing mothers, especially if the enterprise did not have a nursery. A British delegation to Soviet Russia noted in the mid-1920s that 'this rule has not yet been carried out in all factories, but it is already observed in a large number of them'.[8] The 'nursing breaks' were to be counted as work time. Fines, and possible imprisonment, could be imposed on employers who infringed these provisions; according to Dodge, 'it is believed such penalties were enforced'.[9] Pregnant women and nursing mothers were officially banned from night and overtime work under any circumstances. (See Chapter 6.)

As noted earlier, regulations introduced on 16 November 1920 granted the entitlement to extended maternity leave to a number of female employees in a range of professional occupations, including medical personnel, teachers and educational workers and women employed on night shifts.[10] Further additions were made to the list in the following year, when pharmacists, postal workers and machinists were also granted this entitlement.[11] These provisions were included in the 1922 Labour Code and were reviewed and amended again at the end of the 1920s. According to a contemporary Soviet source, the principal aim of the maternity leave provisions at this time was to protect the health of the newly born child.[12] A completely revised list was subsequently issued in 1930.

Several other measures sought to protect pregnant women and nursing mothers. A decree of 5 September 1920 stipulated that on the notification of pregnancy women were to be transferred to easier tasks. Pregnant women and nursing mothers could also request to be transferred to equivalent employment near to their place of residence.[13] The *Pravda* report on these provisions stated that Soviet Russia, with an infant mortality rate of 260 per 1000, stood in poor comparison with other countries.[14] A decree of 9 November 1920 allowed paid leave to women who had undergone an abortion or experienced a miscarriage, on confirmation by a doctor – three weeks for blue-collar and two weeks for white-collar workers. Leave was also granted to women who had experienced the death of a newborn baby.[15] In accordance with a decree issued on 11 November 1920, nursing mothers were to be given preference in employment near to their place of residence. They were to be transferred to easier work and provided with a child care place near to their home.[16] A decree of 24 November 1920 ruled that pregnant women could not be transferred from their work or sent on business trips without their approval. Women with children under 8 years of age were exempted from labour service if there was nobody else available to look after the child.[17] Another decree, issued the same day, reiterated the ban on overtime and night shifts for pregnant women after the fifth month of pregnancy, and nursing mothers in the first six months after the birth.[18]

All of these provisions were consolidated in the 1922 Labour Code. In contrast to countries which were operating a marriage bar on the employment of women in a number of occupations, employers in the Soviet Union could not refuse to hire women on the grounds of marriage or maternity. The Labour Code regulations also stated, in Article 13, that pregnant women and women with children up to 8 years old, even in instances of redundancy, could only be dismissed in exceptional circumstances and on the agreement of the local labour inspectors. Article 131 reiterated the general ban on the employment of pregnant women from the sixth month of pregnancy and nursing mothers on night shifts and in overtime work. The rights to maternity leave (Article 132) and of pregnant women to transfer to alternative employment

(Article 181), the right of pregnant women, starting from the fifth month of pregnancy, not to be sent on business trips without their consent (Article 133) and the guarantee of regular 'nursing breaks' for a period of nine months and to be counted as part of normal working time (Articles 100 and 134) were all set out in the 1922 Labour Code.[19]

In accordance with the maternal welfare provisions, the financial payments made to a new mother from social insurance funds comprised three separate elements: firstly, statutory maternity benefit equivalent to the mother's full wage for the prescribed length of maternity leave; secondly, a one-off supplementary payment equivalent to one month's salary at local wage rates to meet the immediate costs of the layette, to buy bedding, soap, extra food and clothes, and so on; and, thirdly, a supplementary monthly payment for the duration of the nine-month nursing period calculated at 25 per cent of average local wages.[20] In 1923, the payments to nursing mothers were extended to women who were not breast feeding their babies.[21] In the event of the birth of twins or multiple births the payments were increased. Similar payments were also to be made to unemployed women and the wives of unemployed men, irrespective of their unemployment benefits.[22]

Maternity benefit, therefore, was the only payment calculated on the basis of individual earnings, but only fully insured workers were entitled to receive this. The two supplementary payments were calculated on the basis of uniform local rates and were made available also to the uninsured wives of insured husbands. It has been suggested, however, that the actual payments received in accordance with these two supplementary benefits were substantially below the stipulated local wage equivalents.[23] Eligibility for receipt of the various payments soon came under review.

The provisions of the 1922 Labour Code in respect to maternity benefits and the protection of the rights of pregnant women and nursing mothers were undoubtedly extensive in comparison both with the pre-revolutionary period and with other European countries and the United States at this time. The actual implementation of these measures, however, remained irregular and highlighted the dilemmas faced by many women and their employers in the operation of protective labour legislation. On the one hand, the laws secured significant benefits and privileges for women. On the other hand, the measures placed women in a vulnerable situation in respect to their prospects for finding a job or continued employment once they became pregnant.

A number of employers and enterprise managers, notably in the early 1920s, resisted making such financial payments and practical provisions, or were ignorant of their responsibility to do so. This is demonstrated by the introduction of additional decrees to counter the trend of dismissing pregnant women in order to avoid responsibility for the provision of the benefits. The decree of 8 August 1922 deserves citing in full:

> In view of the recently observed trend of the widespread dismissal of pregnant women in connection with the aim by enterprises of avoiding paying to them benefits for pregnancy and maternity, Narkomtrud decrees:
> Pregnant women may be dismissed only in exceptional circumstances with the agreement secured for each instance of the respective labour inspector or the Conflict Commission of the Department of Labour.[24]

Clearly, such situations frequently engendered conflict between male enterprise managers and young female employees. In some instances employers and labour inspectors were more willing to stick to the letter of the law than to its spirit. In July 1927 the Labour Protection Department of Narkomtrud RSFSR received a complaint from Nadezhda Andreevna Reiss who had been made redundant in May despite the fact that she was four months pregnant. Nadezhda Andreevna explained that she was unmarried and was responsible for the care of her elderly mother. She had no other means of financial support except her wages. She was 25 years old and although she had an employment record stretching back over a decade she had only been in her present job for one year. She had been dismissed, she was told, because of all the workers in her section she had joined most recently.[25] This example also illustrates the potential difficulties which undoubtedly arose not only between employees and female staff, but also amongst women workers themselves if pregnant women were offered specific protection by the labour laws.

The situation of single women with young children was an obvious area of concern for those formulating labour protection measures for women workers in these years. As enterprises shut down or reduced their labour force, this group of women was particularly vulnerable to dismissal. To prevent this, a decree was promulgated on 20 February 1922, under the terms of which the children of women workers made redundant were still to be allowed access to the factory's child care facilities until the mother secured alternative employment.[26] For women workers on the Soviet railways these provisions, and those of 8 August 1922, were reinforced by a circular issued on 6 June 1924.[27] The full provisions of the February 1922 decree were reaffirmed in a decree of 16 July 1925, which stated that 'single women, having children up to one year of age, may be dismissed only in exceptional circumstances with the agreement in each individual instance of the labour inspector'.[28] This provision was further extended by a legal ruling of 27 September 1928 to include women who were the main breadwinner (if their husband was unemployed, for example), whose wages provided the only means of support in families with children up to one year of age.[29]

Official surveys conducted in the years following the introduction of the original maternity leave provisions suggest that an increasing number of women were able to take advantage of these measures. It was reported that the recommendations were being implemented more widely in industries employing a majority of female workers, such as in the textiles and tobacco industries, where the laws proved easier to put into practice. The regulations were more difficult to implement in sectors of the economy where female labour was dispersed.[30] Subsequent studies suggested that in the course of the 1920s more and more women were taking advantage of the legal provisions for maternity leave, the number of days sometimes exceeding those set out in law.[31]

Official reports also suggested that women were being allowed to take time off to feed their babies more frequently than the minimal norms established by the Labour Code.[32] In 1927 the Labour Protection Department of Narkomtrud RSFSR sought to clarify the entitlements to nursing breaks: nursing breaks were to be permitted not only for a set nine months, but for the full actual time of breast feeding; breaks were only allowed to women who were breast feeding, not those feeding by other means; enterprises were encouraged to seek the confirmation of a doctor that breast feeding was taking place; women were entitled to nursing breaks irrespective of their length of service at the enterprise; nursing breaks were to be taken at least every three and a half hours so that women received at least a total of a one hour break during the working day, or they were allowed to finish work one hour earlier.[33]

These official reports may distort the reality. Many employers were resistant to the notion of implementing maternity benefits because of the financial costs involved. Women themselves may also have sought to conceal their pregnancies or opt for abortions if their incomes would be reduced or if they were faced with the possibility of being dismissed, however illegally.

One area of debate in the mid-1920s concerned the entitlement of certain categories of women workers to extended maternity leave. The discussion particularly involved women who were officially classified as professional or white-collar workers (*sluzhashchii* rather than *rabotnitsy*), and were, therefore, entitled to a total of only twelve weeks leave, but who claimed that their work involved a significant degree of physical labour, which would entitle them to the longer period of maternity leave totalling sixteen weeks. A number of different groups of women petitioned the Labour Protection Department of Narkomtrud and the Commissariat of Health's Department of Maternity and Childhood from the mid-1920s, often with the help of their trade union organisations, in order to gain recognition for the physical nature of much of their professional work. The main issue was the interpretation of the term 'physical labour'.

In some cases the Department of Labour Protection was called upon to confirm and verify the entitlement to extended maternity leave. On 5 June 1925 Narkomtrud was asked to confirm the length of maternity leave available to 'comrade Minskaya', a cavalry officer in the Red Army.[34] This was interpreted by the Labour Protection Department as an attempt to reduce the length of maternity leave; the Department swiftly confirmed the need to maintain the entitlement to the extended provisions for this category of workers in view of the physical nature of their employment.[35] A few months later, the Labour Protection Department reiterated the entitlement to a total of sixteen weeks leave for women employed in the militia and as supervisors of corrective labour colonies.[36]

Narkomtrud was also asked to expand the range of professional employments offering entitlement to extended maternity leave. The Commission for the Study of Women's Labour requested that the professional hygiene department should investigate the impact of different types of professional occupations on pregnant women and to study evidence collected at the factory clinics and medical centres.[37] The original list of professional occupations offering entitlement to extended maternity leave was continually reviewed in the 1920s. On 15 July 1924 the list was amended to include additional categories of women working in the health care services.[38] In addition to this, the provision for extended maternity leave for specified categories of women working as telephonists was clarified by a decree of 20 December 1924.[39]

In March 1925 Narkomtrud received a request from B. F. Zorokhovich, an employee at the 'Krasnyi Vostok' textile factory, to consider whether women working on semi-automated machines requiring control by the feet should be entitled to extended maternity leave. In this case, the petitioner was successful in her request. Narkomtrud confirmed the amendment to the list of professional occupations carrying an entitlement to sixteen weeks maternity leave by the addition of 'women, who are working continually throughout the full working day on key operated adding machines'.[40] Stenographers were added to the list on 4 September 1925; and women workers in X-ray departments on 9 September 1925.[41]

By the end of 1926 the administrative body responsible for the provision of social insurance benefits, TsUSStrakh, was called upon by Narkomtrud to review the list of occupations with an entitlement to extended maternity leave. A brief amendment to the original list of professions allowing maternity leave of eight weeks before and eight weeks after the birth was embodied in a decree of 17 November 1927. This decree added three new categories of workers to the list: saleswomen and goods packers in warehouses and trading enterprises; cashiers working on automated tills; and veterinary doctors and doctors' assistants. However, sales personnel at state distribution centres were now removed from the list.[42]

It is clear from archival reports, however, that not all of the requests for inclusion on the reviewed list of professions allowing extended maternity leave were granted. For example, the application by librarians and cashiers working on mechanised tills to be allowed an extra four weeks leave had been refused earlier in 1927.[43] Similarly, the request on behalf of rural school teachers engaged in the eradication of illiteracy was turned down at the beginning of 1928.[44] A more extensive list of projected changes and additions had been drawn up by the middle of 1928.[45] An expanded list of professional occupations offering an entitlement to a total of sixteen weeks maternity leave was finally issued up on 22 December 1928 and this now included thirty-three different jobs in nine separate occupational categories.[46]

With the publication of this list the question of what constituted 'physical labour' now became a hotly debated area of contention between the agencies responsible for drawing up labour protection measures for women and women workers themselves. In the first half of 1929 Narkomtrud appears to have received numerous requests to clarify this point and to take into account the specific working conditions of petitioning groups of workers who considered their jobs to involve a significant amount of physical labour. These jobs included tasks, for example, which involved the operation of mechanised equipment. Women also requested that the physiological demands of their jobs or the dangers posed to their health in employment should be taken into consideration.

Requests from a whole range of different occupational groups were considered, including: laboratory workers at a chemical-bacteriological institute; dental technicians, on the grounds that they worked with mechanised equipment requiring a degree of physical control and in a polluted environment; and teachers, in particular nursery workers whose job involved lifting and carrying young children and feeding and playing with them during a long work day. Teachers in general were reported to suffer high levels of nervous disorders and physiological ailments, including reproductive problems, and were employed in situations where they themselves were easily susceptible to infection.[47] In 1927 the Labour

Protection Department of Narkomtrud RSFSR discussed the possibility of paying financial compensation to teachers who took maternity leave during school holidays.[48]

Women who spent much of their working day standing up were also considered for inclusion on the list, notably here women workers in the glass industry and tram conductors.[49] Health visitors were considered for inclusion on the list on the grounds that they had to climb stairs for much of the day and were themselves also liable to infection. Some of these requests, and others, were granted in a further amendment to the list published on 16 July 1929.[50]

A subsequent decree of 3 August 1930 introduced a new edition of the list of professions carrying entitlement to extended maternity leave. This decree specifically revoked the terms of the 1928 and 1929 amendments and additions and introduced slight changes in wording to the two minor decrees published in 1925 which had allowed extended maternity leave for stenographers and women employed in X-ray departments. The new list now included sixty-seven specifically identified occupations in nine separate occupational groups. By the terms of this decree, women who had previously been entitled to maternity leave of only six weeks before plus six weeks after the birth, who were still on maternity leave and had, therefore, not yet returned to work, could immediately take advantage of the extended amount of maternity leave if their occupation was included on the newly revised list.[51] In later years, several new occupations were added to the revised list, including postal workers and hairdressers on 11 April 1935.[52]

However, as has already been noted in respect to the unlawful dismissal of pregnant women and single mothers, particularly at times when women were vulnerable to unemployment, many of the regulations designed to protect the rights of pregnant women and nursing mothers could easily be ignored, even by the women themselves. The opportunity to take advantage of extended maternity leave, therefore, may not always have been welcomed by all groups of women workers, especially if they were not entitled to receive financial compensation in the form of maternity or sickness benefit.

The transfer to alternative work on notification of pregnancy was not always possible. In 1929, in a letter to

Narkomtrud RSFSR, L. Murasheva Sokolova, a ballet dancer, complained that she had been advised by a doctor not to dance after the fifth month of her pregnancy, but had been denied sick pay to support herself at this time.[53] Undoubtedly also, some women felt disadvantaged by the restrictions imposed on the employment of pregnant women and nursing mothers, especially in overtime work and on night shifts. Yet this was often only partly due to the potential loss of earnings. In the textile industry, for example, many women refused to accept the official ban and continued to work at night. (See Chapter 6.) Some female workers attempted to conceal their pregnancies and, it has been suggested, others may have even resorted to abortions in order to continue working.[54]

A number of different attitudes towards maternity leave are reflected in the following short extract from 'The Womenfolk: Factory Sketches' written by Ekaterina Strogova and published in 1927. On the one hand, the pregnant worker in the story identifies 'total equality' with the complete absence of special provisions and privileges for female workers. Her co-workers, on the other hand, reinforce the official view that the health of the child is of paramount concern:

'I'm going to ask to go to the tie shop', cheeps skinny little Varka, with her short, birdlike little head: a Party candidate. She's pregnant: her huge belly rests on her knees. But pregnancy is not spoiling her looks.

'You're not going anywhere, big-belly! You'll most likely be going on leave in a month.'

'Oh, you swine!' Varka goes pale. She's a mean little bitch herself, when it comes to it. 'Soon as I'm pregnant I'm not a person to you any more, you want to peck me to death! Fling it in my face, see if I care: "Big-belly, big-belly". I don't want maternity leave. I'm a totally equal worker and I'm going to work right up until the birth. You'll see. I'll be standing by my machine.'

'Fool, you'll be the death of the child!'

A bitter sense of insult eats Varka. It's tough enough being pregnant. All those months absent from the workers' ranks! But it's even worse when you discuss the changes with everyone and suddenly feel how helpless you are.

'It's all right, Varka dearie! We've all been through it, after all, we're womenfolk, too. But then what joy you'll have when you give birth, and the baby will be so healthy,' Panya consoles her.

Varka is 26. She's been married since she was 17. And she's given birth every year since, nine times in all. But her children don't survive: they live a few months and die. But she, ever the mother and the mourner, hasn't lost hope: she doggedly keeps giving birth.[55]

Eligibility for the receipt of maternity benefits was critically assessed by the providers of social insurance payments in the 1920s.[56] From 13 January 1927 the payments of the supplementary layette and nursing allowances were restricted to women (or wives of insured husbands) who had been in employment for at least six months during the year preceding the birth. A few months later, from 19 May 1927, payments were only made to those with an income under the fixed maximum established for the receipt of sickness benefit.[57] On 28 December 1927 the eligibility for receipt of income-related maternity benefits was restricted to women (or those with insured partners) who had been in employment for at least six months in the year before taking maternity leave. This criterion was temporarily removed in 1931.[58] On 11 August 1931 the maximum wage in order to be eligible for the receipt of the supplementary maternity payments was set at 300 rubles per month.[59]

The criteria for eligibility for receipt of maternity payments and benefits continued to be debated in the 1930s. In 1932 Narkomtrud reached an agreement with the social insurance administration for the provision of higher rates of supplementary maternity payments to new mothers in selected factories, where the current provision was felt to be insufficient to meet their needs. Lump sum payments for the purchase of baby clothes, cooking items, wash tubs, and so on, were to be paid during the first two months after the birth. The level of benefit was dependent on the category of work in which the new mother was employed. Higher levels of benefit were allocated to areas of work where large numbers of women were employed and to women working in more difficult occupations, in textiles and heavy industry for example. The lowest level of benefit was to be paid to white-collar workers and women not in paid employment. After the first two months regular monthly payments on a fixed level were to be paid to all nursing mothers.[60]

From 17 April 1932 full maternity benefit came to be dependent on length of service. Henceforth, statutory maternity benefit was only to be paid to women (or the wives of insured workers) who were members of a trade union and who had been in employment for a minimum of three years, having spent at least two years in their most recent job. Other workers were to receive a reduced payment. The receipt of supplementary payments also came to be dependent on length of service, set at four months for shock workers, engineers and technicians, eight months for other trade union members and twelve months for all other workers. At the same time supplementary payments were no longer to be calculated according to local rates, but were set as uniform sums of 32 rubles for the layette and 5 rubles per month for the nine-month nursing period. The supplementary payments were increased on 27 June 1936 to 45 rubles for the layette and 90 rubles for the nursing period.[61] It should be noted that prices had risen considerably during the previous few years.

The entitlements to paid maternity leave and financial benefits were further restricted towards the end of the 1930s. Yet even before these more restrictive changes were introduced, reports began to appear in the Soviet press of the violations of the rights of pregnant women and working mothers. It is clear from the number of complaints reported in the Soviet newspapers and journals in the 1930s that many of the provisions designed to protect the rights of working mothers were being ignored. Solomon Schwarz, in an extensive study of labour in the Soviet Union in this period, has noted that although such complaints may not have been common neither were they accidental. Such incidents, he argues, proved symptomatic of trends in labour protection in the 1930s:

> The argument that these conditions were not general cannot minimize their tragic significance. They were certainly not the rule; in many plants, such abuses were unknown.

But neither were they accidental. They were the natural consequence of changes which the whole Soviet labor protection system underwent in the 1930s, and to this extent they were representative of the general trend.[62]

Newspaper articles and reports in magazines and journals suggested that pregnant women were experiencing difficulty in being hired for work and were not being transferred to easier tasks by their employers on notification of pregnancy. This led some women to terminate their pregnancies. Such reports were critically reviewed and commented on by western observers of Soviet employment practices in the 1930s. For example, British Foreign Office documentation for July 1935 notes that:

> One of the boasts of the Soviet system is the care taken of workers before and after childbirth. The press recently published an interesting sidelight on this claim. In an article entitled 'At the Doors of the Abortaria' attention was drawn to a practice that seems to be prevalent in most workshops of insisting that women seeking employment must produce a doctor's certificate that they are not 'enceinte'. If they are, they are refused employment. After a vain endeavour to find work in several places the women go to the 'Abortaria' and have the child removed, whereupon they once more enter the ranks of the acceptable. The managers of enterprises maintain they have no choice in the matter. They must show as much profit as possible, and obviously, if they take on all and sundry, the enterprise becomes liable for the payment of wages while the women are off work, before and after childbirth.[63]

The ambiguities over the operation and terms of the protective labour measures with regard to maternity provisions are reflected in some of the letters printed in the trade union newspaper, *Trud*, which for a short while ran a section entitled 'Consultation on Labour Law'. A selection of queries and answers from this column demonstrates the diversity and complexity of issues in connection with the judicial implementation of the maternity provisions. These examples also demonstrate the resistance on the part of enterprise administrators which was experienced by many women workers in trying to secure their full legal entitlements to maternity leave and associated benefits. Examples of the infringements of the rights of pregnant women and nursing mothers were also reported in the popular women's magazine, *Rabotnitsa*, and the trade union journal, *Voprosy profdvizheniya*.

In July 1934 *Trud* was asked to clarify the entitlement to maternity leave for a woman who, on the eve of leaving work to begin her statutory period of maternity leave, had fallen over at work and had subsequently lost the baby in a miscarriage.[64] The question revolved around whether this woman was still entitled to the full amount of post-birth maternity leave. The reply to the letter indicated that women who experienced a miscarriage during the first 196 days (twenty-eight weeks) of pregnancy would be considered for temporary leave and associated benefits in accordance with ill-health regulations as stipulated by their medical doctor. After this period, however, women who had experienced a miscarriage were entitled to the full amount of maternity leave, in this instance 56 days (eight weeks) for a shopfloor worker. Cases were reported elsewhere of enterprise managers who refused to allow working mothers to return to their job at the end of their maternity leave and, under threat of dismissal, these women were forced to accept lower paid work. In a further example, the worker Solov'eva wrote to *Rabotnitsa* that her employer complained that she was misusing her work time when she took her statutory nursing breaks. The Rates and Conflicts Commissions, who dealt with workers' complaints in this period, did not always decide in the women's favour.[65]

In November 1934 *Trud* published a short article by Kletskina, the labour inspector at the 'Krasnyi Treugol'nykh' factory in Leningrad.[66] Kletskina complained that 'the relationship of the adminstration with working women is heartless'. The director of one of the departments, Khodash, did not want to employ women who were nursing mothers. The situation in other departments at the factory was little better. No special place had been identified where women could feed their babies. The report also noted that there were attempts to reduce the wages of women taking statutory 'nursing breaks'. One female shock worker, Naezdnikova, had received wages of 132 rubles a month before the birth of her baby, but once she had become a nursing mother she was being paid only 86 rubles. Kletskina complained that tens of qualified women workers at the 'Krasnyi Treugol'nykh' factory, having become mothers, were being forced to leave the factory.

Not all of the articles, however, reported only bad news; at least some offered mixed blessings! In a few areas substantial improvements were noted in the services and provisions being made for pregnant women and nursing mothers. It is important to note, however, that these were the results of an important state-directed pro-natalist drive in the mid-1930s. In March 1936 *Trud* reported that the establishment of a special 'women's hygiene room' at the 'Krasnyi Perepletchik' factory in Rostov-on-Don in the previous November had significantly improved the maternity and child care services at the enterprise. Since that date, the article noted, there had not been a single instance of a reported abortion.[67] In the following month *Trud* praised the Soviet Union's extensive network of child care institutions which had cost millions of rubles to establish.[68] The article pointed out that many factories had set aside rooms so that nursing mothers could feed their babies at work.

The example of the 'Kutuzov' factory in Gorkii, however, demonstrated just how effectively women were being provided for in reality. Most of the 2000 workers at the factory were women. There was one room for nursing mothers attached to the nursery and this was reported as working well. The bad news, however, was that the room was available to far from all working mothers because only those with children in the nursery were allowed to use it. This meant, the article argued, that women working at the factory either had to leave their babies for seven or eight hours a day without feeding them themselves, or the women had to give up their jobs.

One worker, Fadeeva, was reported as having left the factory after four years of employment there because the nursery would not accept her child and she had no place at work to take her nursing breaks. Occasionally also, the article noted, these rooms were open only during the first shift so that no provision was made for working mothers on the second and third shifts. In order to secure places on the first shift (and thereby the hope of a place in the nursery) some working mothers, such as Migunova at the 'Kutuzov' factory, had had to transfer to less skilled jobs and consequently had incurred a loss of pay.

The *Trud* reports further highlighted the dilemmas faced by many pregnant women in taking advantage of their full legal entitlements in respect of welfare provisions and to payments of maternity and supplementary benefits. In March 1936 in an article entitled 'Deplorable Lack of Coordination' *Trud* reported that some women were reluctant to notify employers of pregnancy and to transfer to easier work as they were entitled to do by law after the fifth month of pregnancy.[69] This provision would allow the pregnant worker to be employed for at least two months in the alternative job before taking maternity leave. These 'easier tasks', however, were often paid at a rate lower than their previous earnings. Subsequent calculations for the payment of maternity benefit were made on the basis of average earnings for the two full calendar months before taking leave. It is important to note, however, that the original decree stipulating the right to transfer to easier work after the fifth month of pregnancy also guaranteed this transfer at the previous rate of pay. This article would suggest, therefore, that this earlier provision was not commonly known or practised. Many pregnant women obviously did not want to see any reduction in their entitlement to benefit under such circumstances.

The issue of the level of payments for maternity benefits was raised again later in the year. In October 1936 *Trud* published an article by Z. Mokhov entitled 'In the Interests of Mothers or at the Convenience of the Accountant'.[70] Mokhov reported the difficulties experienced by one worker, Maria Afanas'evna Karakulina, in securing her maternity benefit. After Karakulina had given birth she approached the accountant at her factory for payment of her maternity benefit. The accountant argued that Maria was not entitled to maternity benefit because she was already in receipt of a substantial income, over 300 rubles. Although Maria herself only earned 200 rubles a month, her husband was paid 450 rubles, totalling 650 rubles in all, twice the maximum level for receipt of the supplementary maternity payments. The accountant argued that the couple was ineligible for benefit as they already had a substantial income. Maria, however, turned for advice to a legal representative who clarified the point that only the mother's own income was to be taken into account in calculating payments of maternity benefit and that the family income should be of no concern to the factory committee responsible for dealing with such matters.

The article, however, proceeded to highlight the anomaly of such a ruling by identifying the circumstances of another worker in a different factory. Mokhov pointed out that the law was quite right in taking only the income of the mother into account in calculations of maternity benefit but pointed also to the problems which this may have caused for single mothers or for a married woman with children whose husband did not work. The chair of the factory committee at the 'Nepreryvka' factory in Moscow had pointed out that a worker at their enterprise earned between 324 and 350 rubles a month but her husband was not employed. The couple already had two children, aged 6 and 3, and they were expecting their third child very soon. The mother, however, would not be entitled to the benefits because she herself was paid over 300 rubles.[71]

In contrast to this, the *Trud* article noted yet another example where a worker at the very same factory was paid 280 rubles a month and her husband, who worked elsewhere, earned 1250 rubles a month. The couple had only one child but were technically eligible for the supplementary payments. The chair of the factory committee had tried to reconcile the two cases by calculating the average income for each member of the family. In the first example this had totalled 70 rubles for each member of the family, but in the second example this had resulted in an income of over 500 rubles per month for each family member. The article concluded that a variety of criteria needed to be taken into account in calculating entitlement to benefits so that payments were made to families which most needed financial support, not purely on the basis of simple guidelines of entitlement.

A few months later, an article in *Voprosy profdvizheniya* also took up the issue of entitlement to benefits.[72] This article suggested that only the income of the parent who was first to register the claim for maternity allowance should be taken into account when assessing the claim. In this event, therefore, if only one of the parents earned below 300 rubles, then the couple would still be entitled to benefits, irrespective of gross income and the number of children in the family.

This issue was soon resolved. According to a decree of 23 March 1937, from 1 April 1937 maternity benefits were to be paid irrespective of income limitations. This was also to apply to women already on maternity leave.[73]

In 1935 a period of statutory maternity leave was introduced for women workers on collective farms. Female collective farm workers were entitled to leave of one month before plus one month after the birth of a baby during which period they were to receive a maternity payment equivalent to half of their usual income.[74] During the following year official Soviet social policy reflected a significant shift in attitudes in the direction of pro-natalist visions of family life and women's reproductive functions.[75] Abortion was criminalised and this undoubtedly had repercussions on women's working lives.

In accordance with a decree issued on 27 June 1936, the period of paid maternity leave for all industrial workers and professional employees was set at sixteen weeks, thereby equalising the entitlement of blue- and white-collar workers (section 2, point 8).[76] In addition to these measures, the amount of maternity benefit was increased (section 2, points 5 and 6). A pregnant woman, on transfer to easier work, was to be paid a wage equivalent to the average of her previous six months' earnings.[77] From 5 October 1936 it was also made a criminal offence to refuse to hire pregnant women or to reduce their wages in connection with their transfer to easier work (section 2, point 9).[78]

By the later 1930s, however, there was a general tendency to cut back on maternity provisions, especially with the growing threat of war. From 1937 women had to be employed in the same enterprise for at least one year to be eligible for the full maternity provisions. At the end of the following year, on 28 December 1938, the period of paid maternity leave was reduced to five weeks before plus four weeks after the birth, allowing a total of only nine weeks. Women now needed to have worked consecutively for at least seven months before becoming eligible for maternity leave and benefits.[79]

The growing threat of war by the late 1930s meant that increasing demands were placed on the use of female labour in industrial employment, especially as enterprise managers sought to retain normal working practices and to maximise utilisation of available resources and potential output.

This resulted in some of the protective measures for women workers introduced in the previous decade being officially revoked and overruled. For example, a decree published on 19 January 1938 allowed pregnant women from the sixth month of pregnancy and nursing mothers in the first six months of breast feeding to be employed on night shifts in the cotton textiles, knitwear and tobacco industries.[80] This was work from which such women had been specifically excluded in 1929.[81] The 1938 decree was introduced with the intention of ensuring the continued operation of the three-shift pattern of work in these industries. The children of women workers affected by these provisions were to be given priority in access to nursery and child care facilities. Women working on these shift patterns were to be allowed an additional holiday entitlement of one extra day per month.

Further minor adjustments were also made to working practices by this decree. Nursing mothers were still entitled to take the statutory 30 minute 'nursing break' at the end of their shift, but now the worker on the next shift was allowed to start work 30 minutes earlier and to be paid for this as overtime work. Directors of tobacco and *makhorka* factories, however, were still instructed to transfer pregnant women after the fifth month of pregnancy from work on crumbling machines to alternative easier work. The number of machines operated by pregnant women in other areas of the production process was to be reduced and the output norms for certain categories of other pregnant workers were to be reduced by 15–20 per cent. Controls were to be placed on the lifting of tobacco by pregnant women. Pregnant women transferred to alternative employment under these regulations were to be guaranteed payment equal to the average of their wages received in the previous six months and in accordance with the proportional fulfilment of their output norm in the new task. The over-fulfilment of norms was also to be rewarded.

According to reports of complaints printed in *Trud* in 1937, the restrictions on the employment of pregnant women were often ignored. It was reported that of twenty pregnant women at one enterprise, twelve had not been granted the provisions sanctioned by law. Employers, it was argued, disregarded the stipulations which required the transfer of pregnant women to lighter duties. Nothing was done when the complaints were registered at the local Public Prosecutor's office.[82] It was reported that many enterprises did not have a designated space for nursing mothers and women were forced to feed their babies on the street.[83]

In the following year, the popular women's magazine, *Rabotnitsa*, published an article which reaffirmed these complaints. It was claimed here that the laws protecting women as workers and as mothers were misinterpreted and ignored, and that party and trade union officials did nothing to counter this tendency. At one machine-building enterprise the following infringements of the protective labour laws were recorded: nursing mothers were not receiving full benefits; pregnant women and nursing mothers were still working on night shifts, having refused transfer to day-time shifts and easier work through fear that their wages would be reduced; incidences of reduced wages were also reported, especially where women had been transferred to jobs paid by piece-rates; and pregnant women were not permitted the full extent of their maternity leave, particularly antenatal leave, sometimes because the women themselves had not given sufficient notification of their pregnancy. Here it was pointed out that there were not enough doctors to attend to women's needs. Other infringements of the protective labour laws, unrelated to the maternity provisions, were also recorded.[84]

Despite the extensive legal provisions for maternal welfare introduced in the Soviet Union before the Second World War, these regulations were not always rigorously adhered to or enforced. Early Bolshevik legal enactments proved insufficient to undermine prejudices against working mothers on the part of some employers. The maternal welfare provisions were often expensive to implement. Moreover, it appears that women themselves often flouted the terms of the more restrictive elements of the laws and were reluctant to assert their rights if doing so would put at risk their continuation in employment or would result in a reduction in wages. By the end of the period under review, social and legal changes had come to identify women increasingly with motherhood, and as such working mothers continued, officially at least, to be offered special privileges by the protective labour laws.

6 Hours of Work

One of the earliest initiatives of the Bolsheviks when they came to power in October 1917 was to introduce regulations which limited hours of work. Four days after the Bolsheviks came to power, on 29 October (11 November) 1917, a decree introduced a universal prohibition on the employment of women in night work. In practical terms this was defined as falling between nine o'clock in the evening and five o'clock in the morning. Overtime work by women was also banned.[1] These prohibitions were reiterated in the 1918 Labour Code, which stated that women should be excluded from employment under such conditions in any circumstances. At the same time a seven-hour shift was established for night workers, compared with eight hours for daytime shifts.[2] The intention at this time was that the employment of women on night shifts would be reduced steadily and that it would be totally eliminated over the following three years.

The stringent regulations on the hours of work for female labour, despite their limited application in reality, had some unfortunate consequences. A Soviet commentator, Astapovich, has noted that in the tumultuous economic circumstances of the immediate post-revolutionary period, such protective measures helped to foster an unfavourable attitude towards working women in general in some enterprises and that women soon became an easy target for dismissal at this time. Astapovich cited a number of examples of married women being dismissed from work altogether in 1918, after the ratification of the night work regulations. The metallurgical workers' trade union successfully protested against this practice in their industry and secured the return to work of women made redundant. In fact, many trade unions and local workers' organisations sanctioned the employment of female labour on night shifts despite the legal prohibition.[3]

The Bolsheviks quickly came to realise that such a stringent prohibition was neither practical nor desirable. It soon became obvious that a whole range of essential services which were reliant on the employment of female labour around the clock could not function properly without the employment of women on night shifts. On 4 October 1919 the formal prohibition was revised by the introduction of a decree, which permitted the employment of women at night temporarily in a number of specified occupations, thus making provision for the continuous operation of essential services. These were to be jobs where women formed an important element in the labour force, such as medical personnel and communications staff, and which could not operate effectively without the continuation of a night shift.[4] Further adjustments to lift the prohibition temporarily could be made with the consent of the respective trade union organisation and on agreement with Narkomtrud. The consent was also required of the local trade union committee for the protection of labour and the labour inspectorate.[5]

In many respects the limitations of night work by women in most industrial and professional occupations were difficult to enforce during the chaotic years of war communism and civil war. For example, a decree introduced on 25 December 1919 permitted women to be employed for up to six hours on night shifts in the tobacco industry when the erratic supply of electricity disrupted daytime production.[6] One young Bolshevik reformer, S. I. Kaplun, suggested that the requests for exemption from the restrictions on night and overtime work by women in these years were anyway only a mere formality.[7] A Soviet commentator on the legislation also argued that many workers were unaware of the existence of such laws or did not understand the terms of the decrees. They had little time or desire to find out about their provisions.[8]

A few days after the decree on the tobacco industry, on 29 December 1919 the restrictions were relaxed on the employment of women in overtime work in state institutions. The decree stated that female labour could be employed in overtime work temporarily if the local labour inspectors and trade union organisations were satisfied that it was impossible to extend any further overtime work by male employees.[9] However, the prohibition on the employment of pregnant women after the fifth month of pregnancy and nursing mothers in overtime work and for both pregnant women and nursing mothers at night was reiterated and reinforced by two separate decrees issued on 24 November 1920.[10]

In a study of contemporary problems of female labour in the early 1920s, Kaplun, who was active in the campaigns to introduce legislative protection of female labour, argued that overtime work by women was rarely used in industrial sectors of the economy but was a common feature of rural employment. He offered an optimistic picture of the elimination of night shift working by women at this time and put forward medical evidence to support the further implementation of the prohibition. In the second edition of his study, published in 1925, Kaplun calculated that women constituted 45 per cent of workers in industries operating a night shift but comprised only 7 per cent of those actually working at night, and these were in such sectors as transport, medical-sanitary services and mining enterprises.[11]

In support of his argument, Kaplun cited a study conducted in 1920 in Odessa, which revealed that the rates of illness amongst female night workers were 50 per cent higher than amongst women working on daytime shifts. In comparison, male night workers recorded a 36 per cent higher level of sickness. Kaplun suggested that if women were to be employed at night it should be in the non-heavy sectors of the economy and in non-hazardous jobs. In industrial enterprises, he argued, predominantly men should work at night.[12] On such evidence Kaplun praised the successes in the implementation of laws on the protection of female labour in regard to the regulation of their hours of work. Another contemporary commentator, Bukhov, also noted that 'soviet law rightly forbids night work to women as it is more difficult'.[13]

The prohibition on night shift employment and overtime work by women was reiterated in Articles 130 and 131 of the 1922 Labour Code, which added that adult women should only be employed in these conditions 'where there is a special need'. Such work was to be considered only under exceptional circumstances and as a temporary measure in tasks specifically identified by Narkomtrud and the ACCTU.[14] In some instances the official prohibition on night work by women was subsequently reinforced by individual decrees. For example, a decree of 9 November 1922, which dealt with night work in bakeries, reiterated the ban on employment of women and young workers at night 'under any circumstances' in Article 8.[15] As a result of such measures, the controversies before the revolution about the regulation of hours of work for female labour were renewed and continued throughout the 1920s, with many women themselves again vociferously opposing the ban on night and overtime work.

The early retractions of the 1922 Labour Code were operative on a sectoral level, and again came into force particularly in service industries which required around the clock operation. For example, a decree of 2 February 1923 reiterated that women were permitted to work temporarily at night as telegraph and telephone operators because of the 'uninterrupted nature of this work' and the difficulties experienced in these tasks of substituting male workers for female employees.[16] It was also argued that this was an area of work for women 'where night duty is necessary and cannot be undertaken by male workers alone' and that 'few men are acquainted with this profession'.[17]

On 27 November 1923 a decree was issued, which, in view of the uninterrupted nature of service in the transport sector and the difficulties experienced in transferring women from night work, permitted women workers to be employed at night in nine different tasks in transportation, largely as cleaners, guards, ticket and luggage cashiers and clerks. The decree maintained the prohibition on the employment of pregnant women, nursing mothers and young workers in these occupations.[18] A subsequent decree, issued on 2 April 1924, supplemented this list with two further categories of permitted employment specifically on the railways, as watchwomen on stations and level-crossings. The decree also noted the temporary nature of these provisions.[19] Women were permitted to work at night as seasonal workers in accordance with a decree passed on 4 June 1926.[20]

Growing concern over the rising levels of female unemployment during the years of the New Economic Policy (1921–28) led to the prohibitive principles of the 1922 Labour Code concerning hours of employment being reviewed so that future retractions would encompass all categories of night work by women. By the mid-1920s some campaigners for the lifting of the ban on night and overtime work were beginning to question the general benefits of laws prohibiting such work by women. There was also some recognition of the fact that the alternatives for female labour to employment in night and overtime work offered no more favourable conditions of work. These alternatives, as women themselves pointed out and as a number of contemporary commentators were beginning to recognise, could, indeed, be grim.[21]

On an informal level at least, the restrictions on night work by women were beginning to be relaxed by 1924. In fact, despite the official prohibition on night and overtime work by female labour embodied in the 1922 Labour Code there is much anecdotal evidence to suggest that women continued to be employed widely under such circumstances throughout the 1920s and 1930s, although the extent of this would be impossible to quantify, and that women were often the most active opponents of the prohibition. For example, in a short article published in 1925 in *Rabotnitsa*, Lavrova reported that women were employed on night shifts at the 'Vyksun' metallurgical factory'.[22] It is important to note also, however, that night work itself was not without its dangers for women. In her study of the male-dominated printing industry, Koenker has noted that recorded complaints of sexual assault were much more common amongst night shift employees. She has suggested, pointedly, that 'perhaps women who worked at night were considered to be outside the protection of the law'.[23]

A circular issued by Narkomtrud RSFSR on 23 February 1924 clearly illustrated some of the contemporary concerns of the reformers. The circular itself questioned the practical utility of restricting night work by women in circumstances of widespread female unemployment. The protective nature of the prohibition under such conditions, the circular pointed out, was being undermined and that this 'gives rise to justifiable criticism from women that prostitution, hunger and depravation, to which they are doomed by unemployment, have a more pernicious effect on them than night work'. The circular proceeded to indicate that present conditions were also leading to a lowering of qualifications amongst women because when they were transferred to daytime shifts they were being allocated to less skilled jobs or they were otherwise faced with the threat of redundancy.[24]

This circular is important because it set out the instruction that women should not be transferred from night shift production if it would result in their dismissal or their transfer to less skilled employment. Local trade unions and departments of labour were sanctioned to permit enterprises temporarily to allow women to work at night, on the submission of the relevant supporting documentation, before official confirmation was received from Narkomtrud. As in previous legislative revisions, however, the circular reiterated the prohibition on night work for pregnant women and nursing mothers.

The question of the necessity of night work by women, however, had clearly not been resolved even within Narkomtrud. A few months later, in June 1924, the newly established Narkomtrud Commission for the Improvement and Study of Women's Labour in Production reported that the removal of women from employment both on night shifts and in hazardous occupations was taking place too slowly. The Commission called for the circulation of instructions recommending that women should be transferred immediately from such employments. The meeting also pointed out the need for an increased number of female labour inspectors to be employed, especially in the textile districts, to promote the enforcement of such legislative regulations.[25]

The question of the impact of the prohibition on night shift employment by women on the rising levels of female unemployment was raised at the VI All-Union Trade Union Congress in November 1924. The People's Commissar for Labour, V. V. Shmidt, himself acknowledged that protective labour legislation did not always serve women's immediate or best interests.[26] Melshchenko, a delegate to the Congress from Rostov-on-Don, argued that the low levels of skill amongst women resulted partly from the night work prohibition. In the printing industry, for example, some highly skilled and technical tasks were conducted only on night shifts, from which women were legally excluded. Women's labour, it was argued, was devalued by the ban on night-time employment. In addition to this, extra men had to be recruited to work at night and this could prove expensive to enterprises and disruptive to production.

Melshchenko argued that a relaxation of the prohibition could only prove beneficial for female labour. Women would be able to pay for their own 'crusts of bread' and would not be forced to sell themselves on the streets.[27] In one of the closing sessions, Shmidt proposed a resolution which argued that the prohibition on night work was resulting in women being forced out of jobs and that this contributed towards widespread unemployment amongst female labour. The Congress was called upon to review the existing laws on night work. The trade union organisations and labour inspectors were called upon to pay particular attention to the observed tendency for women to be replaced by men in some jobs.[28]

The revision of official policy on night work, it has been argued, owed more to the practical demands of enterprise managers and to the workers themselves than to any fundamental change in attitude amongst the contemporary Bolshevik reformers. Waters, in her study of family policy and motherhood in the 1920s, has argued:

> It was not that the regime had been suddenly converted to a feminist critique of protectionist legislation and to an appreciation of the ways in which labour policy reflected and reinforced traditional notions of masculinity and femininity. Concessions to managerial prejudices were preferable to the implementation of radical changes in the training and deployment of the female labour force.[29]

It is evident from this that the fundamental legal provisions of the 1922 Labour Code were being gradually eroded from the mid-1920s, allowing increasing numbers of women to work on night shifts and in overtime employment, whilst at the same time officially retaining the prohibition for pregnant women and nursing mothers.

A circular issued by Narkomtrud SSSR on 13 April 1925 upheld the principles of the February 1924 Narkomtrud RSFSR circular on a union-wide basis. This circular argued that in view of the potential for women to be excluded from production, female labour could henceforth be employed on night shifts in all branches of production with the exception of those areas of employment from which women were already generally prohibited because of the hazardous nature of the work. Again agreement was to be sought from the local agencies of labour protection and trade unions and was dependent ultimately on subsequent ratification by Narkomtrud. These revised regulations were to apply not only to enterprises currently working a night shift but also to enterprises where night work was a new element in the production process as a result of the expansion of plant or the opening of new departments. Pregnant women and nursing mothers, however, were to be transferred to daytime shifts.[30] The relaxation of the night work regulations was noted in the report of the British women's delegation to the Soviet Union in the summer of 1925.[31]

Writing during the course of these revisions, however, Kaplun again reiterated his support for maintaining the protective measures on night work by women and observed:

> Throughout last year different opinions were voiced which wanted to subject to theoretical 'revision' even in essence the very question of the utility of the law generally prohibiting the night work of women. Such a position is fundamentally misdirected and cannot be substantiated from any point of view.[32]

Yet Kaplun proceeded to concede that, according to recent research, night work did not have as negative an impact on the female organism as some of the alternative, more hazardous employments. He clearly felt that whilst it was important to avoid a situation where women would be removed from the productive sphere altogether by such legislative regulations, there was still a need to offer some form of protection to female labour. By 1925, however, he seemed to be defeated in his goal of prohibiting women altogether from working at night and on overtime. In future, the enforcement of these restrictions in practice was to apply most strictly only to pregnant women and nursing mothers, who were to be transferred immediately to work exclusively on day shifts. In March 1927 the head of the Labour Protection Department of Narkomtrud RSFSR sent a note to the labour inspectors in Tver which conceded that women should be allowed to work at night, with the exception of pregnant women and nursing mothers and in the restricted occupations.[33]

The regulation of the hours of work for pregnant women and nursing mothers remained an area of contention. A commentary on the protective measures of the maternity provisions with regard to Articles 130 and 131 of the 1922 Labour Code noted that the original statutes did not establish the length of time in which the employment of pregnant women and nursing mothers would be prohibited at night and in overtime work.[34] This had clearly been interpreted in some cases to encompass the entire duration of the pregnancy and time spent in breast feeding. Subsequent decrees also did not always set out the duration of the prohibition for pregnant women and nursing mothers when women had been permitted temporarily to work at night. The provisions of a decree issued on 8 February 1926 established that women should not be employed as domestic nannies or sick nurses at night after the sixth month of pregnancy.[35] In theory, at least, this extended the period in which pregnant women could work at night by one month over the November 1920 provisions. However, no mention was made in this decree of restricting the hours of nursing mothers.

The restrictions on the hours of work for pregnant women and nursing mothers were not clarified until the end of the decade. On the basis of the findings of a government commission into the impact of the seven-hour working day, a decree was issued on 2 January 1929 which introduced amendments to various articles of the 1922 Labour Code. This decree determined the hours of night work as falling between ten o'clock in the evening and six o'clock in the morning. It reiterated the legal prohibition on the employment of pregnant women from the sixth month of pregnancy and nursing mothers during the first five months of breast feeding on night shifts and in overtime work specifically in enterprises operating a seven-hour working day.[36] In the following month, on 22 February 1929, the duration of the prohibition on the employment of nursing mothers on night shifts and in overtime work was extended to six months.[37] Similar regulations were introduced in the Russian republic on 27 May 1929.[38]

The debates on the potentially harmful impact of night work on women workers in general continued into the later 1920s when the scientific-research institutes undertook to investigate this issue. In 1928 the sum of 2695 rubles was requested by the Department of Labour Hygiene to work in collaboration with Moscow State University to conduct research into 'the influence of night work on the organism of women'. The study aimed to highlight the physiological impact of night shift employment on women working in the textile industry. Comparison was to be made of a control group of forty women and men. The proposal included an indication of distribution of expenditure. The money was to be spent in the consultation of specialists, payments for the workers to undergo physiological tests over the course of three months and a final medical examination. There is no indication in the archival reports of whether this money was allocated in reality or of the results of the investigation if such experiments were conducted.[39] However, a number of articles on the topic of the proposed research are to be found in some of the handbooks of the scientific-research institutes and in the journals of the period.

In 1928 the annual plan of work of the Narkomtrud Commission on Women's Labour included a clause to examine how night shift workers spent their non-working hours and leisure time.[40] Earlier studies into workers in the garment industry conducted by Narkomtrud in July 1925 had revealed some interesting but not surprising results. Although women worked in paid employment fractionally fewer hours per week than men, they spent substantially more time on housework and less time sleeping, eating, resting and on hobbies and other activities than men.[41] It is probable that many women who were employed at night also had a range of domestic tasks and family responsibilities which reduced their time available for sleep and rest during the day. It is possible to infer from this also that such demands on women's time during the day would have had a negative impact on their effectiveness in paid employment by reducing their levels of labour productivity and increasing levels of wastage.

Towards the end of the 1920s the debates on the introduction of the seven-hour day and the continuous working week, especially in the textile industry which had a predominantly female labour force, also showed recognition of the specific impact of the legislative regulation of hours of work on the employment of women workers.[42] Some contemporary commentators were sceptical of the utility of the proposed new work regimes and they themselves put forward arguments that set out the limited economic benefits and the potentially negative social consequences of night shift employment.

For example, in an analysis of the impact of the introduction of the seven-hour day in the textile industry, where every third week workers were required to work at night, N. E. Akim, a Moscow-based sanitary inspector, argued that 'the night shift results in the greater fatigue of the worker, in a lower productivity of labour and to a greater level of spoilage in comparison with day time shifts'.[43] Akim proceeded to elaborate a complex plan for the distribution of work hours over the course of a three-week period, which was designed to minimise the necessity for each individual worker to be employed at night whilst, at the same time, maximising the operational capacity of the factory. It was hoped that such a regime of work would allow the textile industry not only to raise labour productivity and reduce levels of wastage, but also to conserve electric energy and significantly protect the health of workers. Akim also set out a different scheme of work for pregnant women and nursing mothers with the intention of minimising the number of hours that they would be required to work at night over a two-week period.[44]

In reality, the proposed changes to established work regimes, which were debated during the early years of the Soviet industrialisation drive and introduced in practice from 1928, significantly undermined the provisions of earlier legislation which had, in theory at least, restricted the hours at which women could be employed. The introduction of the seven-hour day, three-shift system and the continuous working week would, in practice, increase the number of workers employed at individual enterprises and, in addition to this, required that women should be employed at night alongside male colleagues. For the textile industry, there were discussions also of the possibilities of operating a split-shift system, on the basis of two separate blocks of work in one day. In reality, however, multi-shift and split-shift working patterns were not widely adopted in Soviet industry. As Granick has pointed out in his study of the metalworking industry, there were a number of problems to be overcome. These involved not only labour supply, especially the difficulties in recruiting night shift workers where no public transport was available at night, but also administrative, technical and managerial issues.[45]

The possibility of transfer to the new work regimes also gave rise to a number of additional concerns relating to the employment of female labour. In terms of labour supply, the extension of total hours of work at individual enterprises meant that additional labour would be required to work the new shifts. It was suggested that up to 10 000 new workers would be employed with the implementation from January 1928 of the new work regimes in fourteen textile factories alone. Additional labour was to be recruited from unemployed textile workers and from the grown children of textile workers already in employment. At the same time there was some concern that the proportion of the total labour force constituted by women should not be reduced by the recruitment of additional workers to the industry.[46]

The increase in the operational capacity of industry by the extension of total working hours was also to have an impact in terms of both industrial output and labour development. It was argued that the transfer to the new work regimes should not result, on the one hand, in reductions in labour productivity or, on the other hand, in increases in the prices of industrial goods.[47] The reduction in the working day for individual workers to seven hours would, it was suggested, make additional time available to conduct more effective political and cultural educational campaigns, particularly amongst female workers. Women workers would also be given the opportunity to enter training programmes and, thereby, to raise their levels of skill.[48]

In a speech to the II ACCTU All-Union Meeting on Work amongst Women in June 1928, Tolstopyatov, the deputy Commissar for Labour, drew attention to some of the issues concerning the employment of female labour under the conditions of 'rationalisation' of production and the introduction of the seven-hour working day. He pointed out that more generally on a practical level women had been laid off more readily than men as enterprise managers considered them to be less profitable. He called on the trade unions to stem the trend of female unemployment. The prohibition on night work for female labour had undoubtedly contributed to the levels of unemployment experienced in the 1920s and, as he was aware, a government commission to investigate the impact of the seven-hour working day had decided to permit women to work at night. He proceeded to indicate that the introduction of the third shift at night in the textile industry had already reopened the question of night work by women, and especially by pregnant women and nursing mothers. He also called on the trade unions to enforce more effectively the regulations in regard to pregnant women and nursing mothers, who, he pointed out, 'as experience has shown, quite often themselves circumvent this decree'.[49]

It is clear from these examples that the potential impact on female labour of changes in working practices was being widely debated in the later 1920s. As an outcome of these debates, one line of argument suggested that the transfer to a seven-hour day would be beneficial as it would result in a reduction in the amount of time labour was required to work on night shifts to six hours, thus making night work more suitable for women. The trade union newspaper, *Trud*, called for an expansion in the use of female labour at night as early as the beginning of 1928.[50] Enterprises in the textile industry were transferred gradually to the new patterns of work from 15 January 1928 and these factories came to provide the focus for a range of studies on the impact of the rationalisation measures.

Particular concern in the contemporary discussions, as had been evident also in the earlier debates and actual legislative enactments, was directed towards maintaining the prohibition on the employment of pregnant women and nursing mothers on night shifts and in overtime work 'under any circumstances'. The prohibition on the night shift employment of pregnant women and nursing mothers was maintained, at least officially. Attention was also given to the needs of working mothers with young children, who constituted a significant proportion of the workers employed on night shifts.[51] It was considered important that these women should be able to sleep soundly during the day and have access to child care facilities when they were working at night. It was also felt to be disruptive for working mothers to finish a shift at one or two o'clock at night and then to interrupt their children's sleep when they came to collect them from the nursery.

For working mothers on night shifts, therefore, child care provision needed to be extended throughout the night so that mothers could wait to collect their children in the morning.[52] A report in the official women's journal, *Kommunistka*, noted that in one factory already operating a three-shift system, in weeks when women were employed at night, mothers did not take their children out of the child care facilities at all.[53] All efforts were to be made to maintain child care provision on a three-shift basis in order that children could be cared for at all times when their mothers were working. The factory women's departments were instructed to ensure that such provisions were made.[54] *Trud* reported that expenditure on child care was to be offset by the People's Commissariat of Health, or by the enterprise itself if it proved to be economic.[55]

The difficulties encountered in implementing protective labour legislation in the face of widespread resistance on the part of women workers themselves were clearly demonstrated by the example of various practices which were initiated in the textile industry in this period. These applied particularly to the prohibition on night work by pregnant women and nursing mothers. Norton Dodge has argued that 'the textile industry, for one, seems to have generally ignored these provisions, with the reported concurrence of the mothers'.[56] A detailed analysis of the actual impact of the revised work regimes and of the debates surrounding the question of the employment of women on night shifts in the textile industry is provided by Ward's study of cotton workers during the New Economic Policy.[57] Ward expresses some of the objections put forward by the workers themselves to the operation of the ban on night shift employment for female labour. Some male workers clearly felt that if selected categories of employees were exempted totally from night work, then others would be condemned to working permanently at night. Women workers themselves objected to being excluded from night shifts and Ward cites reports of female textile workers in the Ivanovo district refusing to obey the terms of the legislative regulations.

Official pleas to the workers, however, continued to urge the women to think first of their own health and that of their children before insisting on working at night.[58] Local party cells and committees at individual enterprises were instructed to ensure that women workers complied with the terms of the prohibition in order to safeguard the health of both the mother and child. A case was reported where at one factory a nursing mother who had been employed on the night shift for one week ceased to produce any milk to feed her baby. On the basis of such reports, local departments for the protection of women's labour and party cells at the factories were instructed to speed up the rates of transfer of pregnant women and nursing mothers from night shift employment.[59]

However, as Ward points out, pregnant women and nursing mothers themselves could be the most vociferous of the protestors.[60] In Rodniki, where special arrangements had been made for the employment of pregnant women and nursing mothers exclusively on daytime shifts, women won the concurrence of their local trade union organisation in ignoring the restrictions on their employment at night. Further to this, Ward notes that the newspaper of the textile industry, *Golos tekstilei*, reported cases in which pregnant women were forced to conceal their pregnancies and that some women may even have resorted to backstreet abortions in order to avoid the legal prohibitions on their hours of work. As has already been indicated, however, official policy maintained that pregnant women and nursing mothers should not be employed at night.[61]

More generally, women raised a number of important objections to the suggestion that they should be excluded from night work. A series of articles in *Kommunistka* drew attention to their complaints. Loyalties to other workers on their shifts, attachment to the operation of specific equipment and machinery and fears of reductions in wages, as Ward has also pointed out, all influenced the demands which women put forward to be allowed to work on night shifts. Women feared that by not working at night they would lose access to their machines and tools and pregnant women and nursing mothers in particular argued that their wages would be lower if they were only allowed to work during the day.[62]

The habits of set work patterns proved difficult to break. It was argued that 'on other machines output decreases. They fear that pregnant women and nursing mothers will not be allocated to the best machines. In addition, they do not know with whom they will be working.'[63] Payment by piece-rates meant that workers wanted to ensure being placed with the most efficient colleagues on alternate shifts. One report noted that 'they are afraid of losing their own machines or their work mates on their shift, or they consider that it would be more convenient to work at night'.[64] The ban could also have a detrimental effect on family relations and many women disliked having to work a different shift from their husband.

Despite the wide-ranging discussions on expanding night shift employment by women more generally, the prohibition was maintained officially for the employment of pregnant women beginning from the sixth month of pregnancy and nursing mothers in the first six months of breast feeding.[65] The most difficult period of night work, from which such workers were to be excluded entirely, was regarded as falling between one and four o'clock. Women themselves argued that with the efficient organisation of shifts, working at the most difficult hours of night could be avoided and that these hours could be reserved for special work brigades or used for maintenance and running repairs on the machines.[66] On the basis of this argument it was suggested that the first daytime shift should not begin before four o'clock in the early hours of the morning and the late shift was not to finish after one o'clock at night. Needless to say women were to be employed on only one shift per day.

On the other hand it was argued that by not starting the first shift until six o'clock in the morning factories were still able to run two full daytime shifts on which pregnant women and nursing mothers could be employed.[67] Individual factories continued to operate their own policies on shift arrangements, some of which facilitated the employment of pregnant women and nursing mothers for a minimum number of hours at night. In Shuya, for example, pregnant women and nursing mothers were given the option of working at night. Pregnant women and nursing mothers, according to one account, were being admitted to night work in Ivanovo-Voznesensk, Vladimir, Tver and parts of the Moscow region.[68] Another report suggested that women were more likely to be found working at night in factories which operated a split shift system but did not tend to work at night where an unbroken seven-hour shift was operational.[69]

The disputes arising over the prohibition on the night shift employment of pregnant women and nursing mothers in the textile industry are also illustrative, to a limited extent, of the continuing competitive economic rivalry between the two major industrial centres, Moscow and Leningrad, at the end of the 1920s. The Labour Protection Department of Narkomtrud RSFSR, officially at least, clearly regarded the transfer of pregnant women and nursing mothers from night shifts as an urgent matter by 1929. In Leningrad, however, various objections were raised. In this region most of the textile factories operated on an eight-hour, two-shift pattern, with the second shift running from four o'clock in the afternoon until midnight. It was argued that if women were to finish work by ten or eleven o'clock in the evening then their machines would be left standing idle for the final part of the shift and the norms of output for the remaining workers would have to be raised. In Leningrad also women complained of being taken away from their machines and being transferred to lesser paid jobs.[70]

A handbook on the work of the state scientific-research Institute for the Protection of Labour published in 1930 provides some indication of the outcomes of their early observations into the impact on workers of night shift employment. It is interesting to note that the Institute was headed by Kaplun. The report suggested that if employment stopped before two o'clock at night and did not begin before five o'clock in the morning, and that if workers were able to gain sufficient rest at home after their shift, then the negative consequences of night work, such as lower productivity and greater fatigue, could be significantly ameliorated. Moreover, the observations conducted by the Institute revealed that night work did not seem to have such a detrimental impact on women as it did on men:

> The woman's organism is more easily adapted to night work than men's, which is apparently a consequence of the fact that women generally before all else are mothers, they have a much greater reason than men to accustom their bodies to sleeplessness.[71]

The report argued that where factories already operated a night shift there would be no benefit in prohibiting night work to women. It was now suggested that the problem of night shift employment for women workers was not one of biology but of 'the socialist organisation of labour'.[72] In 1931 the economic newspaper, *Za industrializatsiyu*, reported changes to RSFSR labour laws which confirmed that the duration of night-time employment should be one hour shorter than daytime shifts and determined that night shifts were considered to fall between the hours of ten o'clock in the evening and six o'clock in the morning.[73]

Lili Korber's account of life in a Soviet factory confirms the continued employment of women on night shifts in the Leningrad metallurgical factory where she herself found temporary employment at the beginning of the 1930s.[74] It seems that even the provisions prohibiting the employment of pregnant women and nursing mothers were being ignored by the beginning of the 1930s. Dodge has claimed that 'illegal overtime and night work for pregnant women, as well as underground work for all women, seem to have been fairly common during the 1930s'.[75] Despite the widespread discussions in the 1920s and early 1930s on the question of the regulation of the hours of work for female labour and the introduction of the legislative prohibition on night work, it is evident that not only in these decades but also throughout the entire Soviet period women were widely employed on night shifts, often in greater proportions than men, and in overtime work in a whole range of sectors of the economy in direct contravention of the Soviet Labour Codes.[76]

7 Provision for 'Menstrual Leave'

The debates concerning the extent to which women's differing physiological constitution and biological functions should be recognised by the terms and coverage of protective labour legislation in the 1920s and 1930s were no more clearly exemplified than in the discussions which took place in these decades on the question of allowing women workers a specific number of days release from paid labour during menstruation. Special protective labour laws which set out the terms for 'menstrual leave' were introduced in 1922 and 1931. The study of menstruation and its impact on women's work capacities remained an important topic of scientific research and an area of concern for labour hygiene specialists throughout the interwar years.

Passing reference was made to the menstrual leave provisions in some of the contemporary published sources on protective labour legislation and in the personal reminiscences of visitors to the Soviet Union in the 1920s and 1930s. The more detailed findings of the scientific research into the impact of heavy physical labour and industrial employment on the menstrual cycle and the official discussions about the categories of women workers who should be included in the terms of these laws are to be found in the contemporary journals and archives. These sources suggest that the practice of allowing women workers a few days release from paid labour in the form of menstrual leave was fairly common in the 1920s and 1930s and, as such, the Soviet Union probably presents a unique example in the history of the labour protection of female workers. The research outlined here is interesting also because it highlights some very different attitudes towards the role and application of protective labour legislation with specific reference to the significance of the menstrual leave provisions for the future employment of female labour and for more general notions of the equality of women workers.[1]

Alice Field, writing in the early 1930s, was clearly aware of the potential conflicts which faced both the female labour force and employers if due regard was to be paid to women's reproductive functions. In her study of the 'Russian system of Protection of Mothers and their Children', Field showed support for the equality of opportunity offered to women by the Bolsheviks' introduction of various laws on women's rights after 1917. Yet she proceeded to question the viability of the employment of women in the industrial labour force, firstly, because of the supposed weaker physical constitution of the female sex and, secondly, because of the expense which would be incurred in training workers who, Field argued, were likely to require time off work in relation to their reproductive capabilities:

> The real problem came when women joined the ranks of industrial workers. It is all very well to say that women should have the same social and cultural advantages as men, for that is comparatively easy to accomplish; but, it is quite another matter when industry must be burdened with persons who are not always up to physical standards...Any employer who hires women has an especially difficult and expensive task before him. In the first place, a women's efficiency fluctuates throughout the month, but more important still, every woman is liable to become pregnant, which means that she will have to leave her work to someone else who will require expensive training in her place.[2]

In the years following the October revolution one Bolshevik reformer, S. I. Kaplun, a leading proponent of the legislative protection of female labour in the 1920s, emphasised the harmful effects on young women of early entry into the industrial labour force. This, he argued, resulted in their internal organs being placed under strain and blood disorders, such as anaemia. The unhealthy, poor and inadequate working conditions experienced by female labour in industrial employment were seen to delay young women's physical development. This situation, Kaplun suggested, was later reflected in painful and irregular periods and complications arising in pregnancy and childbirth. Protective labour legislation to improve conditions of work, therefore, was regarded as an essential element in preserving women's health and that of future generations.[3]

It is clear from this that the potentially damaging effects on the menstrual cycle of the industrial employment of women were being discussed by the Bolsheviks at the beginning of the 1920s. These debates emphasised the need to protect the health of women workers in order that they should be able to fulfil their reproductive and maternal functions. This was an important concern for the Bolsheviks, especially after the population losses incurred in the First World War and during the civil war years. The debates also reflected the pro-natalist stance of the Bolsheviks with regard to women's roles and duties in the process of socialist construction, which were later rearticulated more strongly with the publication under Stalin of the 1936 Constitution.[4]

In 1922 one of the labour journals, *Vestnik truda*, published an article which discussed the possibility of releasing women workers from their jobs for two or three days at the beginning of menstruation.[5] The author of the article, Ts. Pik, a leading figure in the field of professional hygiene, outlined some of the physiological changes experienced by young women at the onset of menstruation and argued for the necessity of physical and psychological rest at this time. Pik also argued that women should not be employed in occupations which involved contact with the types of industrial substances which could penetrate the bloodstream and, thereby, cause irregularities in the reproductive functioning of the female body. The environmental conditions of the workplace and the logistics of seating or standing at a machine were also to be taken into account.

In principle, Pik argued, it would be desirable to release all women from work during menstruation, irrespective of the specific nature of their job. In practice, a short-term 'menstrual leave' would have to be introduced gradually in those sectors of the economy which employed the greatest numbers of women. By the beginning of the 1920s the Narkomtrud Department of Labour Protection and the professional hygiene sub-department of the ACCTU were already considering the introduction of such measures for women workers in the garment industry, where some areas of production were almost exclusively female and where higher levels of illness amongst women, including dysmenorrhoea (painful periods), had previously been recorded.[6] Two particular groups of women workers were singled out by the research: workers on the cutting machines and women involved in the operation of ironing presses. This investigation suggested that the inadequate seating arrangements for these workers, which resulted in congestion and tension of the abdomen, meant that 38 per cent of cutting machinists and 30 per cent of ironing press operators experienced problems during menstruation.[7]

Far from reducing the levels of output in these sectors, it was argued that the provision of menstrual leave would help to preserve the health of women workers and would result in raising the intensity of their work. These initiatives, therefore, would simultaneously improve well-being and raise productivity. No other country in the world, it was argued, had discussed the introduction of such sanitary-hygiene and labour protection measures. At the time of publication the matter was under discussion by the presidium of the ACCTU.

Although most general studies of protective labour law for women workers published during the 1920s and 1930s did not discuss this issue, one author, M. Bukhov, has noted a decree of 11 January 1922, which allowed women workers engaged in specified tasks in the garment industry to take two days leave at the beginning of menstruation on the production of a medical certificate. The length of time between menstrual leaves was to be no less than 21 days. Whilst on leave women were to be paid wages, not subject to deductions, equivalent to a two-day average of their monthly earnings.[8]

Waters has questioned the extent to which these legal provisions were likely to have been applied in practice. She has emphasised the important point that:

> Given the private ownership of many of the sewing establishments, the small number of the workers at each enterprise, and the weakness of industrial organisation amongst seamstresses, the [sewing workers'] union was in a poor position to fight for the inclusion of such a novel item in work agreements.[9]

However, the law does appear to have been made known to some of the foreign visitors to the Soviet Union in the early 1920s. For example, Jessica Smith noted the fact that 'women working on treadle machines or jobs requiring special strain are permitted two days off a month'.[10] The provision for menstrual leave was also noted in the report of a group of British women trade unionists of their visit to the Soviet Union in 1925.[11]

In addition to the 1922 decree, archival research has also revealed some of the further discussions on the topic of releasing different groups of women from work during menstruation. The protocols of meetings of the professional hygiene sub-committee of the Labour Protection Department reveal some discussion on this topic in the mid-1920s. On 6 February 1924 the committee debated the issue of introducing leave during menstruation for specific categories of artistic workers.[12] The meeting was chaired by Pik.

The meeting started off by debating the basic point as to whether there was a need for the introduction of menstrual leave regulations for particular categories of artistic workers. The secretary to the meeting, Shafranova, put forward the case in support of the artistic workers and the meeting agreed that the introduction of such measures was necessary. On agreement of this point, the length of the proposed leave and the specific workers to be incorporated in the terms of the legislation were debated. It was argued on the example of historical precedent that female theatrical employees had been released from work during menstruation in tsarist times and that such a provision was necessary to protect the professionalism of the performance artists. The committee debated whether such leave should be paid and the extension of this type of legislation to other groups of workers.

In view of the intensely physical and highly emotional nature of their work it was argued that specially designated categories of artistic workers should be allowed three days' leave during menstruation. These workers included acrobats, tightrope walkers, horseriders, dancers and gymnasts. However, the committee specifically rejected, amongst others, the inclusion of jugglers, impersonators and impressionists in the terms of the regulations, but no reason was offered for this decision. Shortly after the meeting the proposals were passed to the ACCTU for agreement.[13] Despite these discussions, there is no evidence to suggest that the provision for menstrual leave for performance artists was ever included in the terms of any of the officially published labour protection laws, although it seems to have been operative in practice. Evidence of this is provided by requests for clarification on this issue from the artistic workers' trade union to the Labour Protection Department of Narkomtrud in 1929.[14] The issue of extending the provisions for temporary leave during menstruation, however, was not included in any of the lists of annual plans of tasks drawn up by the Commission for the Improvement and Study of Women's Labour in the second half of the 1920s.[15]

Debates on the subject of menstruation reveal some interesting insights into the Bolshevik discourse on the female body and the role envisaged for women in the new Soviet society. Very often, in writing on this topic, reference was made to the 'physical distinctiveness of the female organism' (*fiziologicheskie osobennosti zhenskogo organizma*) and, invariably in comparison with men, women were considered more delicate and vulnerable to work-related illnesses. In reality, also, comparative studies of occupational health sometimes recorded higher levels of illness amongst women than men. It is important to note, however, that if menstrual problems and pregnancy-related 'illnesses' were excluded from these calculations, women often reported far lower levels of ill-health than men.

The impact of different work regimes on the menstrual cycle constituted an important area of research in the interwar years. An occupational survey of women workers conducted in the Orel region in the mid-1920s revealed that of the 391 textile, leather, print and medical-sanitary workers questioned, 87 (approximately 22 per cent) reported irregularities relating to menstruation. Of the total number of women workers included in the survey, 231 (58 per cent) were involved in the lifting and carrying of weights. Irregularities in menstruation amongst these workers were reported by 77 women (33 per cent). The study concluded that the professional work being undertaken by women in this area could have a negative impact on menstruation.[16]

It is important to note, however, that not all of the studies on women's health issues published at this time attributed irregularities in menstruation to the poor conditions of employment of the female labour force in which many women found themselves. It had long been recognised that heavy physical labour, especially amongst seasonal agricultural workers, and strenuous exercise could cause temporary disruptions in menstruation. Barbara Engel, in her study of Russian peasant women, has noted that:

> So demanding was the agricultural labour that when women engaged in it, their biological cycles were sometimes interrupted. During the thirty to sixty days of the *stradnaya pora* [harvest time] a 'significant minority' of women in the words of one physician, the 'great majority', according to another, who were neither pregnant nor nursing ceased to menstruate altogether.[17]

A brief article on women's illnesses in the women's magazine, *Rabotnitsa*, noted that menstrual problems were not always a cause for concern in themselves but that they were sometimes a preliminary indicator of more serious health problems which could very often be related to women's reproductive functions. This article noted that disorders in the reproductive organs could result from women having insufficient opportunity to rest and recover after giving birth or after an abortion. Women were also warned against the dangers of illegal abortions for their future reproductive health. Problems with the reproductive organs, it was noted, may have resulted from women undertaking heavy physical tasks in the last stages of pregnancy or in the early days after giving birth.[18] It was with such concerns in mind that the provision of information and the education of pregnant women and new mothers provided a major focus of social policy for the Women's Department (*Zhenotdel*) of the Bolshevik party in the 1920s and 1930s.[19]

However, by the mid-1920s the harmful impact of heavy physical labour and industrial employment on the health of women workers and particularly on menstruation was treated as an undeniable and well-established fact by some commentators. For example, in 1926 the Leningrad Medical Journal published an article by B. A. Libov which examined the influence of industrial employment on women's reproductive capacities. Libov cited a range of evidence to support the suggestion that professional employment had a negative impact on the health of women and particularly on the menstrual cycles of the female labour force. Libov argued that women's physical and intellectual capacities were reduced by up to 50 per cent during menstruation and that this was reflected in the loss of muscular strength and powers of concentration. Both of these factors, it was argued, resulted in a significant decline in the productivity of women workers.[20]

According to this research, one of the most common and especially serious examples of work-related illnesses amongst women was dysmenorrhoea. Libov argued that from a sample of 8000 women workers 10 per cent regularly required leave of absence from work because of this; 80 per cent of the women had been absent from work because of dysmenorrhoea at least once over the course of a year; and 'many workers systematically every 28 days were absent from work'.[21] In the conclusions to the article, dysmenorrhoea, amongst other illnesses, was identified as one of the industrial diseases suffered by workers in the textile mills, printing industry and in other sectors of the economy. The most common cause of menstrual problems, Libov argued, was the fact that large numbers of women were engaged in heavy physical labour, which lengthened the time between periods, made the periods painful or disrupted the menstrual cycle altogether. Such findings must undoubtedly have influenced the contemporary discussions on the range of jobs involving heavy physical labour in which women workers should be employed. (See Chapter 9.)

The major causes of menstrual problems were believed to be located in the labour process itself. In these debates, little consideration appears to have been given to women's diets, their general physical constitution or overall levels of physical fitness. It was argued that, for women workers in some industrial employments, the unfavourable positioning of the body during physical labour led to congestion and disruption of the internal organs. Most women included in the research, Libov noted, had not experienced dysmenorrhoea before taking up industrial employment. The very monotony of industrial production processes, which meant that workers spent most of the day either sitting down or standing up in the same position and with little opportunity to move around, was also identified as a major cause of menstrual problems. Libov cited women workers in the garment industry as providing a particular example of this. Under such conditions of employment the circulation of blood through the body was inhibited and this resulted in menorrhagia (excessive blood flow during periods) or metrorrhagia (intermittent bleeding between periods). Young workers were especially susceptible to such symptoms and in older women industrial employment under such conditions could lead to the premature onset of the menopause. In addition to Libov's report, a specialist article on questions of women's health concerning menstruation was also published in *Rabotnitsa* in 1926 in which it was suggested that it was dangerous for women to undertake heavy physical labour during menstruation.[22]

Such reports and their consequent recommendations must have had a significant impact on the thinking of those involved not only in the study and recruitment of female labour but also in designing labour protection measures for women workers in the 1920s and 1930s. The reaction of male workers, especially those employed in skilled trades, was also taken into account. Some male workers did not always hold a favourable opinion of the potential for women to undertake specialised industrial tasks.

For example, one metal worker, cited in an interview in *Rabotnitsa*, argued that every month women were weakened by menstruation and that women's additional family duties demanded a great deal of time. In the opinion of this male worker, women lacked the precision and keenness of mind, as well as the physical strength, to take on skilled jobs in the metalworking industry. The editor of the magazine solicited the opinion of readers on this issue. The replies from female readers published in subsequent issues of the magazine confirmed the hostility from male colleagues which many women encountered in the workplace and underscored women's determination to prove themselves capable of undertaking industrial employment.[23]

It is important to note also that, despite the extensive and wide-ranging findings of research into the impact of employment on women's reproductive functions, the generous terms of the menstrual leave provisions were not always welcomed by women workers themselves. The British trade union delegation report noted some reservations about the operation of the law and its reception by women workers:

In view of the fact that these extra days off make the labour power of women more expensive than that of men, there is a tendency on the part of the women in the trade unions to demand the abolition of this rule, substituting for days off during menstruation the transference of women workers during this period to other employment in the same factory.[24]

The right to transfer to easier work had already been enacted for pregnant women and nursing mothers. (See Chapter 5.)

In fact, there was some discussion in the Russian republic of the need to introduce retractions in the application of the menstrual leave regulations as early as the end of 1926.[25] The final decision was ratified by the Narkomtrud Department of Labour Protection at union level the following January. It was argued that the 1922 decree had found only limited application, specifically in the garment industry, despite the fact that female labour was employed in analogous working conditions in other branches of industry. This had given rise not only to a number of enquiries regarding the scope of the application of the regulations and but also some unfavourable criticism on the part of other women workers.

In view of this, it was felt to be 'expedient' and 'opportune' to modify the 1922 decree to allow time off during menstruation in future only to those who suffered menstrual pains, confirmed by a local clinic or factory doctor.[26] Henceforth, time off work during menstruation was, therefore, to be treated as any other form of sick leave. The debates, however, were by no means over. At the beginning of 1928 the Labour Protection Department of Narkomtrud RSFSR received a number of enquiries requesting information on issues relating to menstrual leave, such as whether women workers were to be transferred to alternative tasks or to take days off work altogether and on what basis the level of pay during menstrual leave should be calculated.[27] The provision for menstrual leave via sickness certification was still available to women decades later.[28]

Maya Gordon, in her study of *Workers Before and After Lenin*, argued that women's different biological constitution and reproductive functions should definitely be recognised and accommodated in the law. From this perspective, menstruation was to be treated as a particular type of illness, which required specific consideration. Gordon noted that 'instructions from

the Commissariat of National Health forbid physicians to
permit women "to absent themselves from work because of
diagnosed menstruation"'. In decrying the subsequent retraction in the terms of the original decree, Gordon argued that:

> People in and out of Russia knew quite well that to become
> economically independent it is not at all necessary for
> women to work in the coal pits or to remain at their tasks
> when they are periodically ill, contrary to the opinion of the
> Communist physicians. The instructions of the Commissariat
> of National Health carry Russia back a hundred years. For
> that matter, it is difficult to imagine that even the Russian
> female serfs, once the master consulted his physician, were
> compelled to continue at work when the doctor found
> them too ill to do so. In no country where the trade unions
> are free would such enslavement of women be tolerated.[29]

Comparative levels of sickness between different groups
of workers and the impact of industrial employment on the
female menstrual cycle continued to be important areas of
concern for many of those interested in labour protection
issues in the later 1920s. In November 1928 Narkomtrud
held a meeting to discuss questions of female labour and
the agenda included a report on the impact on the health of
175 young women, between the ages of 14 and 18 years, of
training and employment in the Moscow metallurgical industries.[30] The report noted that the levels of ill-health recorded
by young male workers exceeded the levels of sickness
amongst female trainees and that young women in the metallurgical industries reported levels of illness comparable to
those of women in other sectors of the local economy.

The report offered a profile of the female trainees. Thirty-
seven were between the ages of 14 and 16 years, the largest
sample (115 workers) were between the ages of 16 and 18 years,
and the remaining twenty-three women were over 18 years
old. The vast majority of the young women had started training for work at the age of 15 years. Many of these young
women, unlike their male counterparts, reported having to
do housework in addition to their paid employment and that
this could take up several hours each week. Forty of the
young women reported spending more than twelve hours per
week doing housework and on average most of the sample

spent up to two hours every day on household chores.[31] This additional engagement in housework was cited as the cause of higher levels of fatigue amongst the young women. The report was concerned with some of the indicators of change in the general health of the young women involved in the survey, such as height and weight. Only just over half (54 per cent) of the 175 women involved in the survey were reported to be in good health. Anaemia was noted as a common symptom of ill-health.

The report noted that one of the training schools had made the provision to allow young women regular leave for one or two days during menstruation. A questionnaire was circulated to the sample group which requested information on their menstrual cycles. The majority of those surveyed reported no abnormalities in menstruation. Five of the trainees had not yet started to menstruate. Of these, three were between the ages of 14 and 16 years and two were between the ages of 16 and 18 years.[32] A small number reported that their periods were irregular or late, and this was especially the experience of the youngest age group. Of the forty-one respondents who reported problems or irregularities in menstruation, variations were recorded in relation to the type of job being done, the length of time in training and the timing of the onset of menstruation, in order to determine if this was before or after taking up employment. Higher levels of menstrual problems were recorded amongst the young women who had been employed for more than two years and who had started to menstruate before taking up paid work and amongst those who were mostly engaged in strenuous physical tasks.

The report, however, was unable to come to any concrete conclusions on the basis of this specific study and recommended that further investigations be undertaken with the help of the Institute for Labour Protection. The recommendation was made that attention should be paid to the positioning of the body during training and employment. It was recommended also that trainees should not be made to stand up for long periods of time, as this was believed to affect the development of the reproductive organs, and that seating should be provided for female employees during work breaks. The report also recommended that girls younger than 16 years

should no longer be permitted to enter training schools in the
metallurgical industry in order to allow time for them to go
through puberty before starting industrial employment.[33]

At the end of the 1920s research was also being conducted
by the Institute for Labour Protection into the employment
of women as conductors, and in other tasks, on trams.[34]
A detailed study was made at this time of the employment of
female labour on Moscow and Leningrad trams and of the
impact of such employment on women's health. The research
noted that the vibrations caused by the motion of the trams
could prove detrimental to women's health and cause disruptions of their reproductive organs.[35] One of the ways in which
the working conditions of female tram workers could be
improved, it was suggested, was by releasing women from
work during menstruation on notification confirmed by a
doctor.[36] A brief article in *Rabotnitsa* reported that some
female tram workers already refused to work during the first
few days of menstruation in the winter months through fear
of catching cold. This situation did not appear to give rise to
any cause for concern and women's absence during menstruation was regarded as a professional illness alongside other
common ailments, such as sciatica and other inflammations,
experienced by tram workers.[37]

Despite the earlier retractions in the regulations governing
menstrual leave, the initiative to allow women paid leave during menstruation was given legislative backing again in the
early 1930s. At this time some experiments were already
being conducted by the scientific research institutes into the
seating arrangements for female tractor drivers.[38] A decree
'on the working conditions of women tractor and lorry drivers'
was issued on 9 May 1931, which stated in clause 3 that:

> Women tractor-drivers working on wheel tractors without
> soft spring seats must during menstruation on submission
> of a certificate from a physician or an assistant be trans-
> ferred to easier jobs for three days with retention of aver-
> age earnings, and if not allowed to work at all they shall
> receive temporary disability allowance.[39]

The levels of the practical application and utility of such a
protective provision would be difficult to gauge. Only a small
minority of collective farms would have had access to a tractor

in the early 1930s and it is unlikely that many women would have been allowed to work as tractor drivers at this time, despite the popular images of the period. Bonnell has noted that peasant women 'comprised only six per cent of the tractor drivers in the country as a whole in 1932'.[40] The numbers of women working on tractors undoubtedly increased from this time. Chirkov has estimated that the number of female tractor drivers in the Soviet Union rose from just fourteen in 1926, to 18 000 in 1932 and totalled 57 000 by 1937.[41] According to these figures a significant and increasing number of women would have been affected by the 1931 provisions.

Investigations into the impact on women's health of driving tractors were ongoing in the early 1930s. At a Narkomtrud meeting to discuss the entry of women into industrial production held in January 1933 Rabinovich, of the Institute of the Protection of Motherhood and Childhood in Moscow, reported on a study of 272 female tractor drivers, most of whom had as least one year's experience in the job. 251 worked on wheeled tractors, which were considered to be more injurious to women. Many reported menstrual irregularities and headaches. Nearly one-third of young women and well over half of adult women in the sample reported symptoms of menorrhagia. The report noted that women should be transferred to alternative employment during menstruation and recommended the redesign of seats for wheeled tractors.[42] In 1935 the ACCTU discussed the possibility of extending the menstrual leave provisions for female tractor drivers from three to five days but this change in the regulations does not appear to have been enacted in the law although it may have been in practice.[43]

Women workers themselves, however, often objected to the restrictions imposed by the terms of the protective measures and to the underlying assumptions of the menstrual leave provisions. Lili Korber, for example, argued that women could never expect to be regarded as equal with men if they were offered special treatment in view of their biological distinction. Her account suggests that the revised 'menstrual leave' provisions were still operational in practice in the early 1930s. This example also demonstrates that the revised regulations were applicable to a broader range of workers than was envisaged by the original debates on the legislative enactment of menstrual leave conducted in the early and mid-1920s.

Korber, an Austrian visitor to the Soviet Union, spent two months in July and August 1931 working as a machinist in the metalworking plant of the Putilov Works in Leningrad. On 4 August she complained of 'violent stomach and hip pains that attacked me about mid-day. I found it hard to go on working my machine.' She could barely wait for the lunch break, which offered a chance to rest: 'I crouched down on a low form near the teapots and huddled up my legs. In such cases warmth always helps.' This allowed some opportunity for her to recover and, in contrast to Gordon's attitude to the release of female labour from work during menstruation, Korber proceeded to note:

> From the din of the machinery I noticed the mid-day inter-val was over, and got up. I felt better. Varya asked me where I had been and suggested I should go to the 'Medpoint' and get leave off, but I jibbed at doing that. In the first place my low piece-work record had been posted on the blackboard where the numbers of tractor parts that are urgently needed appear; in the second, we women can never expect to obtain equal treatment with men if we cry off once a month.[44]

Concern for the impact of industrial employment on women's reproductive health remained an area of concern for the scientific-research institutes. In January 1933 Margolin, of the Belorussian Institute of Sanitation and Organisation of Labour, reported on the study of 707 women workers employed in the leather industry and wood processing: 59 women reported that they had developed menstrual disor-ders since taking up their jobs when previously they had not experienced problems; 85 reported an increase in menstrual flow on taking up work; and 72 noted a level of discomfort. Despite these symptoms over half of the women reporting menstrual problems considered themselves to be healthy in general and few really considered that their job was the main cause of their menstrual irregularities. The report concluded that there was no evidence to indicate that women should be prohibited from working in these occupations, although restrictions should be placed on the weights of loads women were required to lift and carry.[45]

A brief synopsis presented in a journal of labour hygiene and technical safety of some experimental work conducted at the 'Red October' confectionery factory by the health protection division of the Central Scientific-Research Institute of Physical Culture indicated that research into the influence of various work regimes on female physical development and menstruation was still being conducted in the mid-1930s.[46] This report noted that up to 60 per cent of the women included in the experiment found work 'difficult' or 'worse than usual' during menstruation.

The research for this report was conducted over a number of days, at different stages of the menstrual cycle and at varying times during the working shift. Most of the women included in the experiment were reported as taking no exercise during menstruation. As a result of a controlled experiment conducted over six months, the investigation demonstrated that the introduction of a short, five-minute, break for exercise twice a day, could improve women's health and physical development as well as contribute towards increasing productivity and reducing absenteeism. Such breaks were observed to be especially important for women during menstruation when labour capacity was believed to be reduced significantly.[47] By the end of the experimental period, the number of women recording no problems with menstruation had increased by 23.6 per cent.

Research into the impact of industrial labour on menstruation was conducted in a number of countries before and after the First World War, but does not appear to have had a direct influence on legislation.[48] In the Soviet Union, the decision to allow selected categories of women workers paid leave of absence for two or three days during menstruation was a significant point of discussion in labour protection debates throughout the 1920s and even in the early and mid-1930s. The Soviet Union, therefore, provides a unique contemporary example of enacting this practice and in incorporating the initiative into its protective labour legislation.[49] The contemporary theoretical discussions and the practical implementation of the menstrual leave provisions aroused a significant controversy. The extent to which such a provision was operable in reality and the numbers of women able or willing to claim release from paid work during menstruation, however, would be impossible to determine.

8 Weights of Loads

What should be the maximum limits to be placed on the weights of loads to be lifted or transported by women at work? No such regulations had existed in Russia before the revolution when women had been employed in many heavy and arduous tasks.[1] The post-revolutionary debates on this, like other issues, were framed in terms both of the relative frailty of the female organism and of the need to preserve women's reproductive capabilities. A number of factors were taken into account. Girls under the age of 16 were prohibited altogether from employment in jobs specifically requiring the transportation of loads. A lighter set of norms was established for young women between the ages of 16 and 18 years and for girls under the age of 16 years in other tasks. The norms for adult women were initially set as equivalent to those for young male workers between the ages of 16 and 18 years. In some cases, the legislation set out the amount of time which women should spend in the carrying and transporting of loads in the course of their shift. The agreement of labour inspectors and the local labour protection organisations was to be sought if women were to spend more than one-third of their shift in transporting loads.

The tasks in which women were employed comprised a range of processes. These included the lifting and placing down of items in loading and unloading jobs and the carrying and transporting of these loads over various distances. Consideration was also given to the different means of carriage. The norms for working with loads depended, firstly, on whether the weights were to be carried by hand or transported in various types of barrows or hand carts and, secondly, on the gradient of the surface over which the load was to be transported. Although not specified in the norms set out in legislation, some consideration in the investigations and scientific research was also given to the distance over which the load was to be carried or transported and to the length of the return journey without a load. The longer the distance of transportation, the lesser the time that was spent in loading and unloading tasks. It was the responsibility of

112

local commissions for labour protection and enterprise administrators to publicise the norms of weights for loading and unloading work.

The restrictions, which were first introduced in the 1918 Labour Code to prohibit female labour from heavy and arduous jobs which were considered to be detrimental to their health, were already being retracted in the early 1920s. For example, the fuel crisis, arising from the privations and disruption of the civil war and war communism, led to the introduction, on 20 May 1920, of regulations permitting the employment of young female workers between the ages of 16 and 18 years in a limited number of tasks involved in the preparation of peat.[2] The employment of women as labour conscripts was permitted in the procurement of wood fuel from 27 March 1920.[3] Further retractions came after the publication of the first full set of norms on the maximum weights of loads.

After the introduction of the NEP in 1921, rising levels of female unemployment were witnessed. Some consideration in the protective labour debates during this period was given to preserving and not undermining further women's likelihood of finding or retaining jobs. In practice, it has been argued, the maximum weights of loads established by these provisions were unrealistic because if they were strictly enforced they would have unduly restricted female workers already in employment and may also have contributed towards the high levels of female unemployment in the 1920s.[4] The extent to which the regulations were enforced in practice, however, is difficult to determine.

A number of social and scientific studies were conducted during the 1920s with the intention of revealing the impact of the lifting and transporting of loads on women's physical well-being. In the same year as the initial set of regulations was introduced the labour journal, *Vestnik truda*, published an article which discussed some of the issues relating to the legal restrictions placed on the carrying of weights by both women and young workers.[5] The author of the article, A. Letavet, pointed to the absence of any real scientific foundations for the legal regulations on loads, despite the identification by labour inspectors of the large numbers of women who were employed in tasks which required significant physical strength. Letavet was concerned that the legal regulations should be supported by scientific study into the physiological characteristics of the female organism.

Calling on research conducted by Dr A. F. Nikitin on the employment of young workers in loading jobs in the Volga, Letavet pointed to the physical damage which could be done to workers involved in the lifting and transporting of weights if they took on such work at an early age before the skeleton had stopped developing.[6] Nikitin, in the results of a survey involving 758 loading workers, pointed to the close correlation between the high levels of professional injury and the young age at which heavy work was started. He identified the widespread incidence of curvature of the spine, displaced vertebrae, flatfootedness and varicose veins amongst loading workers, the vast majority of whom had started work in such tasks before the age of 25 years.

For young women, the situation was further complicated by the fact that the lifting and carrying of loads placed great strain on the pelvic bone, which led to a narrowing of the pelvis and resulted in complications during pregnancy and childbirth. Similar problems were noted also for older women. A major focus of concern at this stage was the impact of the lifting and transporting of loads on female reproductive functions. Letavet argued that women engaged in such jobs recorded high levels of haemorrhaging and miscarriage during both the early and later stages of pregnancy. Women were also reported as suffering shifts in the normal positioning of the womb and prolapses of the womb. Disruption of the menstrual cycle was also noted in terms of women suffering menorrhagia and dysmenorrhoea.

Letavet argued that the number of adult women and young workers employed in jobs involving loads should be reduced. One radical solution, it was suggested, was to be found in the complete mechanisation of tasks involving the lifting and transporting of weights following the example of the Ford factory in America. The Soviet economy in the early 1920s, however, was not in a position to implement such a costly programme of mechanisation, requiring a high level of capital investment. It is also doubtful that such a programme would have brought about any far-reaching improvements in women's jobs or their employment prospects. The experience of mechanisation in the Soviet economy in later years indicated that it was mainly male workers who were given priority in access to mechanised equipment; female workers were employed predominantly in auxiliary, unskilled and manual jobs, which often involved heavy physical labour.

Letavet pointed to the inadequacies of the tsarist system, with its complete absence of regulations on one hand but widespread employment of women and young workers in transporting loads in many sectors of the economy on the other. He was also critical of the legal regulations introduced by other countries, particularly France, which had the most restrictive practices, but also failed to take into consideration issues such as maximum daily norms for the carrying of loads or the surface on which the load was being transported.

In Letavet's opinion, crude empirical data derived from practical observation were an inadequate foundation for legal regulations. Letavet examined in some depth the different physiological specificities of young female workers and adult women and measured their expenditure of energy in terms of calorific values. Young workers, Letavet argued, worked at between 60 per cent and 62.5 per cent of the rate of adult workers and, therefore, their norms of work should be reduced by 40 per cent. As young workers were observed to tire more easily, he argued that their work day should also be reduced from eight to six hours. Letavet argued further that the limitations on loads for adult women should conform to those of young male workers and should, therefore, be set at between 60 per cent and 70 per cent of adult male norms.

Finally, Letavet argued that, ideally, women and young workers should be prohibited entirely from jobs involved exclusively with the lifting and transporting of loads. Juvenile workers, under the age of 16 years, should not be employed under any circumstances in jobs involving loads. On the basis of such arguments, Letavet called for a clear segregation of the labour force by suggesting that jobs which involved the carrying of loads as an integral part of the profession, for example porters and couriers, should be undertaken only by adult male workers. Clearly, Letavet's early study of such issues opened the way for more in-depth research.

Legislation was introduced on 4 March 1921 which established the conditions of work and norms of weights for

Table 8.1   Norms of Loads, 1921

	Adult women	Young women
By hand	16.4 kg (40 funt)	10.25 kg (25 funt)
Wagons on rails	492 kg (30 pud)	328 kg (20 pud)
Single-wheeled barrow	49.2 kg (3 pud)	prohibited
2-wheeled barrow		
Flat surface and shallow incline	114.8 kg (7 pud)	prohibited
Steep incline	57.4 kg (3.5 pud)	prohibited
3- or 4-wheeled barrow	82 kg (5 pud)[a]	57.4 kg (3.5 pud)[b]

[a]on an uneven surface where the gradient does not exceed 0.01.
[b]only on a flat surface (asphalt, wood, etc.) where the gradient does not exceed 0.02.
Source: 'O predel'nykh normakh perenoski i peredvizheniya tyazhestei podrostkami i zhenshchinami', decree of Narkomtrud RSFSR, *Byulleten' trudovo fronta*, 1921, no. 5, pp. 14–15.

women engaged in the lifting and transporting of loads. Table 8.1 sets out the norms which were introduced for the maximum weights to be carried and transported by adult and young women workers.[7]

The established norms of loads were to include the weight of the barrow or wagon used in transportation. A maximum load of 10 funt, or 4.1 kg, was established for both adult and young women employed in the constant carrying and transporting of loads. According to one group of contemporary observers writing in 1927, however, 'as is well known, the 10 funt norm never became a reality'.[8] The State Scientific-Research Institute for the Protection of Labour also argued in 1930 that the 4.1 kg maximum load was never properly implemented.[9] In other occupations the time spent in the lifting and transporting of loads, except with the agreement of the local labour inspectorate, was not to exceed one-third of the shift and was to be interspersed with other tasks. Nursing mothers were permitted to work in jobs involving heavy weights only on the agreement of their doctor. The regulations of 4 March 1921 became applicable on a union-wide basis from 14 November 1923.[10] In the previous year, on 15 January 1922, in a circular of the ACCTU, the norms for loading work established for women had been set at half those of male workers.[11]

The basic principles of 'weights of loads' legislation were further reinforced by Article 129 of the 1922 Labour Code, which prohibited the employment of women in 'especially heavy tasks' and in jobs which required a significant degree of physical exertion.[12] (See also Chapter 9.) Such measures were underpinned by a belief that women's differing physiological constitution meant that they were weaker than men and, therefore, that they should not be employed in occupations which required a significant degree of physical strength.

Further legislation noted here, however, specifically limited the physical labour of pregnant women, nursing mothers and young workers. For example, on 12 April 1923 pregnant women, nursing mothers and young workers were prohibited from working individually or as part of artels in the loose floating of timber. Presumably, therefore, all other adult women could be employed in such tasks. At the same time, however, all adult women and young workers were prohibited from employment in identified rafting tasks.[13] In two subsequent minor decrees women and young workers were prohibited from working in bakeries in connection with the hand kneading of dough and carrying of loads above established norms on 10 March 1924, and pregnant women, nursing mothers and young workers were prohibited from employment in the hand washing of wool on 22 May 1924.[14]

A decree issued on 14 February 1924 reiterated the restrictions on the employment of women and young workers in loading and unloading tasks and in the transporting of loads in the transport sector. The decree also stated that workers employed in these tasks should be permitted regular work breaks and have priority in access to the use of mechanised loading equipment in the transfer of heavy loads.[15]

One of the problems with the existing regulations was that they were believed by many to limit the employment opportunities of women and young workers and this argument in itself provided a sufficient impetus for their revision. The Supreme Council of the National Economy (VSNKh) was unhappy about the situation whereby strict adherence to the existing norms resulted in economic organisations restricting their employment of women and young workers. In January 1925 a request was sent to the Labour Protection Department of Narkomtrud SSSR to oversee the introduction of changes to the regulations.[16] Conversely, another problem lay in the very implementation and enforcement of the regulations, which, it may be assumed, could be easily disregarded and ignored.

In March 1925 the Labour Protection Department of Narkomtrud contacted various trade union organisations and similar departments in a number of the union republics to notify them of their intentions and to ask for their help in reviewing the existing regulations:

> In considering in the near future the revision of the Narkomtrud compulsory regulations published in 1921, 'on the maximum norms for the lifting and transporting of loads by young workers and women', and with the aim of bringing them into line with the actual conditions of work in industrial enterprises, we request that you let us know quickly, in your opinion, of any consequent changes and amendments to be introduced to the stated compulsory regulations.[17]

The existing regulations on the maximum norms of loads for female workers were discussed at a meeting of the newly established Narkomtrud Commission for the Improvement and Study of Women's Labour in Production a few months later.[18] From 1925 the various scientific research institutes which dealt with questions of labour protection were commissioned to investigate the impact on the female body of lifting and carrying weights with the aim of providing guidelines for the revision of the 1921 regulations.

During the course of the revision of the original regulations the People's Commissariat of Post and Telegraph, Narkompit, recommended in 1927 that women should not be employed as postal delivery workers and continued to discuss the employment of women in other tasks involving loads. It was suggested further that the regulations on loads for male workers should also be revised.[19] There was also some limited discussion of the need to rationalise and mechanise tasks undertaken by women workers in connection with the lifting and transporting of loads.[20]

The findings of the investigations into the conditions of work for women in a range of employments involving loading and unloading tasks and in the carrying and transporting of heavy loads suggested that the amount of recorded disorders to women's reproductive organs was directly related to the difficulty of the task in which they were employed. Female loaders recorded the highest level of disorders.

The research into the questions of the influence on the female body of the lifting and carrying of loads and of the maximum norms of loads to be transported by women began in 1925 and continued into the following year. The research programme was headed by Dr I. I. Okuneva of the State Scientific-Research Institute for the Protection of Labour.[21] Okuneva's findings were reported back to the Narkomtrud Department of Labour Protection where they were discussed in detail. An extensive two-part report was published in the labour hygiene journal, *Gigiena truda*, in 1927 and the findings of this research constituted the basis for the revised set of norms for the lifting and transporting of loads by women which were eventually introduced by Narkomtrud in 1932.[22]

Okuneva's reports clearly identified the need to review the regulations on the norms of loads introduced in 1921. The 4.1 kg maximum load was seen as unrealistic when in a number of branches of the economy women were actually frequently required to carry loads of between 40 and 50 kg and sometimes more than this. The aim of the research, therefore, was to examine the damaging impact on the female organism caused by the lifting and transporting of heavy loads. Unlike Letavet, however, Okuneva stressed the fact that the revision of the existing norms should not lead to a reduction in the employment of women, especially in branches of the economy where women worked predominantly as unskilled labour and would otherwise be faced with the threat of unemployment. The task of the research was to establish easily definable and realistic norms.

The issues involved in the revision of the norms of loads were recognised as complex. Field research was conducted in 1926 in the form of a questionnaire and it is the findings of this part of the research which provide the most informative details of the types of jobs and the regimes of work undertaken by women workers in various sectors of the economy dealing with the carrying and transporting of loads. The remainder of the research was conducted under laboratory conditions and aimed to determine the optimum norms for the lifting and carrying of weights without causing harm to the female body. The research was conducted from a range of perspectives, including physiology, gynaecology and biomechanics, under the supervision of experts in each of these fields.

The first part of the research involved a survey by questionnaire of 1450 women workers employed in various types of tasks involving the lifting and transporting of loads.[23] The sample groups were selected with the agreement of the respective trade unions and economic organisations and included both rural and urban occupations. By far the largest group (454) were selected from seven different metallurgical factories in Moscow and Nizhegorodskaya guberniya. The sample also included 128 loaders from Nizhne-Novgorod, 232 peat workers from Elektroperedacha and 173 haulage workers from the mines of the Donbass region.

Included in the original survey were two control groups of women workers who were not directly engaged in loading and unloading tasks, but who, nevertheless, were employed in occupations which required considerable physical strength. 200 workers for each control group were selected from winders in a textile factory and points workers on the Moscow trams. The findings of the survey confirmed the young age at which many women began working with loads, the heavy weights they were expected to lift and carry and the prevalence of physical ailments amongst the selected groups of workers.

Women peat workers constituted a particularly young group of peasant labour engaged on a seasonal basis for seven months a year to cut and dry out the peat, lift it from the fields and pile it into stacks. The peat was carried over considerable distances in baskets lifted onto the shoulders by workers individually. A brief *Rabotnitsa* article in 1924 pointed out that 3000–4000 women were employed in peat production in the Moscow region alone and they were mostly between the ages of 18 and 22 years. The author, Ostrovskii, noted that there had been no protection of peat workers in the pre-revolutionary period, when women had been employed on the same terms as men, and noted also that women with children were no longer employed in this type of work.[24] It was also reported elsewhere that women did not, or were reluctant to train for, work with mechanised equipment.[25] Loading workers were employed no less intensively, usually at the banks of rivers or on the steamboats in the unloading and transporting of firewood and coal in pairs by means of barrows.

Women were engaged in a range of tasks in the metallurgical industries in the breaking up of metals, operating machine-tools and in cleaning up in various departments. Loads were transported by a variety of means, including in barrows, underarm or around the waist. A report in *Rabotnitsa* in 1925 noted that at the 'Vyksun' metallurgical factory women were employed in lifting loads of more than 2 puds (32 kg) and in the loading and unloading of wagons of firewood, which was described as 'no easy matter'.[26] Women employed as haulage workers in the mines of the Donbass region were engaged in dragging wagons of coal from the mine shaft to the coal bunkers. This particular activity was aggravated by the fact that the wagons often tipped over and, in the absence of mechanised lifters, had to be placed upright by the women themselves by hand.[27] Here again, workers were particularly young. (See also Chapter 10.)

The survey revealed that the weights of loads women workers were employed in lifting and transporting were often far in excess of those set out in the 1921 regulations. Young peasant women, who were often used to heavy physical labour from an early age, carried 2–3 puds (32–48 kg) of peat on their shoulders for up to seven hours per day. Women workers in the metallurgical factories often carried loads in excess of these weights. Here, it was argued, the established norms of loads were often exceeded unintentionally by the sheer weight and unwieldiness of the barrows used. Women engaged in the loading and unloading of coal and firewood worked in pairs with loads of between 3 and 5 puds (50–80 kg) and transported these over considerable distances in two-handled barrows. Likewise, haulage workers at the Donbass mines worked in pairs or in groups of three dragging wagons along rails. The wagons themselves, unloaded, could weigh between 25 and 40 puds and were capable of travelling at high speed.

The findings of the research revealed that over 70 per cent of women engaged in work involving the lifting and transporting of weights had experienced some disruption of their reproductive functions after taking up employment in these tasks. The percentages were lower amongst the control group samples, although these two groups of workers recorded a relatively higher level of problems before taking up employment. The lower level of problems reported amongst the peat workers and haulage workers at the Donbass mines, however, could be accounted for by the fact that these were generally younger workers who were less likely to have experienced such problems in the first place.

Most notable and widespread amongst the problems recorded in women's reproductive functions were irregularities in menstruation. Okuneva claimed that the level of irregularities recorded in this survey exceeded those reported in other literature and research findings and that this fact in itself could be used as evidence of the potentially harmful nature of working with loads, especially as the control groups both indicated significantly lower levels of problems before and after taking up employment. (See Chapter 7.)

Particularly notable here were the high levels of reported dysmenorrhoea, indicated by up to 70 per cent of workers in each occupation, and the amenorrhoea (absence of menstrual flow) reported amongst peat workers, who noted no such problems during the winter months when they were not employed in such arduous tasks. Also noteworthy was the fact that disruptions in menstruation were seen to decline as the length of work experience increased. This suggested that physical maturity and acclimatisation to work were likely to reduce menstrual problems. Despite the fact that disruptions in menstruation were seen to undermine women's health, as well as reducing their productivity, the women seemed to be reconciled to these problems and did not allow such issues to interfere with their work.

However, other problems with women's reproductive functions experienced in connection with pregnancy and childbirth were treated much more seriously. A direct correlation was drawn between the lifting and carrying of heavy loads and the high levels of haemorrhaging, prolapses of the womb, miscarriage and premature birth recorded amongst the respondents in the survey. Shifts in the positioning of the abdominal organs during the lifting and carrying of loads were likely to result in prolapses and miscarriages. The incidence of premature birth increased twenty times amongst loaders after taking up employment in these tasks. The numbers of miscarriages and stillbirths were also affected by such work. The very incidence of childbirth itself was reduced by approximately 10 per cent amongst loaders and metallurgical workers. The lower levels of problems recorded by peat and haulage workers can be accounted for again by their relatively young age. It was considered significant that the number of problems recorded in pregnancy and childbirth increased in parallel with the length of work experience.

Other ailments, unconnected with reproductive functions, were also reported by the women questioned in the survey. These ailments included palpitations of the heart, shortness of breath, headaches and migraines, muscular pains and, most commonly, lumbar and stomach pains. Lumbar and stomach pains were noted as long experienced problems. Muscular pains were common after a particularly hard day's work. Other workers indicated less precise but no less serious complaints, such as feeling worn out in general and a certain aching and dullness of the body. The report concluded that attention needed to be paid not only to the weight of individual loads, but also to the daily aggregate level of loads lifted and transported by women as well as their overall regimes of work.

The field survey on the conditions of work for women employed in the lifting and transporting of loads was supplemented by research conducted under laboratory conditions into the influence of these tasks on abdominal pressure.[28] Changes in the positioning of the abdominal organs were seen to be the major cause of problems in the reproductive functioning of women engaged in loading and unloading tasks and in the carrying and transporting of heavy weights. Particular attention during the research was also paid to changes in the patterns of breathing and consequent abdominal pressure amongst women employed in these types of jobs. Special equipment was designed to measure these physiological changes. A control group of those not usually employed in physical labour was also tested.

The results of the experiments indicated that abdominal pressure increased significantly when the load weighed in excess of 20 kg. The process of bending down to pick up the load was in itself seen to increase pressure on the abdominal organs and particularly on the womb and cervix. The impact of lifting loads on the respiratory organs and on the level of pressure on the thorax and diaphragm were also recorded. The lifting and carrying of such heavy loads was seen to encourage changes in the normal patterns of breathing, thereby again increasing pressure on the abdominal organs. It was this abdominal pressure which accounted for the high levels of reproductive and gynaecological ailments reported amongst women employed in the lifting and transporting of loads. Finally, biomechanical studies investigated changes in the pectoral muscles and the thorax in the processes of lifting and carrying heavy weights. In the activity of transporting loads by hand, the reports recommended a 50 kg maximum weight per pair of workers to be carried on a stretcher-like device, which would allow for the weight to be evenly distributed, as the level at which there was the heaviest possible load without causing harm to either worker. 1921 regulations had established a maximum norm of 16.4 kg for individual workers in the manual lifting and transporting of loads.

The findings of the laboratory experiments were later tested and verified in the field with the help of medical personnel by the conduct of in-depth gynaecological studies during the summer of 1928 amongst 550 loading workers in Astrakhan. This practical research experiment also concluded that 'heavy work by women in all professions leads to a number of illnesses and primarily to the disruption of menstruation, to downward pressure on the womb and prolapses of the womb and vagina'.[29]

The lifting of a weight in excess of 20 kg by an individual female worker was seen to displace the abdominal organs to such a degree that reproductive functions were disrupted, and this resulted in complications during pregnancy and childbirth. A 50–60 kg maximum load was suggested for a pair of workers. The preferred method of transportation was seen to be a stretcher-type barrow, which eased the pressure on the body at the point of lifting the load from the ground and allowed for the weight to be dispersed during its carriage. With training, it was argued, most women would be able to work in occupations dealing with the lifting and transporting of loads without threat to their physical well-being. Okuneva's report concluded that 'the organism of women can be adapted to the requirements which are made by the profession of a loader and to the carrying of loads in general'.[30]

These recommendations were welcomed by the Narkomtrud Department of Labour Protection at a meeting held in June 1929 at which Okuneva presented the findings of the research experiments.[31] The meeting directed the research institutes to complete their experiments by 1930 so that the requisite legislative proposals could be drawn up. Amongst other requests, the meeting also asked the Institute of Labour Protection to extend its research into other areas of female employment, specifically to examine the influence of shaking and vibrations on the female organism amongst such workers as drivers and conductors on trams and buses, garment factory workers, and so on, and the conditions of work for women in the building professions.

The Institute of Labour Protection had prepared a report for Narkomtrud by the end of the year. In December 1929 the Institute recommended that only women who had no serious problems with their reproductive systems should be allowed to work in the lifting and transporting of loads. In addition, the report recommended that, in so far as was possible, manual lifting processes should be mechanised, beginning, in the first instance, with tasks in which women were more widely employed.[32]

Despite the findings of such research and the publication of a number of reports and recommendations, Okuneva complained at the All-Union Conference on Work Amongst Women (2–5 February 1931) of slow progress in the area of the protection of female labour. She complained particularly about the disparity between actual conditions of work and the legislative enactments:

> Let's take the question of the transporting of weights. We have a law which allows women to transport weights no heavier than 4 kg, i.e. 10 *funt*, but at the same time we have a huge army of thousands of women who work in heavy labour in the transporting of loads even up to now, despite the fact that the question has already been scientifically studied, despite the fact that our Institute has provided maximum norms, has worked out rationalisation measures for unmechanised tasks, and yet the question of legislation on this question, on the question of the transporting of weights, on the question of physical labour by women, remains at a dead end.[33]

On the basis of the recommendations set out in the research findings of the Institute for Labour Protection and partly in recognition of proclaimed improvements in technology and the general conditions of work, on 20 September 1931 a maximum weight of 20 kg was established for an individual female worker carrying loads by hand on an even surface. A 50 kg maximum load for women working in pairs was also introduced. These levels remained significantly below the 80 kg norm set for adult male workers in loading and transporting tasks. The regulations also set out guidelines for the conditions of work for women engaged in loading and unloading work and in the transportation of loads. Women were to work only in the loading and transporting of packaged goods (sand, clay, grain, vegetables, etc.), light loads (wood chips, packaging materials, fruit in small packets, etc.) and individual items (bricks, asphalt, etc.). Women were also permitted to work in jobs involving the weighing of grains and vegetables and in tasks involving loading grain into buckets, funnels and on to elevator and conveyor belts.[34]

The new regulations introduced in 1932 formed the basis of Soviet legislation on the lifting and transporting of loads by women which remained unchanged for several decades. The proposed full set of new regulations on the maximum norms of loads was discussed at a meeting of ACCTU representatives on 10 January 1932. The meeting also recommended the

Table 8.2   Norms of Loads, 1932

	Weight
By hand on an even surface	20 kg (40 funt)
Single-wheeled barrow	50 kg (110 funt)[a]
3- or 4-wheeled hand cart	100 kg[b]
2-wheeled hand cart:	
On an even surface with a gradient not exceeding 0.02	115 kg
On an uneven earth or paved surface with a gradient not exceeding 0.01	60 kg
Wagons on rails	600 kg[c]

[a]Gradient not to exceed 0.02.
[b]On an uneven surface the gradient should not exceed 0.01.
[c]Gradient not to exceed 0.01.
Source: 'O predel'nykh normakh perenoski i peredvizheniya tyazhestei vzroslymi zhenshchinami', decree of Narkomtrud, *Izvestiya NKT*, 1932, no. 25, pp. 322–3.

mechanisation of tasks where women and young workers were employed in the loading, unloading and transporting of weights.[35] A few months later, on 14 August 1932, a decree was published, which set out a revised list of maximum norms for the carrying and transporting of loads by adult female workers – see Table 8.2. In practice, the new regulations introduced only minor changes to the existing norms.

The revised regulations were applicable on a union-wide basis to women over the age of 18 years. These regulations were not fully revised again until the early 1980s. The maximum norms did not include the weight of the appliance used in the carrying and transporting of the load. A stretcher with handles was recommended for transporting loads by hand. The weight of the load, including the weight of the stretcher, was not to exceed 50 kg for a pair of workers.[36] The 1932 decree specifically revoked the terms of the original 1921 (and 1923 union-wide) regulations in relation to women over the age of 18 years.

At the same time the maximum weight of load to be carried by hand over an even surface by young women between the ages of 16 and 18 years was set at 10.5 kg. For young female workers between the ages of 15 and 16 years, who were permitted to undertake such work only in exceptional circumstances, this norm was again reduced by half.[37] Subsequent regulations introduced on 13 October 1932 forbade altogether the employment of young women under the age of 18 years in jobs exclusively involving the lifting and transporting of loads in excess of 4.2 kg.[38]

From this time, however, there seems to have been some reversal in the general trends towards restricting the employment of women in occupations which involved the carrying and transporting of loads. During the 1930s women were increasingly drawn into jobs which involved heavy physical labour. Some of the earlier restrictions on the employment of women workers in identified sectors of the economy were specifically retracted. For example, in 1937 the restrictions on the employment of adult women in the timber industry were revised so that women were subsequently allowed to work in a broader range of lumbering and floating tasks.[39]

The observations of foreign visitors to the Soviet Union, besides identifying changes in the immediate conditions of employment for women workers in some sectors of the economy, are also useful for their elaboration of the debates on different cultural and social attitudes and assumptions concerning the capacity of women workers for heavy physical labour. Writing in the 1940s and making particular observations about the deployment of the Soviet female labour force during the Second World War, Maggie Jordan argued that Russian women were acclimatised to hard physical labour and although such work may have appeared shocking to a Western observer it was not always considered to be burdensome by Soviet women:

> Russian women have always taken part in hard work. They have always worked on the land ... It is hard physical labour to work in the harvest, but it is not a type of labour which is injurious to healthy, hardy women. Women in Russia work on construction jobs; they are bricklayers; they work with pick and shovel; they push wheelbarrows and carry loads of timber. But this work is not injurious, although it demands a fair amount of physical strength. Therefore, Soviet law

does not forbid a woman, whose strength is equal to the task, from performing it. Many women prefer this work to an inside job in a textile mill.[40]

Jordan argued that women in Russia had for a long time been physically and psychologically prepared for strenuous manual labour and that much of this type of work was not in itself a danger to women's health. The Soviet programme of physical training was, she argued, preparing a new generation of girls for such employment. She noted also that weather conditions were often raised as a point of concern by foreign observers but she argued further that 'Russian women are inured to their climate; and what may seem frightful to a visiting seaman is just ordinary for them.'[41]

As with the other measures introduced for the protection of female labour during the 1920s and 1930s, it is difficult to assess the extent to which the provisions on the maximum weights of loads were adhered to or enforced in practice. In addition to this, McAuley has argued particularly in relation to the restrictions on weights of loads introduced during the interwar years that 'if they had been rigorously adhered to, they would surely have disadvantaged women in competition for loading and unloading jobs'.[42] It is also probable that so many of these types of jobs were done by women anyway that it was unlikely that the regulations could have been put into effect in reality. It is also important to note that the legal restrictions did not cover the unregulated areas of women's lives, such as domestic labour, where women were likely frequently to exceed the established norms for the lifting and transporting of loads. The mechanisation of Soviet industry and production processes in this period was also unlikely to have benefited women a great deal. As with a number of other areas of protective labour legislation for women workers during the interwar years, therefore, it is probable that the restrictions on the weights of loads existed mostly only on paper.

9 Restricted Occupations

In reviewing the conditions of work for women in the period following the October revolution the Bolsheviks discussed the question of restricting the employment of female labour in tasks which were considered to be too heavy or difficult and were considered to be injurious to women's health. Narkomtrud was given the responsibility for drawing up a list of jobs in which the employment of women should be prohibited. The list of restricted occupations formed the basis for controls on the environmental and climatic conditions of female employment and included, for example, jobs which involved working with harmful industrial substances (such as lead, mercury, phosphorus, tobacco, arsenic, benzene), with noxious gases and chemicals or in excessively hot or cold temperatures. A shorter working day was introduced for those employed in exceptionally difficult or harmful tasks and workers in these jobs in practice often received higher rates of pay.

The first Soviet Labour Code, issued on 10 December 1918, included a general prohibition on the employment of women workers in jobs which were considered to be detrimental to their health. At this time it was envisaged that a list of such jobs would be drawn up which would become subject to annual review by the Department of Labour Protection attached to Narkomtrud.[1] As with other areas of the protection of female labour, the disruption caused by the civil war and war communism no doubt meant that the restrictions introduced in these years were widely ignored and proved impossible to implement in practice. Subsequent revisions to the restrictions, therefore, may have served purely to recognise an already existing situation by sanctioning the employment of women in jobs where the prohibition had never fully been enforced. These revisions to some extent also reflected the fact that there were sectors of the economy which were faced with serious labour shortages, especially during the civil war and in the 1930s.

The original provisions themselves were subject to revision in the years immediately following the revolution in direct response to the difficult circumstances of the period. For

130

example, *Izvestiya* reported in October 1919 that female workers, with the exception of pregnant women and nursing mothers, were to be allowed to work in a number of jobs in railway transport, including as stokers and conductors. Women were to be permitted to work as greasers only if they were supplied with the necessary protective clothing.[2]

The prohibitions on the employment of female labour in difficult jobs and tasks considered to be injurious to women's health were reiterated and consolidated further in Article 129 of the 1922 Labour Code. The list of restricted occupations and the norms of loads with which women could work were to be established at the discretion of Narkomtrud in agreement with the ACCTU.[3] The official limitations placed on the scope of female employment by such legislation, in combination with the growing concern over the levels of female unemployment during the NEP (1921–28), may have resulted in a decline in both the actual numbers and proportions of women working in the identified sectors of the economy, although it is important to note that the extent of the impact of the restrictive measures alone would be difficult to gauge. Anecdotal accounts and evidence drawn from individual sectors of the economy do reflect to a limited degree the changes in female employment in this period, some of which may have been brought about by the imposition of the prohibition on the use of women's labour in the restricted occupations. Legislation on the 'restricted occupations' also constituted the legal basis of sex segregationist employment practices which were in evidence especially in industry for many decades.

A circular issued on 6 June 1924 attempted to enumerate and counter the trend of falling female employment in the transport sector.[4] The preamble to the circular stated that railway transport as a whole had witnessed a fall in the proportion of women employed from 13 per cent in July 1920 to 9.1 per cent in October 1923. On balance, there had been relatively little fall in the numbers of women employed in administrative tasks (by 7 per cent), but a much sharper decline in occupations involving physical labour (48 per cent in track maintenance and 45 per cent in supply work); and the employment of young women workers on rail transport had declined by as much as 61 per cent. It is not clear from this study, however, that the decline in the proportion of women workers employed in the railway sector was the result of the strict imposition of the prohibitive legislation or whether it was symptomatic of a more general trend in rising unemployment amongst women in these years.

The circular suggested methods by which the administrative bodies responsible for overseeing employment in rail transport could attempt to redress this decline. These methods included, for example, implementing existing laws which guaranteed the employment rights of pregnant women and new mothers, referring cases of dismissal of more highly skilled and qualified women workers for further review and not preventing night work by women in areas elsewhere identified by law. The circular also suggested raising the levels of professional qualifications amongst women, firstly by increasing the percentages of young women workers in vocational training schools and, secondly, by increasing the numbers of adult women workers on skills-based training courses. In addition, the circular called for further research to be conducted at local levels into the numbers of women employed and the range of their jobs in rail transport as a means of securing a female labour force in this particular sector in the future.

The restrictions placed on female employment by Article 129 of the 1922 Labour Code remained the focus of discussion by the Narkomtrud Department of Labour Protection in subsequent years. On 16 April 1924, for example, the professional hygiene section of the Labour Protection Department, in discussion with representatives from the Moscow print workers' trade union, identified four areas of work in the printing industry where it was recommended that female labour should be banned.[5] Similar restrictions were recommended for the oil industry.[6] In addressing 'measures in the area of female labour protection' a meeting of the Commission for the Improvement and Study of Women's Labour in 1924 heard the report of the Department of Labour Protection. The report outlined the areas of work where the employment of female labour was prohibited and proceeded to recommend a reduction in the number of prohibited jobs in order to increase the scope of women's employment. At the same time the report pointed to the vast numbers of women still engaged in hazardous employments. The transfer of women from these hazardous occupations was noted as proceeding very slowly.[7]

Despite the general statements of prohibition included in both the 1918 and 1922 Labour Codes, a full list of occupations in which the employment of female labour was prohibited was not fully enumerated by Narkomtrud until 1925. Article 129 of the 1922 Labour Code was supplemented by a decree of 30 October 1925, which set out for the first time 'a list of especially hazardous employments in which women are not permitted'. The list detailed thirty specific tasks in nine different sectors of the economy in which the employment of female labour was to be prohibited.[8] The decree stated that the identification of any additional task for inclusion on the list of restricted occupations required an agreement between the relevant economic organisations and trade union bodies and was to be confirmed by the labour inspectorate. In addition to these measures and in accordance with the 1922 Labour Code, industrial safety and hygiene regulations permitted soap and specialist protective garments and clothing, such as masks and glasses, to be assigned to workers in identified hazardous occupations.

The effectiveness of industrial safety and labour hygiene measures can be judged partly by the evidence of western visitors to the Soviet Union in this period, although it is also important to note that these visitors most probably were only invited to witness conditions of work in the most progressive and model factories. For example, a report by six British women trade unionists to the Soviet Union in 1925 includes a comment on the supplementary provisions allocated to workers in the hazardous occupations:

> As regards the injurious trades, such as certain branches of the tobacco trade and those in which poisonous substances are used, the employment of women is, for the most part, prohibited; where it is permitted women are given a certain definite allowance (at the expense of the enterprise) of milk, butter, or other fats to counteract the effects of the injurious materials.[9]

A pamphlet published by the Communist Party in London in 1928 records the observations of five British women who surveyed factory conditions for female labour in the Soviet Union in the later 1920s. These women noted that in the 'Rabochi' textile factory in Leningrad 'great precautions are taken to safeguard the workers' health. Those in unhealthy departments receive one month's holiday a year on full pay, while the rest have a fortnight's on full pay.'[10] On the general conditions of work in 'unhealthy occupations' the women noted:

> Special consideration is given to women in unhealthy occupations. These include very hot or dusty occupations, and certain kinds of printing, dyeing and bleaching, etc.[11]

These delegates also noted the special benefits which were assigned to women working in unhealthy occupations, which included an extended holiday entitlement, noted earlier, and extra supplies of basic foodstuffs and milk. Jessica Smith during her visits to the Soviet Union in 1922 and 1924 observed the operation of a system of night sanatoria in some sectors of the economy for workers who were unwell but not sick enough to be laid off work. The cigarette factory in Rostov had such a provision where the workers, mostly women, could avail themselves of free medical supervision at night to safeguard against the contraction of serious industrial diseases.[12] Environmental and physical working conditions were improving as a result of the consideration being given to ventilation at factories, the supply of protective clothing and the provision of drinking water and washing facilities. Health checks were also being made on raw materials, such as wool fleeces, before they were allowed into the factories and before women came into contact with them. The British visitors were informed that 'such inspections were unknown under the Tsar'.[13] They noted also that:

> although the conditions in Russian factories are not yet by any means perfect, we were assured of the appreciation of the textile workers of the tremendous difference and betterment of their conditions since the revolution.[14]

Despite such observations by western commentators on the improvements in factory environmental conditions and the adaptability of Soviet women to hard physical labour, the prohibitions on the employment of female labour in certain specific occupations were often justified by the bad conditions which prevailed and resulted from extensive scientific research into the impact on women's health of particular jobs and production processes. Contemporary working conditions could prove extremely detrimental to women's health. It may also be assumed that working in such environments was injurious also to male workers, although this did not result in men being officially excluded from any of the industrial occupations.

In a number of industries in which the prohibition on the employment of female labour was imposed toxic substances were widely employed in the production process: lead and hot metals in the printing industry, aniline dyes in the textile industry, nicotine in the tobacco industry,[15] rubber in the manufacture of rubber shoes[16] and phosphorus in the production of matches, for example. These substances could easily penetrate the female body and poison the bloodstream, thereby undermining the health of women workers and increasing the likelihood of complications during pregnancy. Poor ventilation was also recognised as a danger to women's health, in the porcelain industry, for example.[17]

Koenker's study of the printing industry questions the motivations behind the imposition of restrictions in this particular sector:

> In June 1923, the presidium of the [printer's] union central committee resolved that women should not be permitted to work in particularly harmful departments: typecasting, because it required work with hot metal; in the stereotype departments, where hot metal was poured into matrices; in zinc-engraving departments, where poisonous metals were involved; in engraving departments; and on the Monotype typesetting machine. These were constructed 'hazards'. On the one hand, they were no less harmful for men, but, on the other, machine typesetting work in other countries was considered to be especially appropriate for the 'weaker sex'.[18]

Yet the restrictions did not all involve 'constructed hazards'. One contemporary study noted the high levels of consumption and anaemia amongst female tobacco workers, who spent their day surrounded by dust and nicotine in badly ventilated workshops. Working with toxic substances, as scientific research identified, increased the likelihood of miscarriage, premature birth, stillbirths and infant mortality. According to one report, of a total of 100 pregnancies amongst women working with lead-based substances, there were only thirteen live births and only ten of these children survived to the second year of life.[19]

A different investigation noted the far higher reporting of illness amongst women and girls in comparison with male employees working with toxic substances and in hazardous conditions. Of 133 incidences of lead poisoning reported in one particular study 94 cases involved women. 95 per cent of cases of phosphorous poisoning were of women. High levels of infection were also registered amongst female workers in the tobacco industry.[20] Such investigations, however, did not always note the proportion of the total labour force consti-tuted by women in the identified sectors. The higher record-ing of illnesses amongst women workers in these cases may have resulted simply from the fact that female labour consti-tuted the bulk of the labour force in the sectors under review.

Particularly hazardous employments for women were noted in printing, weaving, *makhorka* (a type of tobacco), brush and bristle production, the chemical industry and occupations involving work in high temperatures.[21] Even in cases where the work may not actually have been dangerous, it could still be unpleasant. Lili Korber, for example, complained that 'our work is not actually injurious to health, but the fine metal-dust permeates the skin and stops the pores. One ought to rub one's whole body with machine oil.'[22] Work in indus-tries where the production process involved close contact with toxic and harmful substances formed an important element in the debates identifying hazardous occupations in which the employment of female labour should be prohibited.

The general findings on the danger to women's health of employment in the tobacco industry were confirmed by a 1923–24 survey conducted by the Institute of Labour Protection amongst tobacco workers in the Ukraine. Women constituted 67.7 per cent of tobacco workers in Khar'kov. Many had started work before the age of 14 years, and some had been as young as 8 years old; 70 per cent of employees had work experience of at least six years. The bulk of the labour force, however, remained young; 70 per cent of workers were under the age of 30 years. The relatively young age of the labour force in the tobacco industry was credited to the high levels of invalidity caused by the production process in this industry.[23]

The levels of industrial invalidity and ill-health were particularly marked amongst women. Recorded levels of illness in the Ukrainian tobacco industry were six times higher than in other local industries. In particular, the report noted the higher levels of infertility, miscarriage and infant mortality suffered by female tobacco workers. Around 20 per cent of the female tobacco workers in Khar'kov were reported to be infertile, as compared to 16.7 per cent of workers in Kiev and 20.3 per cent in Odessa. In Khar'kov also there were reported to be 8.7 miscarriages for every 100 pregnancies and 32.7 per cent of babies died in the first year of life. The slightly higher figure of 9.8 miscarriages per 100 pregnancies was reported for Kiev, where infant mortality was recorded at 33.9 per cent. The levels of infant mortality amongst female tobacco workers were compared in the report to local figures of between 8.5 per cent and 19 per cent.

The survey report recommended that both machinery and entire workshops should be properly ventilated, and that the production process should be automated and mechanised. It recommended also that special clothing should be provided to prevent any contact of the tobacco with the skin, and this was subsequently supplied.[24] Despite the findings of this research, however, work in the tobacco industry was not included in the list of prohibited occupations for female labour issued by Narkomtrud in 1925. Subsequent studies continued to highlight the hazards for women of employment in the tobacco industry.

The influence of nicotine on the reproductive processes of women became an important area of investigation for the research institutes involved in labour protection issues from the mid-1920s.[25] An article published in the labour hygiene journal, *Gigiena truda*, in 1927 reported on the findings of an investigation into the impact of infection by nicotine of breast milk.[26] This report also noted that the levels of infant mortality experienced amongst nursing mothers working with nicotine-based substances in the tobacco industry were higher than for women working in other sectors of the industry and significantly exceeded the average levels of infant mortality for the population as a whole.[27]

The article, based on the examination of women at the Odessa maternity home in March–April 1926, reiterated the high levels of infant mortality reported in the 1923–24 survey and emphasised that infant mortality amongst women working directly with nicotine was double that of other women in the industry. The author of the article, Dr Vol'ter of the Odessa department of the All-Ukrainian Institute of Workers' Medicine, argued that nicotine penetrated the breast milk of working mothers and impeded the development of the immune system in nursing babies. Vol'ter argued further that nicotine diminished both the quality and quantities of breast milk, which resulted in babies being inadequately nourished.

A further investigation was conducted by Narkomtrud RSFSR at the end of the 1920s into the conditions of work for women at three different tobacco factories in Moscow. Women constituted around two-thirds of the total labour force. A number of infringements of the protective labour law provisions were noted in the report. Women were employed on an overtime basis to clean and maintain machinery. Special brigades, composed entirely of women, worked at night to clean the machines. There were no reported infringements of the protective measures for the employment of pregnant women and nursing mothers, but all the factories noted examples where women were employed in especially difficult jobs and in the carrying of loads. The working conditions were generally unhealthy. Illnesses, such as tuberculosis and nervous disorders, were recorded. The high level of ill-health in the tobacco industry was partly blamed on the fact that women spent much of their work time in one position and that this inhibited the circulation of blood and encouraged reproductive disorders.[28]

Unlike the example of the tobacco industry, in 1925 Narkomtrud identified nine tasks in the metallurgical and metal working industries in which the employment of women was to be prohibited, including occupations involving the movement and treatment of molten and hot metals and employment in conditions with very high temperatures. In April 1927 the metallurgical industry trade union allocated 600 rubles a month for up to six months for an investigation to start immediately into the conditions of work for female labour in the industry under the guidance of the Institute of Labour Protection.[29] The investigations were to encompass workers in three broad areas of production: the tool shop (locksmiths, lathe turners and cutters), mechanised production (as in the tool shop plus drillers and plane operators) and machine fitters (on lathes, cutting machines, etc.).[30] The intended study was directed, amongst other tasks, towards investigating the physiological and biomechanical impact of these jobs on the female organism and it aimed to record the levels of traumatism and ill-health amongst female workers. The findings of this research, however, have not been located.

The environmental and climatic conditions of female employment formed the basis of some of the research undertaken by the various museums and institutes for labour protection in the 1920s. The rationale behind such research, at least in theory, was to expand the scope of female employment by introducing changes to the working environment rather than restricting further the number of occupations in which women could be employed. Investigations were conducted into the impact on the female organism of employment in different temperatures and humidity and the impact of lighting, ventilation, dust and toxic substances on women's health. The maintenance of the health of workers appears to have been a central concern in the research into labour protection in this period.[31]

Research was also directed towards improving seating arrangements for female machine-operators and drivers in order to minimise the impact of vibrations and to relieve the congestion of the internal and reproductive organs. Specific research in this area was conducted into the potential for the employment of women as tram conductors and tractor drivers. As Bonnell's research has shown, the 'woman on the tractor' image, represented on posters and in art, has come to epitomise the process of women's emancipation and economic achievements in the Soviet Union in the 1930s.[32] It has also been used in socialist realist formulations to symbolise the technological advances of Soviet agriculture in this period and the subordination by women workers of family life and femininity to the liberating processes of socialist labour and industrialisation. In reality, however, the suitability of employing women as tractor drivers was the subject of much debate from the late 1920s.

Some of the research into the employment of female labour on tractors was conducted at the Institute of Labour Protection. The aim of the research was to identify the potential dangers of tractor driving for women and to recommend changes in tractor design and construction rather than restricting the employment of female tractor drivers. Research was conducted in conjunction with the Saratov Institute of Professional Diseases and fieldwork was conducted on a state farm in the lower Volga in the summer of 1930. The limited experience of female tractor drivers in this particular region, however, meant that the fieldwork was supplemented by a study conducted with the help of the Institute for Motherhood and Childhood in the central Volga region. The report on the research recognised that such employment could potentially be injurious to both women and men but experiments were conducted to examine the particular impact of tractor driving on women's reproductive functions.[33]

Research focused on the level of vibration generated by different types of tractors. Consideration was given to the positioning of levers and seating arrangements. Measurements were taken with the different types of tractors operating at a variety of gear speeds. The actual degree of movement of both the tractor and the driver was determined by fixing a series of lights to the tractor and to different parts of the driver's body (head, shoulders, etc.) and the level of vibrations was plotted by means of various horizontal and vertical markings on a graph. Tractors with caterpillar tracks were found to operate at lower levels of vibration and jolting than wheeled tractors, thus reducing the potentially harmful impact of this work on the female organism. The published report noted that 'caterpillar tractors do not shake, although the tractor oscillates with small vibrations over its whole frame, but wheeled tractors (such as the "International") encourage jolting movements which greatly intensify the impractical positioning of the seat'. The report recommended, therefore, that 'the most expedient use of female labour in the first instance is on caterpillar tractors'.[34] However, there were very few such tractors in operation at this time.

The report also recommended that changes should be made to the seating arrangements on wheeled tractors in order to minimise the level and impact of vibrations. Starter mechanisms were also the subject of discussion. Preliminary findings into the impact of driving a tractor on the placement of the womb and abdominal breathing also formed part of the report and influenced the legislative outcomes of the research. Okuneva, of the Institute of Labour Protection, clearly identified the importance of the findings of this research in her speech to the meeting of the All-Union Trade Union Conference on Work amongst Women in February 1931.[35] The growth in the socialised sector of agriculture, she argued, had generated a great demand for women to become involved in all areas of mechanised labour, including as tractor drivers.

Okuneva pointed out that there were two major types of tractors: wheeled tractors, such as the 'International' and the 'Fordson', which required less skill to operate; and caterpillar-track tractors, which required a higher level of skill but were less harmful to operate. Work on wheeled tractors, research had revealed, was more damaging to women's health. Okuneva recognised that large numbers of wheeled tractors were being produced in the Soviet Union at the Stalingrad and Khar'kov works. She recommended that different types of seats (presumably with soft springs) should be manufactured for the 'International' tractor, thus making them more suitable for operation by women workers. She argued 'thus, by this practical measure, we will ensure the widespread introduction of female labour into the mechanised branches of agriculture'.[36] The concern here, therefore, was to broaden the scope of female employment in skilled and mechanised work whilst at the same time reducing the potential for injury.

However, the seating arrangements and the constant vibration in operation of certain types of tractors were deemed by Narkomtrud to make them unsuitable for the employment of female labour. A decree of 9 May 1931 required women to undergo a medical examination before beginning training to drive these vehicles. Women were to be given priority in access to caterpillar tractors once trained and were to operate wheeled tractors only if caterpillar tractors were not available. Women were also to be given priority of access to tractors with automated ignition.[37] (See also Chapter 7.)

A few years later, in September 1935, the discussion on the employment of women as tractor drivers was renewed at a meeting of the ACCTU labour inspectorate with representatives from agricultural organisations. A draft decree drawn up at this time revealed the intention of the trade union organisation to forbid entirely the employment of women on all types of wheeled tractors and to gain the consent of the Council of People's Commissars for this restriction. The draft decree reiterated the clause that women should be given priority in the operation of tractors with automatic starter motors and other equipment which facilitated the ignition of the tractor.[38] These draft proposals, however, do not appear to have been incorporated into the published statutes. During 1935 there was also extensive discussion of expanding the range of occupations in which women could be employed in river and sea transport.[39] Unlike the discussion on tractor drivers, these proposals were later incorporated in the law.

Somewhat earlier, on 17 May 1930, a revised decree was published which reiterated and extended the prohibition on the employment of women in especially heavy and dangerous jobs and occupations. As had been the case since 1925, the identification of additional restricted tasks required the agreement of the relevant administrative bodies. This new decree, however, also supplemented the terms of the 1925 regulations by stating that any specified occupation listed under any particular individual industrial sectoral heading in the decree should also be prohibited in all other branches of the economy. For example, the decree stated that the prohibition on women working as stokers in the metal-processing industries was to apply also to the deployment of female labour in transport.[40]

By the terms of the 1930 regulations, in exceptional circumstances and depending on local conditions of production, republican level labour commissariats could permit the employment of women in the restricted occupations and professions. Special conditions of work were established for female engineering-technical workers and practical experts. Special terms were also set out for women machine operators, including regular rest periods and the supply of protective clothing. Significantly, Article 6 of the decree stated that women already working in a restricted occupation, as identified in the newly revised list, should not be made redundant on account of this legislation. The appended list identified seventy-nine specific tasks and occupations in ten different sectors of industry.

Faced with growing labour shortages during the First Five-Year Plan and the need to implement the goal of encouraging women into industrial employment, on 6 September 1930 the Council of People's Commissars authorised Narkomtrud to draw up a list of tasks which should be reserved predominantly or exclusively for female labour. The attempt to encourage growing numbers of women into industrial employment was also reflected at this time, on the one hand, by renewed attempts to improve the provision of communal services and child care facilities to relieve the burden on working women and, on the other hand, by the raising of quotas for the numbers of young women in vocational schools and on industrial training courses.

In view of the need to meet the requirements of a rapidly expanding economy and with the aim of attracting more women into the process of socialist construction, a decree of 8 December 1930 set out the intention of expanding the use of female labour in all branches of the economy. The decree suggested that this would allow the maximum use of available labour reserves at a local level as well as the establishment of permanent cadres of women workers. The stated intention of the decree was to identify areas of the economy where women workers were completely absent or where female labour was being under-utilised.[41]

By this decree, Narkomtrud RSFSR was authorised to draw up a list of jobs in specific industries (metallurgy, electrical, chemicals, mining, paper, leather, garments and textiles) and occupations in state and cooperative organisations to be reserved 'exclusively' and 'predominantly' for women (as had been requested at union level a few months previously). Narkomtrud RSFSR was to liaise with other labour and economic organisations to ratify the list and with other administrative bodies to work out ways of implementing the terms of the legislation, taking account also of the substitution of male workers by female labour which was necessitated by this process. The remainder of the decree identified the need for the expansion of the cultural and social services available to women, especially in terms of child care facilities.

Soon afterwards, on 16 January 1931 Narkomtrud RSFSR issued two lists outlining jobs which were to be reserved, firstly, 'predominantly' and, secondly, 'exclusively' for women. The first list identified 190 tasks in seven different industrial sectors. The second list identified 137 tasks in seven different industrial sectors.[42] These lists, however, were soon superseded by union-wide regulations outlined in a decree of 19 May 1931, which identified areas of the economy in which the employment of female labour was to be expanded. This decree listed 329 jobs in twelve different industrial sectors.[43] The list was subsequently further expanded by a decree of 10 April 1932 which specified the addition of another 108 tasks in four different sectors of the economy.[44]

In keeping with earlier restrictive practices, however, a revised list was issued also on 10 April 1932 of especially difficult and dangerous jobs in which the employment of women was to be prohibited, thereby replacing the list published in May 1930 and introducing changes in wording to other minor legislative enactments. The revised list was issued with the intention of taking into account factories which had been newly built on the basis of protective labour requirements, the mechanisation and rationalisation of various labour processes and the improvements in the conditions of labour in existing enterprises. These developments, the decree claimed, now permitted the broader assimilation of women into jobs in all branches of the national economy. The 1932 decree, however, reduced the number of restricted occupations only very slightly, from seventy-nine to seventy-two, and even increased the number of restricted tasks in the chemical industries (from nine to sixteen).[45]

In addition to reinforcing the ban on underground work in mining by women, the employment of female labour was also prohibited in tasks in the metallurgical industries, largely involving handling molten metals, in jobs involving work with dangerous chemicals, in hazardous employments, such as fire fighting and work involving the continuous lifting of heavy weights, such as stokers on the railways and loading jobs on water transport. Prohibitions were also reinforced on the employment of women in specified tasks in more traditional areas of female employment, including in the textile and leather industries.

In view of the rapidly changing development in the nature of some of the occupations listed in the decree and the introduction of changes in the production process itself, it was intended that the list should be periodically reviewed. Serebrennikov observed that:

> More than fifty different kinds of work that might be harmful to the female organism are prohibited to women. But there is nothing permanent about this prohibition. As the result of widespread industrial reconstruction, of the increasing mechanisation of labour, and of the vast improvements that are being made in industrial hygiene, the possibility of employing women without injury to their health is continually being extended to new kinds of labour.[46]

With the exception of a few amendments resulting from such mechanisation of various labour processes and technological developments, however, the 1932 list remained the basis of prohibited tasks for women's employment in the Soviet Union until the Labour Code was completely revised in 1978.

It would be difficult to determine the degree to which the terms of the 1932 protective labour provisions were implemented in practice, or their subsequent impact on the levels and structure of female employment in the 1930s. On reviewing the terms of these measures McAuley has pointed out that 'no mention of provisions for retraining or relocating those displaced by the new law' was made and that 'the most important effect of the 1932 decree ... was to inhibit the training of women for skilled jobs in heavy industry – although the evidence even for this conclusion is not substantial'. He goes on to argue that 'given the apparent frequency with which the law was disregarded under Stalin, I suspect that the 1932 decree had little direct impact on women's employment before the mid-1950s' but that the 1932 decree probably contributed to the increasing levels of horizontal segregation in the labour force.[47]

In December 1931 further in-depth research was authorised into the use of women's labour and the levels of productivity in a variety of industrial sectors with the aim of expanding the scope of female employment.[48] The research programme was initiated in the following month. The findings of the research were published in 1933 and challenged some of the earlier assumptions concerning the dangers of industrial employment for the female organism. For example, research conducted in Leningrad into women's employment in the machine-building industry suggested that levels of ill-health amongst women employed in this sector were no higher than the average levels of sickness amongst women workers elsewhere in Leningrad industries and did not significantly differ from the levels of sickness amongst male colleagues. Changes adopted as a result of these findings allowed the number of women employed in machine-building in five different factories to double in the second half of 1932.[49]

The findings of the research also proposed that both technological developments and the dilution of the labour process were greatly facilitating the expansion of female employment. Mechanisation of the production process and the breakdown of complex and skilled manual occupations into a variety of unskilled tasks reduced the need for highly trained and qualified labour. These changes in the production process resulted in the deskilling of the industrial labour force which increased the scope for women's entry into the heavy industrial sectors of the economy. For example, this was noted to be the case in the machine-building industry cited earlier, and in the timber industry, where the transfer to a system of labour organisation based on brigades facilitated the employment of women in a broader range of tasks and reduced the number of jobs reserved exclusively for men.[50] The research findings, therefore, formed the basis for the expansion of women's employment in the 1930s and especially in the heavy industrial sectors of the economy and, it could be argued, may have helped to justify the less rigid enforcement of the prohibition on women's employment in the restricted occupations in this decade.

Despite the legislative prohibition on the employment of women in the restricted occupations it is evident that the 1930s saw a radical shift in the nature of female employment in the Soviet Union with women being employed in a range of different jobs which had previously only been undertaken by male workers. During the 1930s, and especially with the growing threat of war later in the decade, specific operations in various sectors of the economy came to be identified as tasks in which female labour should no longer be excluded and these were gradually removed from the list of prohibited jobs by a series of separate decrees, although the full list itself was not officially revised. The imminence of war predictably, therefore, allowed for a significant expansion in the scope of female employment, in drilling and boring work in the oil industry and a broader range of jobs in the metallurgical industries, for example.[51]

The official list of jobs in which women could be employed on steam locomotives was revised by a decree issued on 1 November 1938.[52] This decree allowed women to be employed as engine drivers and assistants on steam locomotives, stokers and as repair workers in the routine maintenance of locomotive engines.[53] In his study of the Soviet locomotive industry in this period, Westwood has noted that in the campaigns to recruit women as locomotive drivers candidates were usually selected from amongst those already working in the repair shops, where they would have built up familiarity with the engines. By the end of 1938 the 'Stalinsk' railway had 119 women attending night schools with the intention of becoming drivers. After three and a half months of training these women were qualified as assistant drivers, which allowed them to drive locomotives independently in times of need. After five years of training women were able to take exams in order to become fully qualified locomotive drivers. Yet, Westwood has noted:

> one such recently qualified driver, taking the driver's seat on the FD for the first time, was removed on the instructions of the chief of traction because 'in the depot there continues to be respected the false "theory" that women cannot drive locomotives'.[54]

In response to proposals dating back as far as 1935, on 13 June 1940 the restrictions were lifted on the employment of female labour in river transport. In 1935 it had been proposed that women should be allowed to work, amongst other tasks, at the helm and as sailors on ships with mechanised equipment. In 1940 the prohibition was maintained for women working in only a few specified tasks. These included jobs as stokers on steamboats powered by solid fuel, sailors on cargo ships or at the helm of ships with manual steering controls.[55]

It is worth noting here that such legislative changes, which were introduced from the later 1930s to expand the scope of female employment, did not in themselves remove the long-standing prejudices of male colleagues and managers towards the physical capabilities of women workers, as has been demonstrated particularly by the example of railway transport. The sex segregation of the labour force was reflected also in differentiated levels of skill, and thereby wages, and the continued sectoral concentration of women in the light industries and men in heavy industries. It could be argued, however, that legislative initiatives did pave the way for women workers to play a more extensive and 'equal' role in Soviet industry and transport during the Second World War.

10 Underground Work

An investigation into the employment of women in underground work in the Soviet mining industry is illustrative of a number of important questions relating to the protection of female labour in the 1920s and 1930s.[1] These questions include in this specific example the debates surrounding the physical capabilities of the female labour force and the fact that whilst the enactment of protective labour laws was perceived to be entirely in women's interests by some, others argued that such legislative practice discriminated against women in that it prevented them from working in jobs which they themselves wanted to do. Women were clearly employed in a whole range of tasks in mining, including in underground work, throughout the interwar years.

As Friedgut's study of 'Iuzovka' has revealed, a small number of women were employed in the mining industry in the tsarist period.[2] Women were employed more widely in the mining industry, including underground work, during the First World War from 1915.[3] Female mine workers even attracted the attention of artists.[4] The law allowing women to work underground was repealed by the Provisional Government in July 1917.[5]

A formal prohibition on the employment of women in underground work was introduced by the Bolsheviks in the 1918 Labour Code as part of the restrictions on the employment of women in heavy labour and in tasks considered injurious to their health.[6] The prohibition was reiterated in Article 129 of the 1922 Labour Code.[7] There was clearly some uncertainty amongst mining officials in the mid-1920s over the extent of the prohibition as is demonstrated by the exchange of letters and requests for information between economic administrators, trade union personnel and the Labour Protection Department of Narkomtrud in 1925.[8]

It is unlikely, however, that the legislation was ever fully enforced in practice. For example, Narkomtrud's own journal, *Voprosy truda*, noted that included in a survey conducted on 1 September 1925 of 49 000 underground workers in the Donets coal basin, there were 'only' 168 women.[9] There is no indication of the types of jobs in which these women were employed, but in view of the fact that women received little technical training or professional education this was more likely to be in unskilled tasks.[10]

The North Caucasus labour department reported in 1926 that in the previous year there had been a number of infringements of the laws dealing with the protection of female labour but that the enforcement of these laws had reached nearer 100 per cent in the current year.[11] The article also noted that at this time the shorter working day introduced for some categories of mine workers had also not been fully implemented in the Donbass region, where coal-hewers were still working an eight-hour day, plus overtime in some cases, instead of the decreed six hours.[12]

The legislative prohibition on underground work by women was further reinforced by a decree issued on 30 October 1925. Included in the list of jobs prohibited to women was a section on the mining industry, which identified four areas of work in which the ban on the use of female labour was to be enforced. The specifically identified tasks, in addition to the prohibition on all underground work, included work directly connected with the manual crushing, firing and smelting of ores containing sulphur and arsenic, employment in the primary processing of precious metals involving cyanide compounds and chlorine, and jobs involving the loading of baked coke.[13] At the end of 1925 Narkomtrud undertook to investigate further the possibility of employing women in underground work.[14]

One of the important concerns in the official debates on the introduction and retraction of protective labour legislation for female labour in the interwar period was the access which women had to the operation of mechanised equipment. Technological advances would, in theory, reduce the number of difficult and heavy jobs from which women were legally excluded. In 1927 a meeting of the scientific-technical council of the mining industry discussed the possibility of allowing women to operate hoisting mechanisms in the mines of the Krivoi Rog region, although this would contravene Article 568 of the safety regulations issued by Narkomtrud in 1925. It was argued that such a move would help to raise the level of skilled work undertaken by women. The meeting was caught between the need to secure the maximum safety conditions of work in the mining industry on the one hand and the desire, on the other hand, to raise the level of qualifications amongst its female labour force.

Narkomtrud's Labour Protection Department supported the suggestion that women should be allowed greater access to mechanised equipment, given the appropriate training for such work, but solicited the opinion of the scientific and technical experts. One representative, A. P. German, argued that although women could be trained for this work it would have negative consequences for their physical well-being. The meeting recommended changes to the wording of the safety regulations to satisfy both the technical and sanitary requirements of the rules. These changes would allow women to be employed in work formally prohibited by Article 568.[15] The outcome of this meeting, therefore, indicated recognition in principle of the potential for employing women in a range of mechanised tasks in the mining industry by the end of the 1920s. The findings of a preliminary investigation were reported on 13 March 1928.[16]

The claim that a substantial number of women were still being employed in underground work in the mining industry in the late 1920s, despite the official prohibition, is confirmed by Narkomtrud's own schedule of work in the area of labour protection for 1928/29.[17] A similar schedule included the intention to undertake an investigation into the utilisation of female labour in underground work and into the conditions of life and work for women in a number of different regions of the country, including the North Caucasus.[18]

Underground work by women was witnessed and deplored by a number of foreign delegations to the Soviet mines during this period. The contemporary debate on whether Soviet women should be employed in the mining industry in any capacity was noted by the American writer, Jessica Smith, who argued in 1928 that:

As opposed to the discrimination against women in some quarters, is the tendency to push women into all kinds of work irrespective of whether they are fitted for that type of work or not. Thus an attempt was fostered by the Miners' Union to raise the percentage of girls in the mining schools

to ten percent. And some women have demanded the abro-
gation of all laws protecting women, claiming that they
always result in discrimination.[19]

A number of other western studies which outline the
changing position of women in Soviet Russia in the years
immediately following the October revolution and in the
1920s note the growing employment of women in various
sectors of the economy, including the mining industry.[20]
Maggie Jordan noted that:

> Women, even in peacetime, work in the mines – but not as
> miners proper. They do not hew coal, but they may be seen
> operating the electric switchboard underground which con-
> trols the haulage trucks, and doing other work.[21]

Central Statistical Administration (TsSU) figures on the distribution of women workers by branch of industry for the
period 1926–29 indicate a steady decline in the proportion
of women employed in mining and related tasks up to 1928.
Yet although the percentage decreased, the actual numbers of
women employed in the mining industry increased gradually
over this period. However, no indication was provided in
these data of the numbers of women employed in mechanised tasks or in underground work or for the rate of transfer
of female labour from underground to surface jobs.[22] In some
cases, as was noted elsewhere, women themselves were reluctant to transfer to surface work, not only because of the
potential reduction in their earnings that this would involve,
but also because they did not want to be employed in
unskilled tasks.[23]

The official statistics record an increase in both the numbers and the proportion of women employed in the mining
industry by the beginning of 1929 (after the proposals for the
First Five-Year Plan had been drawn up)[24] – see Table 10.1.

Even before the introduction of the First Five-Year Plan
there was growing concern about the conditions of work and
particularly the effectiveness of labour protection measures
for women in the mining industry. One report cited in the
archives offers a critical account of the protection of female
mine workers in the Donbass region in 1927.[25] The report
noted that women were employed at the mines predominantly

Table 10.1   Women in the Mining Industry, 1926–29

	Actual number of women	% of total
1 January 1926	33 492	7.4
1 January 1927	38 177	7.2
1 January 1928	36 256	6.7
1 January 1929	41 178	7.0

Source: GARF, f. 5515, o. 13, d. 6, l. 31.

as haulage workers and in the extraction of rocks. Yet in virtually every mine women complained of the inadequacy of labour protection measures. Haulage workers were not provided with overcoats despite the fact that they worked in temperatures of extreme cold and rain for eight hours a day and their meagre wages of 25 roubles per month would be unable to cover the cost of a 12–15 rouble coat. Gloves, which were supposed to last three months, wore out after one month and women were left to haul wagons with their bare hands.[26]

More serious incidents were also noted in the 1927 report. The haulage tracks on the slopes were often rotten, they were not always guarded with barriers and were badly illuminated. The report cited cases of women falling over and breaking their legs and mutilating their hands. One woman at the 'Trud' mine had lain for two hours in the snow waiting for an ambulance after falling down one of the slopes. Another woman at a different mine had worked to the last minute of her pregnancy, despite officially being on maternity leave, and had given birth in the mine shaft.[27]

The report also pointed to the increasing use of female labour in underground work in the mining industry. At the same time the report showed concern for the fact that the actual enforcement of the labour protection laws would exclude women from underground work and leave them unemployed. In these areas there was no alternative employment. At the same time men were being employed in haulage and other surface work and could be transferred to underground tasks. The reassignment of women to surface work and men to underground jobs, the report continued, would need to proceed with caution so as not to upset the women or disrupt production. In reality, however, this transfer of women from underground work appears not to have taken place.

The Narkomtrud journal, *Voprosy truda*, published a second report on the protection of labour in the mining industry in 1929. This report commented on the results of a survey into conditions in the Shakhty district in the North Caucasus.[28] The article noted that 'concerning the protection of women's labour...there are no cases of admitting women to underground work'.[29] There had been an occasion, however, where women had been employed at night as sorters in the 'October Revolution' mine. One women had subsequently sustained a serious injury to her foot. The article also noted that an annex to the women's bath-house was under construction at the 'Proletarian Dictatorship' mine.[30] An earlier report on conditions of work at the 'Proletarian Dictatorship' mine noted that women were employed 'only above ground: in haulage and grading' in jobs which were 'difficult and dirty'.[31]

Foreign visitors and western delegates to the Soviet mining regions in the 1920s and 1930s provide a more detailed picture of the conditions of work and life in the mining areas. They reveal also evidence of the increasing numbers of women employed in a range of tasks in the mining industry in this period, including in underground work. In addition, they note the improvements in the use of mechanised equipment and the overall technological level of the industry, which, it could be argued, facilitated the employment of women in greater numbers and in an even broader range of jobs.

Five British working women, some of whom were the wives of miners, travelled to the Soviet Union in October 1927 to attend the All-Russian Congress of Women and to celebrate the tenth anniversary of the revolution. Their report provides a very positive and enthusiastic account of developments and the conditions of life in the Soviet mining regions. After a tour of some of the factories in Moscow and Leningrad, the women proceeded to visit the Donets basin, where some of the representatives themselves went down two coal mines. The conditions underground compared favourably with those in England, which they had also observed first hand, and the visitors reported that the workers 'assured us that the conditions of their mines were typical of the whole minefield, and that where production had been increased it was due to the modernisation of the plant'.[32] The visitors were surprised to find a communal bath-house, where the miners could clean themselves before returning home, and a pit laundry for their clothes. They noted also that facilities such as these were not available in their home communities.

A far less optimistic account of work and conditions in Soviet mines, including a brief observation on women workers, is provided by two male delegates from the Tilmanstone Colliery in Kent accompanied by a local male school teacher to the Soviet Union in August and September 1929.[33] These three observers also visited the coal mines in the Donets basin and, in addition, witnessed work in a nearby salt mine. This group was far more critical of the day-to-day conditions in the mining districts and noted that 'the quarters for the single men comprise sleeping accommodation, a dining hall and a reading room. The single women's quarters were on the same lines and were good and clean, but here again "awful sanitary arrangements" were noticed.'[34] Although new housing was being constructed, the visitors noted that 'the modern houses which had just been built were an improvement on the old but still very primitive'.[35] They noted later that 'although clothes and boots were free, they are of a type that our miners would not wear'.[36]

The two mining delegates descended with some difficulty to the actual coal face at one mine shaft and noted that 'if the men at Tilmanstone had to work under these conditions there would be hell to pay. Both said that apart from working a six-hour shift, two hours would be too much for them.'[37] They saw no evidence of a bath-house for the miners, such as the one that the women's delegation had utilised two years previously, but they themselves were allowed to use the bath in the officials' bathroom.

In other pits, including the salt mine, the conditions of underground work were commented upon much more favourably. At the surface of the 'New Economic' mine, however, they noted that 'the women work on the mines eight hours a shift, five shifts per week, and they saw them pulling tubs of coal out of the cage in their bare feet'.[38]

The dangers posed by underground work and the potential for injury, for both female and male workers, were not topics which were openly discussed in the Soviet Union at the beginning of the 1930s. Despite the legal restrictions on underground work by women and the openly hostile reception to such a practice vocalised by some of the western visitors to the mines, a number of arguments were put forward from the later 1920s to support the lifting of the ban on underground work by women. This was partly in recognition of the increased levels of mechanisation and technological advances experienced in the mining industry. Some of the work of the scientific-research institutes dealing with the protection of female labour was directed to studying the potential for employing women in underground tasks. It was also argued at this time that the shortage of child care places was inhibiting the further expansion of female employment in the mining industry.

Archival reports suggest that women were being employed in increasing proportions in a whole range of tasks in the mining industry, and in growing numbers in underground work, by the late 1920s and especially in the early 1930s. After the introduction of the First Five-Year Plan in 1928 the demand for labour increased significantly, especially in the heavy industrial sectors, including mining. Serious consideration was given in these years to finding ways of increasing the numbers of women employed in the mining industry and to the more general question of the viability of employing female labour in underground tasks. At the ACCTU meeting on work amongst women in March 1929, Amosova, of the Mineworkers' Union, complained that the protective labour laws were inhibiting the further employment of women in the mining industry, especially in underground work, and criticised both the trade unions and the Bolshevik Party Women's Department for doing nothing to challenge this situation.[39]

In some regions individual mines developed their own policies on underground work by women. From November 1929 women workers in the Novosibirsk region were allowed to work underground in the distribution of lamps, an exclusively female task above ground, as the mine operators did not wish to place restrictions on women in this particular task.[40] Some of the areas of work in which women came to be employed in the mining industry during the years of the First Five-Year Plan required a degree of technical expertise.

Nina Popova, who became secretary of ACCTU after the Second World War, noted that amongst the whole range of jobs which required much skill now being done by women were coal-cutting machine operators and that the women 'learned to run the most complicated machinery'.[41]

Narkomtrud's Committee for Improving the Work and Life of Women in June 1930 discussed the rate at which women were being absorbed into the industrial labour force. Koshedeva, of the Mineworkers' Union, complained that the numbers of women workers allocated to the mining sector during the First Five-Year Plan were very low:

> Such a meagre percentage, which Narkomtrud has envisaged for the mining industry, is, in my opinion, insufficient. There will be big discrepancies between our figures and those from Narkomtrud. The fact of the matter is that the mining industry is located in an exceptional position, i.e. outside the towns, mainly in outlying districts and the question of accelerating the utilisation of female labour is necessary. Narkomtrud must raise the percentage of drawing female labour into the mining industry.[42]

The meeting even considered the very necessity of labour protection measures as they concerned female labour, especially as the demand for industrial labour was increasing. One member of the committee, Ignat'eva, cautioned against making hasty decisions on such matters and argued that employment in underground work could be easier than surface work:

> We are now considering the introduction of female labour into industry; we need to study this; we need to attract the attention of scientific institutes to this matter; and we need to put off for the present committing ourselves to points on the protection of labour, so that we do not end up with the same situation as for underground tasks, when we agreed that women were forbidden to work underground, whereas it has been shown that underground work is easier by far than work above ground, when women are required to drag heavy wagons and they often exhaust themselves.[43]

There was still a great deal of reluctance in some quarters, however, to admit more women to underground work. Speaking in April 1931 at the ACCTU meeting on the preparation of materials about the entry of women into the production process, Tsyrlina argued that if women were encouraged to work underground in mining then this would have repercussions for their colleagues. Men would be forced into even heavier and more dangerous jobs, at the coal face for example.[44]

Targets established for the First Five-Year Plan aimed to maximise the employment of women in surface work in the mining industry and to utilise female labour in a restricted range of tasks in underground work. The plan indicators showed the proportion of the labour force in the coal mining industry constituted by women rising from 7.8 per cent in 1929–30 to 14.1 per cent in 1932–33.[45] On 19 May 1931 Narkomtrud published a list of professions and tasks in which the use of female labour was to be significantly expanded. This list included twenty-six specifically identified tasks exclusively in surface work in the mining industry. These included a number of jobs as machine-operators, working with pit ponies, as supervisors, storekeepers and winch-drivers.[46]

Yet despite the on-going research into conditions of work in the mining industry and the fact that there was significant debate about lifting the ban on the employment of women in underground tasks by the beginning of the 1930s, the official prohibition was reiterated on 10 April 1932.[47] In accordance with this decree women were to be employed underground in the mining industry only in tasks which did not involve physical labour. The number of notes sent to Narkomtrud RSFSR for clarification on this issue suggest that a degree of uncertainty remained over the extent of the prohibition.[48]

As part of the drive to expand the levels of female industrial employment, and to increase the production of coal, plan figures for 1933 indicated that women were to constitute 18 per cent of workers in the mining industry. In order to facilitate this end, further improvements were to be made in educational and vocational training and in the area of social and cultural provisions, including nurseries, canteens and laundries.[49]

In reality, it seems very probable that the actual numbers of women employed in the mining industry, including in underground work, exceeded the plan targets. The fact that women were being employed in increasing numbers and proportions in the mining industry by the early 1930s is clearly illustrated by the reports of periodic surveys into the conditions of employment for female mine workers. One report on the employment of women in the coal industry cites the growth in numbers of women employed in coal mining as set out in Table 10.2, which points to the expansion of female labour dating from October 1929.

Alongside figures from a similar report 'on work amongst women', it is possible to trace the increase in the employment of female labour in the coal mining industry specifically in the Donbass region – see Table 10.3.

The overall growth of female employment in the mining industry was reflected also, it was argued in both of these

Table 10.2   Employment of Women in Coal Mining, 1929–31

	All workers	Women	Women as % of all workers
October 1929	326 068	32 780	10.1
October 1930	324 603	39 279	12.1
April 1931	407 409	55 301	13.5

Source: 'O massovoi rabote sredi zhenshchin po soyuzu rabochikh ugol'noi promyshlennosti', GARF, f. 5451, o. 15, d. 360, l. 208, dated 1 October 1931.

Table 10.3   Employment of Women in the Donbass Region, 1930–32

	All workers	Women	Women as % of all workers
1 November 1930	227 236	28 179	12.4
1 April 1931		36 751	13.7
1 August 1931		39 655	14.1
1 November 1931	321 788	51 799	15.6
1 January 1931	386 146	59 720	15.5

Sources: 'O massovoi rabote sredi zhenshchin po soyuzu rabochikh ugol'noi promyshlennosti', GARF, f. 5451, o. 15, d. 360, l. 208; and GARF, f. 5451, o. 16, d. 557, l. 30.

reports, in the level of mechanised work undertaken by women. Included in the lists of occupations in which the employment of women was to be significantly expanded, which were issued for the Russian republic on 16 January 1931 and made applicable on a union-wide basis on 19 May 1931, were a number of automated tasks. The decrees stipulated, however, that these should be performed above ground.[50]

An unpublished report suggested that the further expansion of female labour in the coal mining industry was inhibited by shortages of accommodation and the lack of child care facilities. The increased provision of child care institutions, however, according to this report, had allowed the proportion of women employed in coal mining to increase from 15.1 per cent on 1 January 1932 to 17.2 per cent five months later (1 June 1932).[51] Spivak, the East Siberia delegate speaking at the All-Union Trade Union Conference on Work Amongst Women in February 1931, complained that women were badly paid in mining and were provided for last in the distribution of protective clothing. The complaint was made that women often worked in conditions of extreme cold without gloves, as other reports had also noted. This situation, Spivak argued, resulted in women absenting themselves from the mines as they were unable to work under such conditions.[52]

There is further evidence to suggest also that women were being employed increasingly in underground work. One report on the coal mining industry from a collection of sectoral studies on work amongst women noted that:

> The composition of the staff of women workers employed underground has taken place by the transfer of women workers from surface to underground tasks...
> The actual use of female labour in underground tasks took place in the first half of 1931 and has continued uninterrupted.[53]

According to unpublished data, overall figures from ten different mines for the period 1 May 1931 to 1 February 1932 revealed an increase in the proportion of women employed in underground work from 3.2 per cent to 11.7 per cent. The proportions are slightly higher for the Donbass region – 5.4 per cent on 1 May 1931, 12 per cent on 1 October 1931 and 12.5 per cent on 1 January 1932 – and also confirm the rapid growth in the underground employment of women from the second half of 1931.[54]

Significantly higher figures, ranging from 15–19 per cent, were reported for the employment of women in underground work in other regions. A report on the recruitment of women workers into industry during the first half of 1931 confirmed the employment of female labour in thirteen separately identified underground tasks in the coal mining industry.[55] In the Donbass region a rapid growth in the numbers of women employed underground was noted from July 1931, with over 1300 women taking on underground work in seven different mines, compared to a total of only five women in the previous six months. In some mines, it was argued, the transfer of women to underground work was delayed because of the shortages of workers to take their place in surface jobs.

At the same time, despite the predominance of female labour in unskilled jobs, the numbers of women employed in skilled work and mechanised tasks underground were also increasing. These skilled and mechanised tasks, on the whole, it was argued, conformed to the list of permitted tasks in underground work in mining published by Narkomtrud.[56] 769 women in the ten mines under review had taken on jobs as winchdrivers, machinists and assembly workers by the beginning of February 1932.[57] Hundreds of other adult and young women were taking part in training programmes and short courses to improve their level of skill. At this stage it was reported that the rate of substitution of female labour for male labour was progressing very slowly.[58]

As a result of an extensive survey conducted in 1931 into the recruitment of new groups of women workers into the mining industry, detailed figures are available for the numbers of women workers employed at the 'Il'ich' mine in the Donbass region in that year.[59] The data offer a breakdown according to the specific task undertaken and length of service.[60] The figures reveal a total of 342 women employed at the 'Il'ich' mine, nearly half (155) of whom were employed as haulage workers. Significant numbers of women were also employed as lamp fillers (53) and sorters (42). Half of the women had been employed at the mine for longer than one year and 26 of these had at least three years' experience of

mine work. Some of the new workers were identified as former housewives. Ten of the women were explicitly identified
as being employed in underground work, including three as
haulage workers, three winchdrivers and two concrete layers.
Of the two remaining women, one was a medical worker and
the other a telephonist. In reality, it is clear that many more
women than this were actually employed in underground
jobs. The conclusions to the report indicated that special
campaigns were being organised to encourage women to
take on mechanised jobs underground. One 16-year-old girl
was reported to be working underground alongside adult
workers.

The report offered an insight into some of the difficulties
experienced by managers in trying to transfer women from
underground work. As the report noted, women continued to
be employed in the mining industry after the First World War
and even during periods of high unemployment during the
NEP. At the 'Il'ich' mine plans had been drawn up to transfer
eighty-three women from underground to surface work, but
in reality only eighteen women had changed jobs. The continued employment of women in underground tasks, it was
argued, pushed men into more difficult and dangerous jobs
at the coal face and men were beginning to view women com-
petitively as rivals for underground jobs. It was suggested also
that women were not being used to their full capacity in surface tasks.[61]

The report also illustrated the fact that very few young
women or adult workers from the 'Il'ich' mine were entering technical training and specialist courses to improve their
levels of skill. Other mines cited in the report, however,
provided better examples of this. Likewise, the 'Il'ich' mine
had no child care facilities, but other mines were able to
report more favourable provision, which facilitated the entry
of mothers of young children into employment. There had
been promises to improve child care provision at the 'Il'ich'
mine but this had not materialised. The mine did have a can-
teen, but it was noted that most of the women did not eat
there, preferring instead to cook for themselves at the bar-
racks or at home.[62]

The survey report also commented on the fact that the
quality of work by women was better than by men and that

labour turnover amongst women was virtually non-existent, though there were a few reported cases of absenteeism. Finally, the detail of the report, as with a number of similar surveys, provided an insight into the social, cultural and political activities of the women mine workers, including participation in various work campaigns and representative committees, levels of literacy and membership of the trade union and party organisations.

A significant shift in the unofficial policy on the employment of female labour in underground tasks in mining can be dated from the second half of 1931. A mass recruitment drive vastly expanded the overall numbers of women in industrial employment and in the mining industry women workers were used in part to counter the high levels of labour turnover. During the course of the next eighteen months extensive investigations were conducted by a number of scientific-research institutes into the employment of women workers in various sectors of the economy, including the coal mining industry.

In January 1933 the Labour Protection Department of Narkomtrud RSFSR, during a meeting on female labour, received the report of Aushev, of the Makeevskii Institute, on the employment of women in the Donbass coal mining industry. By this time, according to Aushev's report, women constituted on average 18 per cent of workers in this sector of the economy and between 4 and 6 per cent of underground workers. A significant proportion of these underground workers were employed in skilled and heavy labour. Aushev argued that the rates of industrial accidents and illness were lower amongst women and that women had a better record of attendance.[63]

This study revealed that women were easily capable of undertaking skilled work in underground conditions, although some mine managers were still reluctant to allow women to take on these tasks and confined them to unskilled jobs. Despite their lower level of formal education and training, under test conditions women had proven themselves capable of operating machinery. Women themselves wanted to work underground as such jobs were more highly paid.

At the same meeting Shcheglova, of the Urals Institute of Labour Protection and the Institute of Motherhood and

Childhood, reported on a 1931 survey of the impact on women's health of employment in underground work. Most women considered themselves to be entirely healthy and only a much smaller proportion reported serious illnesses. On the basis of this study and contrary to earlier policy, Shcheglova argued that there were no health reasons why women should not be employed in underground jobs in the mining industry.[64]

Further studies were being conducted elsewhere and the findings of these were also used to support the industrialisation drive. For example, in the Caucasus an investigation was made of 592 women coal miners, 444 of whom were employed in underground work. The findings of such investigations suggested that the extensive mechanisation achieved in the mining industry during the First Five-Year Plan had broadened the scope for the employment of women workers in a range of underground tasks. These tasks were now regarded as being no more harmful to women than work on the surface of the mines and required no greater effort than similar jobs undertaken by male colleagues.[65] By January 1933 the All-Russian Conference of Labour Research Institutes was calling for a partial abolition of the prohibition on underground work by women in the coal mining industry.[66] Unpublished reports noted research conducted by the Obukh Institute, which revealed that by 1933 women were being employed widely as machine operators, especially in mechanised lifting operations, and that such tasks were being undertaken exclusively by women in some mine shafts.[67]

The reports of foreign mining delegations to the Soviet Union in the 1930s suggest that women were being employed in increasing numbers, including in underground work, by the middle of the decade. Kingsbury and Fairchild's study, arising from two visits to the Soviet Union in 1929 and 1932, suggests that although women were not to be seen at the coal face, female labour was already being employed in a number of mechanised and semi-automated tasks by 1932.[68] It is interesting to note here also that by the mid-1930s women were being employed in underground work in the construction of the Moscow metro.[69]

A British observer, Sam Watson, the Durham area secretary of the National Union of Mineworkers and a member of the

National Executive of the Labour Party, reported in the *Daily Telegraph* in 1954 that 'during my visit to Russia in 1936 I protested against the employment of women in mines and was told it was only temporary'. Watson noted the further increase in the numbers of women employed in underground work in the years following the end of the Second World War and called on the Soviet government to stop sending women miners underground. He argued that 'if they refuse, they cannot be considered a government or party that believes in the dignity of working-class women'.[70]

A French mining delegate, Kléber Legay, also visited the Donets basin in November 1936. Here he was told that very few women were employed in underground work in mines and these women were engaged only in easier jobs. When Legay expressed his surprise to the Soviet officials at discovering that women were engaged in underground tasks under any conditions, the officials responded that they considered this was preferable to prostitution, to which they believed women were condemned in France. This caused an animated discussion between the delegation and the Soviet officials until Legay was reassured that the work of women underground was not considered to be tiresome.[71]

On entering one shaft, Legay counted twenty-two women amongst the forty-five workers he met. Women were engaged in all kinds of work, except in coal cutting, and Legay expressed some scepticism at having been told the previous day that women were only employed in easier jobs. He reported that he had seen two women engaged in heavy loading tasks and one woman working to assist a male colleague, a *stakhanovite*, in the cutting of coal. Legay was told that the women had chosen to do these jobs as they paid more money, although, as he discovered, their wages remained significantly lower than their male colleagues, whose own work often depended on their efforts. Legay deplored the fact that women were being encouraged to take on work which he considered to be unsuitable for them. He argued that there were only two possible ways of making women take on work underground: firstly, by imposing such work by brute force or, secondly, either by refusing to pay husbands a sufficient sum for the family or not paying enough to workers on the surface of the mines. He saw no evidence of violent methods.

In 1935 the ACCTU initiated another major survey into the conditions of work for female labour in a range of industrial sectors, which revealed some interesting data on labour protection issues. The mining industry was included in the survey and some of the findings again are to be found in the trade union archives.[72] The labour inspectors, who were drawn from the local and regional mining trade union organisations, were responsible for conducting the survey and in some of the mining districts formulated a questionnaire to facilitate the quick response to the requests for information. The responses to the survey, therefore, varied in length and detail. The findings of the survey detailed below, for reasons of continuity and comparison, will be based again predominantly on the 'Il'ich' mine. The survey outlined a range of questions to which enterprise administrators were expected to respond.

The survey at the 'Il'ich' mine was conducted on 28 November 1935 and the findings here exemplify to a significant extent the reports of other mines included in the investigation.[73] Women were actively encouraged to work at the 'Il'ich' mine. A total of 4507 workers were employed at the mine, including 984 women, of whom 467 were employed in underground work. Women, therefore, constituted almost 22 per cent of the total labour force. The 467 women employed in underground work constituted just over 10 per cent of the total labour force and over 47 per cent of the total number of women employed at the mine. Of the female workers, eleven were under the age of 18 years, 524 were between the ages of 18 and 25 and 447 were over 25 years of age.[74] A number of the women were not employed directly in mining tasks but instead undertook administrative and technical roles. Thirty-six women were reported to be working in jobs in contravention of the legal prohibitions, including thirteen as coal loaders, four in timbering, three in the extraction of coal, thirteen slate workers, three as scuttle workers and three in the raking out of coal.[75] Later in the report, however, it was noted that women were being transferred gradually from tasks in the restricted areas of employment and a recent example had included all seven women who had previously been employed as workers on the coal wagons.

The 'Il'ich' mine was unable to provide information on the health and physical well-being of its workers. There was no specialist medical service for women at this mine. Many of the other mines, however, were able to supply detailed figures for recorded illnesses and even in some cases serious injuries.[76] At some mines records were also kept of numbers of pregnancies and births, of miscarriages and reproductive disorders. One mine reported two serious injuries, where one woman had broken a leg and another had lost forty-five days' work through incapacity.[77] The levels of medical provision and recording of illnesses obviously varied very greatly between the mines.

Unlike some of the other mines included in the survey, the 'Il'ich' mine by this time, in contrast to earlier investigations, was able to report that 210 children were served by 24-hour child care provision. Other reports noted that child care arrangements needed to be extended, or even initiated in some areas, in order to increase the employment and productivity of working mothers.[78] One mine reported that the absence of child care facilities resulted in working women giving up their jobs to look after their children.[79] In addition to its child care facilities, the 'Il'ich' mine also had a bath-house open around the clock which was large enough for 120 workers at any one time, but the report also noted that this was insufficient to serve the needs of the 984 women employed at the mine.

The findings of this survey clearly confirm both Watson's and Legay's observations on the extensive employment of women in the mining industry, including in underground work, by the mid-1930s. The reports also demonstrate the widespread infringements and often deliberate ignorance of the provisions of the established protective labour laws, which had originally been conceived to ease the accommodation of women into the industrial labour force. Violations were reported not only of the laws prohibiting the employment of women in underground work but also in a whole range of other areas.

Infringements of other labour protective measures were also noted. These included women who did not take the full entitlement of maternity leave because they were late in gaining certification from the doctor. Some nursing mothers were not transferred from underground to surface work and were not permitted the agreed breaks from work for breast feeding.

The 'Il'ich' mine also noted the inadequate provision of protective clothing and that warm clothes for surface workers had not been received. Soap had also not been delivered and this violated the terms of the collective agreement for mineworkers.

Reports from other mines noted a range of other infringements of the protective labour laws and it was often noted in the responses to the survey that women were employed on equal terms with men. Such reports confirm the widespread employment of women in prohibited jobs and extensive infringements of maternity provisions, as witnessed at the 'Il'ich' mine. Other infringements included the employment of women in night and overtime work, and some reports identified the types of jobs most affected by the extended work day. At the 'Stalin' mine, for example, conveyor belt workers often worked longer hours. In fact, the report of the 'Stalin' mine noted that 'cases of this kind of infringement of the law on women's labour are not isolated, they are very common'.[80] A number of the reports noted the lack of provision of specialist protective clothing to women.

It is also worth citing here some of the more general observations of the survey concerning the employment of women in the mining industry. A number of reports noted that rather than recording a reduction in the numbers of women employed and the substitution of male labour for female labour, especially in the more difficult and dangerous tasks, the numbers of women employed in mining, in a whole range of tasks, remained constant or increased and that, contrary to the assumption of the survey, women, in reality, were substituting for men in a number of areas of work, including as winch-drivers, machinists and auxiliary workers. The levels of turnover amongst women workers varied between mines with some reports citing higher levels of turnover in comparison with men and others reporting much lower levels of turnover. However, no reasons were given to explain the levels of turnover. Women were reported as working well with mechanised equipment and were regarded as more disciplined than men. Many women were reported to be acquiring skills in specialist areas of work in the mining industry.

By the end of the 1930s women, especially the wives of miners, were being actively recruited to work in the pits and to voice their support of their husbands.[81] Women were recruited to all types of mining work, including underground tasks and the operation of mechanised equipment, and many were reported to be working in excess of established norms of output.[82] The legal prohibition on underground work by women was not officially lifted until 25 October 1940 by which time the urgency of the war situation required that women should take on jobs previously reserved predominantly for men. The decree noted the expansion of mechanisation and improvements in technical safety in the mining industry. Yet even with this revision women were still not permitted to work in the most arduous underground tasks, such as coal cutting, loading and timbering, etc.[83] Norton Dodge has suggested, however, that this revision served purely to recognise an already existing situation by sanctioning the employment of women in an area of work where the prohibition had never been fully enforced in reality.[84] The findings of this study substantiate his claim.

11 Conclusion

This analysis of official policy towards the legal protection of women workers in the Soviet Union in the interwar period has highlighted in particular two specific areas of labour protection which are insufficiently documented in the contemporary published literature: the provision for 'menstrual leave'; and the regulation of underground work as it was applied in the mining industry. The broad areas of concern in the contemporary debates on labour protection issues can be determined largely from the scope of investigations conducted into the conditions of female employment and the published findings of the various scientific research institutes. Women in the Soviet Union, as in many other countries, were treated as a distinct and separate category in the protective labour debates and scientific research, as were juvenile and young workers. In many areas of the new Soviet way of life (*byt*), the 1920s can be regarded as a relatively experimental, libertarian and proactive decade in terms of social policy, scientific research and legislative enactments.[1] Stalin's declaration in 1930 that the 'woman question' was solved, however, signalled the end to the more radical political and ideological debates on women's liberation which had enjoyed a relatively high profile in the 1920s.

A great deal of emphasis in the debates on the legislative protection of women workers was placed on the differing biological constitution of the female organism. In practice, physiological differences were interpreted in such a way as to identify women as weaker and inferior to men. There seems to have considerable concern about the levels of ill-health and industrial injuries experienced by women, although there is little evidence to suggest that these were higher than amongst male factory workers.

Women were viewed as being in particular need of legislative protection. The fact that many of the restricted occupations, in which the employment of women came to be prohibited, were also potentially injurious to male workers seems to have received relatively little attention in the debates.

170

Also overlooked were the many areas of women's work which remained unregulated. This is strikingly demonstrated in the example of heavy agricultural labour. Scant attention appears to have been paid to improving work environments and production processes in order to make the restricted occupations and other proscribed areas of work more accessible to the female labour force. In the early 1930s Soviet women researchers on issues of female labour themselves complained about this.[2]

The fact that Soviet protective labour laws for women workers were never fully implemented in practice and were irregularly enforced makes a detailed evaluation of their efficacy impossible. There are a number of explanations for the erratic application of the protective labour laws. For most of the interwar period, much of Soviet industry, and the economy as a whole, was in a state of chaos and flux. The channels for the communication of many central government policy goals and legislative enactments, especially those which concerned women, were slow to develop and remained underfunded. The Bolshevik regime had little money or time to invest in the publication and enforcement of the protective labour laws and so it is safe to assume that in many sectors of the industrial economy women workers remained uninformed of the extensive range and detailed nature of their entitlements and of the prohibitive restrictions.

Labour protection and labour inspection were not afforded a high profile or priority on the agendas of the workers' committees which were established at the factories in these decades. This is illustrated by the example of Koenker's study of the Soviet printing industry where 'women trainees were assigned to work in the various factory subcommittees, although more frequently in cultural and labour protection work than in the powerful rates and conflicts commissions'.[3] Moreover, the legislative enactments were not always seen to serve the immediate requirements of enterprise managers whose primary concern was to fulfil production targets. Many of the regulations proved costly to implement. Managers and enterprise administrators sometimes deliberately circumvented and ignored the laws when it served their own interests to do so. The complaints from women workers in the newspapers bear witness to this.

The protective labour laws were not always welcomed by the women workers themselves. The female labour force often remained a stubborn obstacle to the full implementation of the terms of the decrees. In many instances women were able to resist and overturn the application of the protective measures. For example, the high levels of female unemployment during the early years of the NEP resulted in a number of partial retractions being introduced in the strict application of the night work prohibition, in the regulations governing the employment of women in the injurious occupations and, some years later, in underground work. It is important to remember, however, that the protective labour laws were only one factor influencing women's employment prospects in the 1920s and 1930s.[4] The extent to which the retractions in the protective labour laws increased the opportunities for women to find work during periods of widespread unemployment remains unclear.

Theoretically at least, the numbers of women workers covered by the protective labour laws would have increased as the state extended its control over industry. Despite the fact that the regulations may have been 'protective' in intent, in practice they were often viewed by the female labour force as 'restrictive'. Women resented being excluded from the more highly skilled, and therefore more highly paid, jobs listed amongst the restricted occupations and in underground work, for example. Legislation which aimed to protect women from unhealthy working environments served also to safeguard higher wages for men.[5] Women also resented being denied the opportunity to earn more money by extending their hours of work. Female workers argued that they should be allowed to work alongside their husbands and male colleagues on specific shifts and in certain occupations and that pregnancy and maternity should not act as a restraint on employment.

Although in the long term it may not have served women's best interests to work under such conditions, at this time many women workers were able to perceive both the immediate economic benefits to be derived from ignoring the protective labour laws and the necessity for securing their position *vis-à-vis* male workers in the Soviet industrial labour force. One unanticipated consequence of the restrictive regulations may have been that, when they were enforced, women resorted to jobs in the sectors of the economy which were not covered by the protective labour laws, where conditions of work may have been much worse. These unprotected areas of employment were often unskilled occupations, with irregular hours of employment, and involved monotonous and sometimes unclean and unhealthy jobs, which male workers were unwilling to do.

It is clear from the arguments put forward by some of the women themselves that their own notions of equality meant that they should not be treated differently from men and that they considered that their different physiological constitution should not be used as the basis for legislative enactments. In general, Soviet policy towards protective labour legislation for women workers reflected this trend after 1932. It should be remembered also, however, that not all women argued from this perspective and many welcomed the distinct protection which had been, and to a more limited extent in the 1930s continued to be, offered to female workers by the labour laws.

Whatever their impact, the protective labour laws did not bring about the complete withdrawal of women from dangerous, difficult and unpleasant occupations. One western observer, writing in the early 1940s, argued that:

> during the unemployment period the weakening of measures protecting women workers did not improve their employment opportunities, but since 1930 the abolition of essential measures protecting women from work harmful to motherhood has greatly facilitated increasing employment of women in unhealthy work.[6]

However, despite the retractions in the application and enforcement of the protective labour laws, and the mass recruitment of women workers to Soviet industry in the 1930s, heavy industrial labour remained an overwhelmingly male preserve before the Second World War.

It is obvious too that the Soviet regime worked to its own economic and political agenda in respect to the protection of female labour and that this agenda shifted during the course of the interwar years. The government was able and willing to interpret research findings to suit its own requirements. Thus, night shift employment was initially considered to be unsuitable for women in view of the fact that it resulted in higher levels of fatigue and ill-health. By 1930, however, at least one research institute was arguing that women were more suited to night work because their maternal functions accustomed them to broken patterns of sleep. Likewise, underground employment by women was initially prohibited because of the assumed dangerous and difficult nature of such work. Yet by the beginning of the 1930s, it was being argued that underground work was no more harmful to women than some surface tasks.

The underlying trend in official labour policy for women workers can be identified as moving from 'protection' in the 1920s to 'equality' in the 1930s.[7] The active mass recruitment of women workers into the Soviet industrial labour force can be dated from the beginning of 1931. Although it is clear that women worked in contravention of the protective labour laws before this date, and often in quite significant numbers, changes in unofficial attitudes towards the protection of female labour, as identified in the published findings of the scientific-research institutes and as yet not reflected in legislative enactments, also date from this period.

In the 1930s the priorities given by the Soviet regime to rapid industrial development had a profound impact on official policy goals and this resulted in many of the protective labour measures for women workers being overridden and ignored in practice. Henceforth, the economic priorities of the industrialisation programme dominated the regime's agenda. In this decade, therefore, significantly less attention was paid to research into labour protection issues and there were far fewer actual legislative enactments after 1932. Narkomtrud was disbanded in 1933 and the work of the trade unions and the labour inspectorate was downgraded.

The mass entry of women into the industrial labour force was in itself interpreted as an indicator of sexual equality. Underlying the declarations of sexual equality, however, were also very traditional and conservative notions of gender differences, which were reflected not only in family policy but also in cultural life, as Susie Reid has demonstrated in her study of the art and artists of the period:

Notwithstanding the Stalin regime's protestations of its unfailing commitment to sexual equality, artistic images identified man with culture, woman with nature; man with consciousness and rationality, woman with spontaneity and emotion; man with heavy industrial production, and woman with agriculture, food preparation, consumption and reproduction.[8]

However, the 1930s also provided unprecedented economic opportunities for women. By the end of the decade women were working in a wide range of occupations which had previously been reserved for male workers alone. By 1941 the traditional stereotype of the woman worker had been both reinforced and challenged by changes in the protective labour laws. The new laws introduced in the mid-1930s underlined women's primary maternal functions and responsibilities and required women to work in both paid productive labour and unpaid reproduction with inadequate structural and financial support for this dual role. Yet at the same time developments in both official and unofficial policy towards the protection of women workers were beginning to recognise the potential for female labour to be employed successfully in a broader range of industrial occupations. Women's newly assigned 'equal' role as industrial workers resulted in less official attention being directed towards the protective regulation of their work.

Indeed, by the later 1930s, legislative measures were beginning to be introduced which broadened the scope of women's employment into areas of work which, only a few years earlier, had been legally prohibited to the female labour force. However, the opportunities offered by the revised laws did not result so much from the fact that the original regulations had received only limited practical application and had sometimes been met with open resistance by women workers themselves. Nor was the shift in policy the result of a genuine fundamental change in the official perception of the physical capabilities of women workers. Instead, on the whole, the 1930s legislative enactments reflected the economic imperatives of the Soviet industrialisation programme and the preparation for war. No further significant changes in the protective labour laws for women workers were introduced until after Stalin's death in 1953.[9]

Despite the mass entry of women into the Soviet industrial labour force and the fact that many women took up jobs in areas of employment from which they had previously been officially excluded, the 1930s also witnessed the entrenchment of sex segregation in the Soviet labour force. The fact that the Soviet industrial labour force embodied a high level of both horizontal and vertical sex segregation by the end of the 1930s was partly a function of the fundamental principles which underpinned attitudes towards protective labour legislation. It should be acknowledged also, however, that the limited advances in technology, manufacturing and production techniques, the automation and mechanisation of a range of industrial processes and, more importantly, the imminence of war by the late 1930s all had a profound impact on the structure of the Soviet labour force and the roles which women were to play in the Soviet industrialisation process.

The policies on the protection of women workers elaborated during the interwar years continued to have an impact on the structure of the Soviet labour force for many decades.[10] In the period of *perestroika* and after the collapse of the Soviet Union, the segregationist and exclusionary functions of the protective labour laws were further entrenched, rather than challenged.[11]

A number of specific issues arising from this study remain unresolved. It has been possible to provide only a preliminary assessment of the levels of support for and opposition to the protective labour laws. It is evident that the extensive provision of the protective labour laws was only one of a number of factors affecting gendered employment patterns, the sexual division of labour and the economic subordination of women workers in the Soviet Union in the interwar years. The fact remains that the early Soviet attempts to accommodate women into the industrial labour force through the introduction of legislative regulations provided no more for the 'protection' of women workers in the 1920s than they did for their 'equality' in the 1930s.

Appendix 1
Summary of Decrees

29 October (11 November) 1917
On the 8-hour working day, the length and distribution of work time.

31 July 1918
On labour departments.
31 July 1918
On responsibilities of labour inspectors.
31 October 1918
On social insurance of workers.
10 December 1918
Labour Code.

4 October 1919
On night work by women.
8 October 1919
25 December 1919
On night work in tobacco production.
29 December 1919
On time spent in overtime work by women in state institutions.

27 March 1920
On the use of women workers as labour conscripts in the procurement of wood fuel.
20 May 1920
On the use of young and juvenile workers in peat working.
5 September 1920
'Maternity protection'.
9 November 1920
On leave from work after a miscarriage.
11 November 1920
On measures to protect the labour and health of breast-feeding mothers.
16 November 1920
List of occupations, which, equally with physical labour, allow the entitlement to maternity leave of the period of 8 weeks before and 8 weeks after birth.
24 November 1920
On the labour protection of pregnant women and nursing mothers.
24 November 1920
On the prohibition of night work by pregnant women and nursing mothers.

4 January 1921
On the maternity leave of women pharmacists.
4 March 1921
On the limits to the norms of transporting and moving loads by juveniles and women. [RSFSR]

10 March 1921
On maternity leave for postal sorters at post-telegraph offices.
May 1921
On transfers and business trips by women, juveniles and young workers.
9 September 1921
On the maternity leave of machinists.
5 December 1921
On supplementary maternity benefits.

11 January 1922
On the release from work during menstruation of machinists and iron press workers working on cutting machines without mechanised gears in the garment industry.
15 January 1922 (circular)
On maximum norms for women loaders.
20 February 1922 (circular)
On the conditions and procedure for the dismissal of women from work in connection with staff reductions.
8 August 1922
On the procedure for the dismissal of pregnant women.
9 November 1922
On night work in bakeries.
15 November 1922
Labour Code.

2 February 1923
On night work by women on telegraph and telephones.
15 February 1923
On the payment of supplementary benefits for breast feeding.
20 February 1923 (circular)
On the recruitment of women to the labour inspectorate.
12 April 1923
On conditions of labour in floating work.
28 June 1923
List of occupations, which on the basis of especially difficult work allow the entitlement to an extra two weeks' leave.
14 November 1923
On the limits to the norms of transporting and moving loads by juveniles and women. [USSR]
27 November 1923
On night work by women on transport.

14 February 1924
On the labour protection of loaders in loading-unloading and trans-shipping work in transport.
23 February 1924 (circular)
On night work by women.
10 March 1924
On the organisation and maintenance of work in bakeries.

2 April 1924
On night work by women on rail transport.
22 May 1924
On the sanitary regulations of work in the cold hand-washing of wool.
6 June 1924
On women's work on the railways.
15 July 1924
On the length of pregnancy and maternity leave for certain categories of women working in health care services.
20 December 1924
On maternity leave for telephonists.

13 April 1925 (circular)
On night work by women.
16 July 1925
On the procedure for the dismissal from work of single women with children up to 1 year of age.
4 September 1925
On work time and leave for stenographers employed permanently in institutions and enterprises.
9 September 1925
On the labour protection of workers in X-ray rooms.
30 October 1925
On the prohibition of female labour in especially dangerous and difficult occupations.

8 February 1926
On the conditions of work for hired domestic labour, working in the homes of their employers (domestic workers) as a personal service to the employer and his family.
4 June 1926
On conditions of labour in seasonal occupations.
8 July 1926
On procedures for release from work after a miscarriage.

9 May 1927
Rights and applications of payment of benefit for temporary incapacity.
19 May 1927
On changes to the rights to entitlement and payment of supplementary social insurance benefits.
17 November 1927
On additions and changes to 'the list of occupations, which, equally with physical labour, allow the entitlement to maternity leave of the period 8 weeks before and 8 weeks after birth'.

26 May 1928
Establishment of a Commission of the Presidium of TsIK SSSR on the improvement of labour and life of women of the culturally backward peoples.

7 July 1928
Appointment of a chief inspector for women's labour attached to Narkomtrud SSSR.
7 July 1928
Exemplary appointment of a chief inspector of women's labour attached to Narkomtrud USSR and on the inspectors of women's labour attached to the local organisations of Narkomtrud USSR.
18 July 1928 (circular)
On the reorganisation of the work on the study and improvement of women's labour in production.
22 December 1928
On the ratification of the list of professions allowing, equally with jobs involving physical labour, entitlement to leave of 8 weeks before birth and 8 weeks after birth.

2 January 1929
On the 7-hour working day
2 January 1929
On measures for the struggle against infringements of labour laws.
22 February 1929
On amendments to Article 8 of the TsIK and SNK SSSR decree of 2 January 1929 on the 7-hour working day.
4 April 1929 (circular)
On the work of the women's labour inspectorate.
20 April 1929 (circular)
On the work of the inspectorate for the protection of women's labour.
27 May 1929
On amendments to Articles 75, 94, 96 and 131 of the Labour Code and the supplement to Article 97.
16 July 1929
On additions to the list of occupations allowing equally with occupations involving physical labour the entitlement to 8 weeks' leave before and after birth.

17 May 1930
On the prohibition of female labour in especially difficult and dangerous occupations and professions.
3 August 1930
On the ratification in a new edition of the list of professions allowing equally with occupations involving physical labour the entitlement to maternity leave of 56 days before and 56 days after birth.
8 December 1930
On the deployment of female labour in production and in state and cooperative organisations.

16 January 1931
On the ratification of a list of jobs by individual branch of industry, and also a list of occupations in state and cooperative organisations, in which exclusively or predominantly female labour is to be used.

9 May 1931
On the working conditions of women tractor and lorry drivers.
19 May 1931
On the consolidation of the list of professions and occupations in which the use of female labour should be significantly expanded.
30 June 1931
On voluntary labour inspectors.
11 August 1931
On the expansion of the categories of blue- and white-collar workers with the entitlement to benefits for giving birth and nursing a baby.
20 September 1931
On conditions of labour in loading-unloading work.

10 April 1932
Supplementary list of professions and occupations in which the use of female labour should be significantly expanded.
10 April 1932
On the consolidation of a new list of especially difficult and dangerous jobs and professions, in which women are not permitted.
14 August 1932
On the limits to the norms of transporting and moving loads by adult women.
13 October 1932
On the use of juvenile labour.

7 March 1933
On conditions of work for blue- and white-collar workers employed in the timber industry and forestry.
23 June 1933
On the amalgamation of Narkomtrud SSSR and VTsSPS.
10 September 1933
On the conditions for the amalgamation of Narkomtrud SSSR and VTsSPS.

11 April 1935
On granting to women postal delivery workers and women hairdressers entitlement to pregnancy and maternity leave equally with occupations involving physical labour.

26 March 1936
On the research of the VTsSPS scientific-research institutes for the protection of labour in Rostov-on-Don in connection with the article in *Pravda* on 20 January 1936.
23 June 1936
On the work of the Tashkent labour protection institute.
27 June 1936
On the prohibition of abortions, increases in financial help to parents, establishment of state help to large families, expansion of the network of maternity homes, nurseries and kindergartens, the reinforcement of criminal responsibility for the non-payment of alimony and on amendments to the law on divorce.

28 August 1936
On the work of the labour protection laboratories.
2 September 1936
On the work of the labour protection laboratories.
5 October 1936
On the criminal responsibility for the refusal to hire women for work and for reducing their wages on the grounds of pregnancy.
13 December 1936
On the work of the Kazan labour protection institute.

23 March 1937
On changes to the limits of allowances for pregnancy and birth for women employees to a maximum income of 300 rubles.
9 April 1937
On the use of the decree on the criminal responsibility for the refusal to hire women for work, and the reduction of their wages, because of pregnancy.
21 October 1937
On the work of the VTsSPS scientific-research institutes for labour protection.

19 January 1938
On the use of labour of pregnant women and nursing mothers in the cotton textiles, knitwear and tobacco industries.
1 November 1938
On changes to the list of especially difficult and dangerous jobs and professions, in which women are not permitted.
28 December 1938
On measures for regulating labour discipline, improving the practice of state social insurance and the struggle against abuses in this matter.

13 June 1940
On the deployment of female labour in occupations in river transportation.
25 October 1940
On the use of women's labour in underground tasks in the mining industry.

Appendix 2

Number and Percentage of Women Workers in Selected Industries, 1890–1926/27

	No.[a]	%[b]	No.[c] adjusted	% adjusted
1890	193 200	23.8		
1895	219 200	24.2		
1900	299 900	28.4		
1905	359 400	27.8		
1909	428 900	31.3		
1913	565 700	30.7	613 150	25.2
1914	596 200	31.8		
1915	715 000	36.0		
1916	868 200	39.5		[42.1][d]
1917	903 100	39.7		[42.5][d]
1918	740 400	41.2		[43.0][d]
1919	445 800	36.7		
1920	448 200	40.5		
1921/22	356 900	38.0		
1922/23	357 700	34.7		
1923/24	381 300	32.8	453 073	27.7
1924/25	496 400	34.2	559 112	29.3
1925/26	623 900	34.3	707 516	29.3
1926/27	650 400	35.0	751 105	29.5

Notes: [a] Excludes mining and metallurgy (where low nos. women).
[b] All female labour (includes girls and young women).
[c] All factory production and mining but excludes printing.
[d] Excludes war industries.

Source: L. Ye. Mints, 'Ocherki razvitiya statistiki chislennosti i sotava promyshlennogo proletariata v Rossii', *Ocherki po istorii statistiki SSSR* (Moscow, 1957) pp. 203–6, 244–5.

Appendix 3

Percentage of Women Employed in Selected Industries, 1890–1926/27

Industry	1890	1900	1905	1910	1912	1913	1916	1917	1920	1922/23	1923/24	1924/25	1925/26	1926/27
Textiles		43.5				54.1		66.6		58.5				59.4
Metallurgy	1.8	1.9		3.7		4.8						9.8		10.2
Chemicals		26.0	28.4		34.5						26.0			31.2
Silicates		>12.0				18.0		36.1						24.7
Food	13.6	16.0	18.0			21.0	34.6	32.0	47.0					26.8
Wood proc.						>9.0		21.0	30.0					16.4
Paper						>38.0		>48.0			14.0			30.0
Matches	42.0					51.0		55.0						51.5
Mining						8.0					15.1	13.8	14.0	14.5
Coal mining						3.6					10.7	10.1	10.0	9.9
Oil						–					3.4	3.1	2.9	3.0
Ferrous metals						10.1					12.9	10.8	9.6	8.8
Peat						36.5					33.9	36.3	38.0	37.3
% Total						25.2					27.7	29.3	29.3	29.5

Source: L. Ye. Mints, 'Ocherki razvitiya statistiki chislennosti i sostava promyshlennogo proletariata v Rossii', *Ocherki po istorii statistiki SSSR* (Moscow, 1957) pp. 204–10.

Appendix 4

Employment of Women by National Economic Sector, 1929–35 (No. in 000s and %)

	1929		1930		1931		1932		1933		1934		1935	
	No.	%	No.	%	No.	%	No.	%	No.	%	No.	%	No.	%
TOTAL	3304	27.2	3877	26.7	4197	26.9	6007	27.4	6908	30.5	7204	31.7	7881	33.4
including:														
Large-scale industry	939	27.9	1236	29.0	1440	29.3	2043	32.2	2207	34.5	2274	35.6	2627	38.3
Construction	64	7.0	156	9.6	189	10.1	380	12.8	437	16.0	454	18.7	450	19.7
Agriculture	441	28.0	425	27.4	221	23.1	394	21.3	508	24.2	605	25.4	685	27.0
Transport	104	8.0	146	9.7	173	10.2	243	11.6	322	13.8	358	15.1	384	16.6
Trade	97	15.5	179	22.0	233	25.9	374	29.3	432	30.9	408	29.6	473	30.8
Canteens	37	46.4	100	55.5	172	63.8	301	65.6	354	65.9	358	66.8	349	63.0
Education	439	53.6	482	52.3	514	50.4	692	53.6	790	55.7	859	56.6	919	56.6
Health	283	64.6	320	67.1	358	69.0	426	70.2	466	70.8	506	72.2	537	71.2
State Administration	239	19.0	332	22.6	373	24.1	475	25.8	510	27.9	499	29.4	522	31.1
Domestic workers	527	74.6	312	78.1	283	78.4	279	79.6	241	75.7	200	73.7	192	74.3
Other	134		189		241		400		641		683		743	
[% l/s ind. to TOT.]	[28.4]		[31.9]		[34.3]		[34.0]		[31.9]		[31.6]		[33.3]	

Source: Trud v SSSR: statisticheskii spravochnik (Moscow, 1936) p. 25. % large-scale industry to total: own calculations from actual numbers.

Notes

1   INTRODUCTION

1. In America, as in a number of other countries, the divisions amongst women's campaigners over the issue of the protection of female labour had posed a serious threat to a united suffrage movement well before the First World War. Attempts to regulate the hours of women's employment had led to the case of *Müller* vs *Oregon*. The significance of this case in the history of legal reform for women and the development of feminist politics is discussed in N. S. Erickson, 'Historical Background of "Protective" Labour Legislation: Müller v. Oregon', in D. K. Weisberg (ed.), *Women and the Law: A Social Historical Perspective*, vol. II, *Property, Family and the Legal Profession* (Cambridge, Mass., 1982), pp. 155–86.
2. The nineteenth-century British debates are discussed in R. Feurer, 'The Meaning of "Sisterhood": the British Women's Movement and Protective Labour Legislation, 1870–1900', *Victorian Studies*, 1988, vol. 31, no. 2, pp. 233–60.
3. On Britain, see B. Harrison, *Not Only the 'Dangerous Trades': Women's Work and Health in Britain, 1880–1914* (London, 1996); for a study which examines the issue of labour protection alongside other feminist campaigns, see M. L. Shanley, 'Suffrage, Protective Labour Legislation, and Married Women's Property Laws in England', *Signs*, 1986, vol. 12, no. 1, pp. 62–77. On France, see M. L. Stewart, *Women, Work and the French State: Labour Protection and Social Patriarchy, 1879–1919* (London, 1989), and P. Hilden, *Working Women and Socialist Politics in France, 1880–1914. A Regional Study* (Oxford, 1986). Some of the measures introduced by different states in America are detailed in E. E. Witte, 'The Effects of Special Labor Legislation for Women', *Quarterly Journal of Economics*, November 1927, vol. 42, pp. 153–64.
4. A detailed analysis of classic nineteenth-century socialist writings on the woman question is offered in L. Vogel, *Marxism and the Oppression of Women: Toward a Unitary Theory* (New Jersey, 1989).
5. The second edition of Bebel's work was published under the title *Woman in the Past, Present and Future* (London, n.d. [1883]). In his chapter 'In the Present' Bebel curiously asserts that 'of all European States, Russia is the one in which the position of women is freest'.
6. B. Webb, 'Women and the Factory Acts', *Fabian Tract*, 1896, no. 67, extracted in P. Hollis, *Women in Public: The Women's Movement, 1850–1900* (London, 1981), p. 127. Shanley, *op. cit.*, p. 68, notes that 'the opposition of some nineteenth century feminists to protective labour legislation for women aroused a deep-seated resentment and distrust of feminists in such socialists and labour historians as ... Beatrice Webb'.
7. Webb, *op. cit.*, pp. 124–9.
8. See, for example, the work of Elizabeth Gurley Flynn, *The Rebel Girl: An Autobiography. My First Life (1906–26)* (New York, 1973), and

Notes 187

R. F. Baxandall, *Words on Fire: The Life and Writing of Elizabeth Gurley Flynn* (London, 1987).

9. C. Eastman, 'Equality or Protection', *Equal Rights*, 15 March 1924, extracted in B. W. Cook (ed.), *Crystal Eastman: On Women and Revolution* (Oxford, 1978), pp. 157–8.

10. B. Harrison, *op. cit.*, and B. Harrison, 'Some of Them Gets Lead Poisoned: Occupational Lead Exposure in Women, 1880–1914', *Social History of Medicine*, 1989, vol. 2, no. 2, pp. 171–95. See also M. D. McFeely, *Lady Inspectors: The Campaign for a Better Workplace, 1893–1921* (Oxford, 1988), pp. 64–74.

11. The belief that restrictions on the employment of women workers would eventually be of benefit to the industrial labour force as a whole is noted in M. Valverde, '"Giving the Female a Domestic Turn": the Social, Legal and Moral Regulation of Women's Work in British Cotton Mills, 1820–50', *Journal of Social History*, 1988, vol. 21, no. 4, pp. 626–7.

12. Witte, *op. cit.*, pp. 155–7.

13. See, for example, E. Waters, 'From the Old Family to the New: Work, Marriage and Motherhood in Urban Soviet Russia, 1917-31', unpublished PhD thesis (CREES, University of Birmingham, 1985), and E. Waters, 'The Modernisation of Russian Motherhood, 1917–37', *Soviet Studies*, 1992, vol. 44, no. 1, pp. 123–35. See also W. Z. Goldman, *Women, the State and Revolution: Soviet Family Policy and Social Life, 1917–36* (Cambridge, 1993).

14. For the problems experienced in Germany after the Second World War in implementing a 'law for the protection of mothers', see R. G. Moeller, 'Protecting Mother's Work: From Production to Reproduction in Postwar West Germany', *Journal of Social History*, spring 1989, pp. 413–37. Moeller notes, firstly, that 'social policies, which ostensibly address women's needs, may also circumscribe women's capacities and choices', and, secondly, 'protective legislation that acknowledged women's biological difference uncritically accepted women's socially constructed responsibilities to children, husbands, and other relatives dependent on unpaid domestic labor; it aimed at sparing women from certain kinds of work in order to save them for work of a different sort'. See pp. 414, 418.

15. See J. Evans, 'Women and Family Policy in the USSR, 1936–41', unpublished PhD thesis (CREES, University of Birmingham, 1987), and 'The CPSU and the "Woman Question": the Case of the 1936 Decree "In Defence of Mother and Child"', *Journal of Contemporary History*, 1981, vol. 16, pp. 757–75. See also Goldman's chapter, 'Recasting the Vision: the Resurrection of the Family', *op. cit.*, pp. 296–336.

16. For reviews of some of the published literature see B. A. Engel, 'Women in Russia and the Soviet Union', *Signs*, 1987, vol. 12, no. 4, pp. 781–96, B. A. Engel, 'Engendering Russia's History: Women in Post-Emancipation Russia and the Soviet Union', *Slavic Review*, 1992, vol. 51, no. 2, pp. 309–21, and R. Ruthchild, 'Engendering History: Women in Russia and the Soviet Union', *European History Quarterly*,

1994, no. 24, pp. 555–62. Despite the extensive and growing literature on 'women in Russia' listed in these reviews the particular study of women in the Soviet Union in the 1920s and 1930s has received very little attention.

For some recent monograph literature dealing partly or wholly with women in this period see, for example, M. Buckley, *Women and Ideology in the Soviet Union* (London, 1989), and Goldman, *op. cit.* For some recent useful collections of essays see: B. A. Clements et al., *Russia's Women: Accommodation, Resistance, Transformation* (Oxford, 1991), B. Farnsworth and L. Viola, *Russian Peasant Women* (Oxford, 1992), R. Marsh (ed.), *Women in Russia and Ukraine* (Cambridge, 1996), and L. Edmondson (ed.), *Gender in Russian History and Culture, 1800–1990* (forthcoming). See also S. Reid, 'All Stalin's Women: Gender and Power in Soviet Art of the 1930s', *Slavic Review*, 1998, vol. 57, no. 1, pp. 133–73.

17. I include here by no means an exhaustive listing. For standard texts of Soviet economic development in these decades see M. Dobb, *Soviet Economic Development since 1917* (London, 1946), and A. Nove, *An Economic History of the USSR* (first published London, 1969). For more detailed studies see the series on the industrialisation of Soviet Russia by E. H. Carr and R. W. Davies.

D. Filtzer, *Soviet Workers and Stalinist Industrialisation* (London, 1986) devotes five pages to 'the growth of female employment', see pp. 63–7. J. Barber, 'The Composition of the Soviet Working Class, 1928–41', unpublished *Discussion Papers*, SIPS no. 16 (CREES, University of Birmingham, 1978) also includes details of sex composition.

Edmondson, *op. cit.*, includes two chapters on different aspects of gender identity in the 1930s: L. Attwood, 'Rationality versus Romanticism: Representations of Women in the Stalinist Press', and M. Buckley, '"Realities" of "New" Women in the 1930s: Assertive, Superior, Belittled and Beaten'. See also L. Attwood's forthcoming study of *People Made from a Special Mould: Representations of 'the New Woman' in Soviet Women's Magazines*.

18. GARF, f. 5515 for Narkomtrud SSSR, and f. 5451 for VTsSPS. The name of the published journals changed throughout the interwar years and the titles are listed in the bibliography.

19. For Narkomtrud RSFSR, see GARF, f. A-390.

20. *Zhenotdel* representatives sat on a number of the commissions established by Narkomtrud in the 1920s to investigate the life and experiences of women workers. S. I. Kaplun, *Sovremennye problemy zhenskogo truda i byta* (Moscow, 1924), pp. 71–4, offers some insight into infringements of the protective labour laws in the early Soviet period.

21. See, for example, the multiple editions of *Kommentarii k zakonodatel'stvu o trude*, *Sbornik zakonodatel'nykh aktov o trude*, *Sovetskoe trudovoe pravo* and *Trudovoe zakonodatel'stvo*.

22. Such objections are noted in J. Smith, *Woman in Soviet Russia* (New York, 1928), p. 24, and S. M. Kingsbury and M. Fairchild, *Factory, Family and Woman in the USSR* (New York, 1935), p. 100.

This argument was also put forward by the nineteenth-century British feminist, Frances Power Cobbe, 'Criminals, Idiots, Women and

Minors. Is the Classification Sound?' (orig. 1868), reprinted in
C. A. Lacey, *Barbara Leigh Smith Bodichon and the Langham Place Group*
(London, 1987). In the 1970s, the chair of the Equal Opportunities
Commission in Britain identified the treatment of adult women with
young persons as the 'most insulting anomaly' of the existing protective
labour laws. See B. Lockwood, 'Protective Legislation: Who Benefits –
Men or Women?', *Journal of the Society for Occupational Medicine*, 1979,
no. 29, p. 5.
23. In 1939 women constituted 52.1 per cent of the Soviet population
(including the Baltic republics), and 50.9 per cent of those of working
age (between 16 and 54 years of age). 38.4 per cent of the total female
population was in paid employment. By the end of the decade the proportion of women in blue- or white-collar jobs equalled just over 13
per cent of the total female population and around 34.6 per cent of
those recorded as being in paid employment in 1939.

A great number of handbooks, such as the series *Zhenshchiny v SSSR*
and *Trud v SSSR*, detail demographic data for the Soviet Union. My
calculations are based on *Trud v SSSR: statisticheskii sbornik* (Moscow,
1988), pp. 105–7, Goskomstat, *Zhenshchiny v SSSR 1989: statisticheskie
materialy* (Moscow, 1989), pp. 9–10, 15–16, and TsSU SSSR,
Zhenshchiny v SSSR: statisticheskii sbornik (Moscow, 1975), p. 5.
24. P. H. Solomon, 'Laws and Administrative Acts: Sources and Finding
Aids', in S. Fitzpatrick and L. Viola (eds.), *A Researcher's Guide to Sources
on Soviet Social History in the 1930s* (London, 1990), p. 146.
25. See, for example, M. Bukhov, *Kak okhranyaetsa trud rabotnits po sovetskim
zakonam* (Moscow, 1925); A. Pasternak, *Chto dolzhna znat' rabotnitsa ob
okhrane zhenskogo truda* (Khar'kov, 1923); V. V. Sokolov, *Prava zhenshchiny
po sovetskim zakonam* (Moscow, 1928).

2 PROTECTION OF WOMEN WORKERS IN TSARIST RUSSIA

1. G. M. Price, *Labour Protection in Soviet Russia* (London, 1928), pp. 20–1.
See also W. B. Walsh, *Readings in Russian History*, vol. 3 (New York,
1963), pp. 547–64, citing *Twenty-Fourth Annual Report of the
Commissioner of Labor, 1909. Workmen's Insurance and Compensation
Systems in Europe* (Washington, 1911).
2. Price, *op. cit.*, p. 21.
3. D. Pospielovsky, *Russian Police Trade Unionism: Experiment or Provocation?*
(London, 1971), p. 18.
4. For an outline of the developments in this period see *ibid.*, pp. 18–19.
Walsh, *op. cit.*, p. 548, outlines the 1866 law on factory owners' responsibilities to provide medical aid to workers.
5. Much of the historiographical debate has focused on the reforms introduced by Alexander II. The major arguments are summarised in
M. Perrie, *Alexander II: Emancipation and Reform in Russia, 1855–1881*
(London, 1989).

6. Price, *op. cit.*, pp. 29–30.
7. Pospielovsky, *op. cit.*, p. 20.
8. See R. L. Glickman, *Russian Factory Women: Workplace and Society, 1880–1914* (London, 1984), p. 77, which cites I. I. Yanzhul, *Fabrichnyi byt moskovskoi gubernii. Otchet za 1882–83* (St Petersburg, 1884), p. 8, and *Fabrichnyi byt moskovskoi gubernii. Otchet za 1885*, p. 51.
9. Pospielovsky, *op. cit.*, p. 30.
10. *Ibid.*, pp. 33–4.
11. This point is also emphasised with reference to British protective labour law in the nineteenth century by J. Humphries, 'Protective Legislation, the Capitalist State, and Working Class Men: the Case of the 1842 Mines Regulation Act', *Feminist Review*, spring 1981, no. 7, pp. 1–33. Humphries, p. 24, argues that 'employers in regions where female workers were not used had a vested interest in legislation which prohibited such employment elsewhere, requiring other employers to recruit and train substitute male workers, or to shift to a more capital-intensive technology, both of which would cause dislocations in production and place them at a competitive disadvantage'.
12. F. C. Giffin, 'The Prohibition of Night Work for Women and Young Persons: the Russian Factory Law of June 3, 1885', *Canadian Slavonic Papers*, 1968, vol. 2, no. 2, pp. 208–18. A succinct account of the debates and their outcome is also to be found in Glickman, *op. cit.*, pp. 146–9.
13. Glickman, *op. cit.*, p. 148, notes that a strike in the Vladimir province in October 1885 in protest against the night work regulations led to the revision of night shift hours, which were subsequently narrowed down to fall between ten o'clock in the evening and four o'clock in the morning.
14. *Ibid.*, pp. 148–9.
15. See Walsh, *op. cit.*, pp. 548–9.
16. Glickman, *op. cit.*, pp. 124–5.
17. For a detailed study of the complex relationship which developed between the state and the labour movement from this period see T. McDaniel, *Autocracy, Capitalism and Revolution in Russia* (London, 1988).
18. Price, *op. cit.*, p. 31. Pospielovsky, *op. cit.*, p. 34, however, argues that this move paved the way for the establishment of state-sponsored trade unions, under the Zubatov initiative, which were designed to protect the interests of workers.
19. Other amendments to the protective labour laws in the 1890s also further expanded the scope of employment of child labour. See Price, *op. cit.*, p. 28.
20. Glickman, *op. cit.*, p. 149.
21. *Ibid.*, p. 6.
22. See Giffin, *op. cit.*, p. 217.
23. S. M. Kingsbury and M. Fairchild, *Factory, Family and Woman in the Soviet Union* (New York, 1935), p. 9.
24. See Glickman, *op. cit.*, p. 89.
25. In the following decade, the attempt to restrict the daily employment of women workers in America to ten hours resulted in a protracted legal battle and clearly vocalised feminist opposition. See N. S. Erickson,

'Historical Background of "Protective" Labor Legislation: Müller v. Oregon', in D. K. Weisberg, *Women and the Law: A Social Historical Perspective*, vol. II, *Property, Family and the Legal Profession* (Cambridge, Mass., 1982), pp. 155–86.

26. A. S. Kalygina, *Prava rabotnits i krest'yanok v SSSR* (Moscow-Leningrad, 1925), p. 24, claims that many factories were able to evade the law, often operating 12–13 hour shifts.

27. Price, *op. cit.*, p. 28, notes that this was an argument put forward by Lenin.

28. Kingsbury and Fairchild, *op. cit.*, p. 102.

29. S. I. Kaplun, *The Protection of Labour in Soviet Russia* (Moscow, 1920), p. 2.

30. *Ibid.*

31. V. E. Bonnell, *The Russian Worker: Life and Labour Under the Tsarist Regime* (Berkeley, Calif., 1983), p. 7.

32. H. Seton-Watson, *The Russian Empire, 1801–1917* (Oxford, 1967), p. 541.

33. O. Crisp, 'Labour and Industrialisation in Russia', *Cambridge Economic History of Europe*, vol. 7, part 2 (Cambridge, 1978), pp. 348–9, 356–7. In an index of the growth in numbers of the industrial labour force employed in enterprises subject to factory inspection, Crisp notes an increase of 34.9 per cent for the period 1901–14. The figure was slightly lower (27.9 per cent) for the mining and metallurgical sectors, where few women were employed. Between 1900 and 1914, however, the proportion of women working in enterprises subject to factory inspection grew by 64.1 per cent.

34. See the more detailed arguments on these issues put forward by McDaniel, *op. cit.*, pp. 150, 153, 280.

35. V. Andrle, *A Social History of Twentieth-Century Russia* (London, 1994), pp. 100–2.

36. C. Kelly, 'A Stick with Two Ends, or, Misogyny in Popular Culture: A Case Study of the Puppet Text "Petrushka"', in J. T. Costlow et al. (eds.), *Sexuality and the Body in Russian Culture* (Cambridge, 1993), pp. 89–90.

37. Price, *op. cit.*, p. 32.

38. Glickman, *op. cit.*, p. 165.

39. *Ibid.*, p. 125, citing *Voprosy strakhovaniya*, 1914, no. 8, p. 6.

40. B. A. Engel, 'Women in Russia and the Soviet Union', *Signs*, 1987, vol. 12, no. 4, p. 784, but she does not cite her source for this information.

41. L. H. Edmondson, *Feminism in Russia, 1900–17* (London, 1984), p. 94.

42. *Ibid.*, p. 94.

43. *Ibid.*, pp. 93–4.

44. For a detailed study of the background to and impact of the 1912 social welfare provisions see R. B. McKean, 'Social Insurance in Tsarist Russia, St. Petersburg, 1907–17', *Revolutionary Russia*, 1990, vol. 3, no. 1, pp. 55–89.

45. R. B. McKean, 'The Bureaucracy and the Labour Problem, June 1907– February 1917', in R. B. McKean (ed.), *New Perspectives on Modern Russian History* (London, 1992), pp. 229–30.

46. See Andrle, *op. cit.*, p. 116.

47. McKean, 'Social Insurance', p. 82.

48. See, for example, G. L. Gullickson, 'Womanhood and Motherhood: the Rouen Manufacturing Community, Women Workers and the French Factory Acts', in R. L. Rudolph (ed.), *The European Peasant Family and Society: Historical Studies* (Liverpool, 1995).
49. See Glickman, *op. cit.*, pp. 151–2.
50. See, for example, the extensive study of peasant and working women by B. A. Engel, *Between the Fields and the City: Women, Work and Family in Russia, 1861–1914* (Cambridge, 1994), *passim*.
51. L. Ye. Mints, 'Ocherki razvitiya statistiki chislennosti i sostava promyshlennogo proletariata v Rossii', *Ocherki po istorii statistiki SSSR* (Moscow, 1957), p. 244. See Appendix 2. Crisp, *op. cit.*, pp. 356–7, gives slightly different figures.
52. See, for example, J. Pallot, 'Women's Domestic Industries in Moscow Province, 1880–1900', in B. E. Clements et al., *Russia's Women: Accommodation, Resistance, Transformation* (Berkeley, 1991), pp. 163–84.
53. Mints, *op. cit.*, pp. 244–5. See also Crisp, *op. cit.*, pp. 356–7.
54. Mints, *op. cit.*, pp. 246–53, and Crisp, *op. cit.*, pp. 356–7, 361.
55. By 1913 the female population of Russia numbered 80.1 million, or 50.3 per cent of the population as a whole. See *Zhenshchiny v SSSR: statisticheskie materialy* (Moscow, 1981), p. 3.

3 WOMEN WORKERS AND SOVIET INDUSTRIALISATION

1. A useful survey of this period is provided by G. W. Lapidus, *Women in Soviet Society: Equality, Development and Social Change* (London, 1978). This source includes some interesting comments on the operation of protective labour law for women workers.
2. The statistical data dealing with women in the Soviet interwar economy are complex and there is not room to discuss this in detail here. Reasonably easily accessible, detailed and reliable data are available for the specific category of worker focused on here. Some useful explanations of Soviet economic and statistical categorisations are provided by A. D. Redding, 'Nonagricultural Employment in the USSR, 1928–55', unpublished PhD thesis, University of Columbia, 1958.
3. A. Meyer, 'The Impact of World War I on Russian Women's Lives', in B. E. Clements et al., *Russia's Women: Accommodation, Resistance, Transformation* (Berkeley, 1991), pp. 208–24.
4. L. Ye. Mints, 'Ocherki razvitiya statistiki chislennosti i sostava promyshlennogo proletariata v Rossii', *Ocherki po istorii statistiki* (Moscow, 1957), pp. 203, 245. Mints' survey includes comprehensive data for twelve selected industries for which a full set of information was available for the period from 1885–1926/27. R. W. Davies, *Soviet Economy in Turmoil, 1929–30* (London, 1989), p. 10, states that these data account for 76 per cent of industrial workers.

   Mints' information includes a breakdown by sex and age. The 1917 figure of 39.7 per cent includes war industries and this total is

increased to 42.5 per cent if war industries are excluded from the cal-
culation. Adult women alone constituted 34.6 per cent of the labour
force in 1917.

5. *Women and Communism: Selections from the Writings of Marx, Engels, Lenin and Stalin* (London, 1950), pp. 52–3.
6. See for example the argument put forward by the Petrograd Council of Trade Unions in April 1918 cited in J. Smith, *Woman in Soviet Russia* (New York, 1928), pp. 15–16.
7. '*Kodeks zakonov o trude*', decree of VTsIK, *SU*, 1918, Article 905.
8. Mints, *op. cit.*, p. 244.
9. A concise account of economic development in the early Soviet period is provided by A. Nove, *An Economic History of the USSR* (London, 1982).
10. See, for example, the account offered by Smith, *op. cit.*, pp. 12–14, of her visit in 1923, and the views presented in *Soviet Russia: An Investigation by British Women Trade Unionists, April to July, 1925* (London, 1925), *passim*.
11. Mints, *op. cit.*, p. 244.
12. Ye. Tsyrlina, 'Rabota komissii po izucheniyu i uluchsheniyu zhenskogo truda', *Voprosy truda*, 1926, no. 2, p. 52. Tsyrlina does not offer data for the actual numbers of women employed in these years but states that the proportion of women amongst large-scale industrial employees declined from 41.9 per cent in July 1921 to 27.4 per cent by 1 January 1924.
13. Gosplan SSSR, *Trud v SSSR: statisticheskii spravochnik* (Moscow, 1936), p. 91, covers only large-scale industry. This source details data according to employment category (shopfloor workers, trainees and apprentices, ITR and white-collar workers), sex, age and industrial sector for the period from 1923–36. By the end of the 1920s large-scale industry accounted for approximately 30 per cent of paid employees.
14. A. G. Rashin, *Zhenskii trud v SSSR* (Moscow, 1928), pp. 6–7.
15. With the addition of cotton textiles and the food industry, these four sectors accounted for over 70 per cent of all male industrial workers. See Rashin, *op. cit.*, p. 7.
16. *Trud v SSSR* (Moscow, 1936). See also Rashin, *op. cit.*, p. 8.
17. Mints, *op. cit.*, pp. 244–5. See Appendix 2. 1913 figures are based on USSR territory. See also Rashin, *op. cit.*, pp. 9–11.
18. *Ibid.*, p. 13.
19. *Ibid.*, p. 14. See also G. Datsuk, 'Zhenskii trud – v proizvodstvo', *Puti industrializatsii*, 1931, no. 2, pp. 39–40.
20. Davies, *Turmoil*, p. 10, notes that 'according to surveys of the central bureau of labour statistics, the average daily earnings by adult women increased from 63.4 per cent of adult male earnings in March 1926 to 67.2 per cent in March 1928', citing Rashin, *Statistika truda*, 1928, nos. 9–10, pp. 2–48.
21. VTsSPS, *Sostav fabrichno-zavodskogo proletariata SSSR v diagrammakh i tablitsakh: itogi perepisi metallistov, gornorabochikh i tekstil'shchikov 1929 goda* (Moscow, 1930), p. 64.
22. Gosplan SSSR, *Trud v SSSR: spravochnik 1926–30* (Moscow, 1930), p. 45. See also S. Davies, *Popular Opinion in Stalin's Russia: Terror, Propaganda and Dissent, 1934–41* (Cambridge, 1997), p. 60.

23. Serebrennikov, *The Position of Women in the USSR* (London, 1937), p. 30.
24. *Ibid.*, p. 31.
25. *Trud v SSSR* (1936), p. 25. By this time women constituted 27.9 per cent of the labour force in large-scale industry. See also Gosplan SSSR, *Pyatiletnii plan narodno-khozyaistvennogo stroitel'stva SSSR*, tom 2, part 2 (Moscow, 1930), p. 181.

  Ye. B. Gruzdeva and E. S. Chertikhina, *Trud i byt sovetskikh zhenshchin* (Moscow, 1983), pp. 17, 21–2, offer a detailed breakdown of numbers and percentages of women employed in the Soviet economy in 1926 based on data taken from the census.
26. W. Z. Goldman, *Women, the State and Revolution: Soviet Family Policy and Social Life, 1917–1936* (Cambridge, 1993), p. 110.
27. Smith, *op. cit.*, p. 21, states that 'unemployment among women increased until 1924, when it reached 600,000, about half the entire number of registered unemployed'. In a report on 'Unemployment and its Character' to the Central Commission for the Improvement and Study of Women's Labour in Production on 12 June 1924, Isaev noted that women constituted 47 per cent of those unemployed in the USSR: see GARF, f. 5515, o. 4, d. 8, ll. 200–1. See also Goldman, *op. cit.*, for a more detailed study of the impact of unemployment on women.
28. *Ibid.*, pp. 110–18.
29. *Pyatiletnii plan* (Moscow, 1930), p. 175.
30. J. Grunfeld, 'Women's Work in Russia's Planned Economy', *Social Research*, February 1942, vol. 9, no. 1, p. 29.
31. See the example cited in Smith, *op. cit.*, p. 27, and the expressed resistance noted by B. Marsheva, 'Zhenskii trud v 1931 godu', *Voprosy truda*, 1931, no. 1, p. 40.
32. Goldman, *op. cit.*, p. 115, for this and other counter-arguments.
33. *Soviet Russia: An Investigation by British Women Trade Unionists, April to July, 1925* (London, 1925), p. 26, argues that 'the women being less organised, could the less protect themselves against unfair discrimination against them by managers with the old ideas of woman's place being in the home'.
34. Vinnikov's report, 'Measures in the Area of the Protection of Female Labour' was read to the Central Commission for the Improvement and Study of Women's Labour in Production on 19 June 1924: see GARF, f. 5515, o. 4, d. 8, ll. 202–3.
35. *Pyatiletnii plan*, p. 181, and Gosplan SSSR, *Pyatiletnii plan narodno-khozyaistvennogo stroitel'stva SSSR*, tom 1 (Moscow, 1930), pp. 94, 129.
36. This issue is discussed in B. Khasnin, 'Vovlechenie zhenshchin v tsensovuyu promyshlennost' SSSR v 1931 g.', *Voprosy truda*, 1932, no. 2, pp. 47–51.
37. *Trud v SSSR* (1936), p. 25. See also P. M. Chirkov, *Reshenie zhenskogo voprosa v SSSR (1917–37 gg.)* (Moscow, 1978), p. 125.
38. *Trud v SSSR* (1936), p. 91. In the same period the number of female shopfloor workers alone, including trainees, rose from 804 000 to 1 826 200.
39. *Ibid.*, p. 25. See also Chirkov, *op. cit.*, p. 124.

40. The research project and findings are outlined in G. Serebrennikov, 'Itogi nauchno-issledovatel'skoi raboty po izucheniyu zhenskogo truda', *Voprosy truda*, 1933, nos. 2–3, pp. 63–7.
41. Chirkov, *op. cit.*, p. 122.
42. VTsSPS report, 'O rabote sredi zhenshchin', GARF, f. 5451, o. 16, d. 557, ll. 19–20.
43. For example, in a Narkomtrud RSFSR report on the recruitment of female labour to production it was noted that in Leningrad industries 67.68 per cent of women were engaged in unskilled tasks. 'Ob itogakh vovlechenii zhenskii trud v promyshlennosti za 1932 g. i o khode vypolneniya plana 1932 g.', dated 26 August 1932, GARF, f. 5451, o. 16, d. 557, l. 1.
44. GARF, f. 5451, o. 16, d. 966, l. 11, dated 10 April 1932. Lapidus, *op. cit.*, p. 99, suggests that women were faced with lower levels of hostility in areas of the country where notions of the sexual division of labour were less entrenched.
45. W. Z. Goldman, 'Industrial Politics, Peasant Rebellion and the Death of the Proletarian Women's Movement in the USSR', *Slavic Review*, 1996, vol. 55, no. 1, pp. 72–3, for this and other examples.
46. See, for example, Datsuk, *op. cit.*, pp. 40–1.
47. GARF, f. 5451, o. 15, d. 357, l. 66.
48. These issues are discussed in passing in B. Marsheva, 'Zhenskii trud v 1931 godu', *Voprosy truda*, 1931, no. 1, pp. 32–41.
49. GARF, f. 5451, o. 16, d. 557, l. 1.
50. See also Ye. Orlikova, 'Sovetskaya zhenshchina v obshchestvennom proizvodstve', *Problemy ekonomiki*, July 1940, no. 7, p. 113. Orlikova's data are fully consistent with *Trud v SSSR* (Moscow, 1936) for the period up to 1935. Khasnin, *op. cit.*, p. 47, offers more detailed figures for the period 1928–31, which reveal that a very high proportion of the total female labour force was employed in the Russian republic, where women workers also constituted a higher proportion (around 35 per cent) of the labour force as a whole.
51. Orlikova, *op. cit.*, p. 114.
52. The draft version of the plan envisaged a net growth of 7.4 million women in paid employment. These totals excluded trainees (*ucheniki*). See Gosplan SSSR, *Vtoroi pyatiletnii plan razvitiya narodnogo khozyaistva SSSR (1933–1937 gg.)*, tom 1 (Moscow, 1934), p. 338, and Gosplan SSSR, *Proekt vtorogo pyatiletnego plana razvitiya narodnogo khozyaistva SSSR (1933–1937 gg.)* tom. 1 (Moscow, 1934), p. 321. See also *Opyt KPSS v reshenii zhenskogo voprosa* (Moscow, 1981), p. 46.
53. S. Schwarz, *Labor in the Soviet Union* (New York, 1952), p. 72.
54. *Opyt KPSS*, p. 45.
55. Chirkov, *op. cit.*, pp. 128–9.
56. *Trud v SSSR* (Moscow, 1988), p. 106.
57. Orlikova, *op. cit*, p. 114, offers data for the distribution of women workers in a range of large-scale industries in this period.
58. *Ibid.*, pp. 114–17. Grunfeld, *op. cit.*, pp. 43–4, also provides a summary of some of Orlikova's findings discussed here and above.

59. See, for example, the speech by Antselovich at the All-Union Trade Union Conference on Work amongst Women on 2 February 1931: GARF, f. 5451, o. 15, d. 358, l. 286.
60. *Opyt KPSS*, p. 48.
61. Grunfeld, *op. cit.*, p. 42.

4   THE ADMINISTRATION OF THE PROTECTIVE LABOUR LAWS

1. See G. M. Price, *Labour Protection in Soviet Russia* (London, 1929), pp. 35–6, and Z. A. Astapovich, *Pervye meropriyatiya sovetskoi vlasti v oblasti truda* (Moscow, 1958), pp. 12–14.
2. The efforts of the Provisional Government are explored in more depth in G. A. Beilikhis, 'Iz istorii bor'by za okhranu zdorov'ya rabochikh v 1917 g.', *Gigiena i sanitariya*, 1957, no. 11, pp. 43–8.
3. See Price, *op.cit.*, pp. 36–7.
4. These administrative changes are dealt with in part by H. Blagg, 'The Development of Soviet Social Insurance From 1917 to the Eve of the First Five-Year Plan', unpublished M.Soc.Sci. thesis, CREES, University of Birmingham, 1981.
5. '*O vos'mychasovom rabochem dne, prodolzhitel'nosti i raspredelenii rabochego vremeni*', decree of Sovnarkom, 29 October 1917, *SU*, 1917, Article 7. The decree also set out regulations for young workers and listed eight days as public holidays.
6. Shlyapnikov and Kollontai headed the Workers' Opposition movement in 1921, which called for a more independent role for the trade unions. By this time Shlyapnikov had already been replaced as People's Commissar for Labour by V. V. Shmidt, who had previously been active in the ACCTU.
7. Astapovich, *op. cit.*, p. 36.
8. '*Ob otdelakh truda*', decree of Narkomtrud, 31 July 1918, *SU*, 1918, Article 619.
9. The weakness of Russian trade unions in this period is described in E. H. Carr, *The Bolshevik Revolution, 1917–1923* (vol. II) (London, 1983), pp. 108–13.
10. Price, *op. cit.*, p. 42, argues that 'these Factory Committees often acted in an irresponsible and incompetent way, tried to enforce rules and regulations which were unenforceable and impracticable, so that much of their activity, regarded as pernicious by some, was curtailed and largely modified', but he offers no real evidence for this.
11. '*O nakaze inspektsii truda*', decree of Narkomtrud RSFSR, 31 July 1918, *SU*, 1918, Article 620. In addition, hygiene inspectors were made responsible for such issues as air quality, ventilation, temperature controls, work which involved dangerous industrial substances, the provision of soap and washing facilities, etc., and technical inspectors were made responsible for the oversight of building and equipment regulations.

12. Astapovich, *op. cit.*, pp. 126–8.
13. L. H. Siegelbaum, 'Okhrana Truda: Industrial Hygiene, Psychotechnics and Industrialisation in the USSR', in S. Solomon (ed.), *Health and Society in Revolutionary Russia* (Bloomington, Indiana, 1990), p. 226.
14. '*Kodeks zakonov o trude*', decree of VTsIK, *SU*, 1918, Article 905. The code set out the obligations of Soviet citizens to work, with exclusions, and general regulatory measures. Section 9 dealt with questions of the administration of labour protection.
15. Price, *op. cit.*, p. 41.
16. *Ibid.*, p. 43.
17. S. I. Kaplun, *The Protection of Labour in Soviet Russia* (Moscow, 1920), p. 12.
18. S. I. Kaplun, *Zhenskii trud i okhrana ego v sovetskom Rossii* (Moscow, 1921), p. 32.
19. *Ibid.*, p. 34.
20. *Ibid.*, pp. 34–5.
21. S. I. Kaplun, *Okhrana truda za 2 goda proletarskoi revolyutsii, 1917–1919 gg.* (Moscow, 1920), pp. 12–13.
22. '*O vovlechenii zhenshchin v inspektsiyu truda*', circular of Narkomtrud and VTsSPS, *Izvestiya NKT*, 1923, no. 8, p. 6.
23. '*Kodeks zakonov o trude*', decree of VTsIK, *SU*, 1922, Article 903.
24. The opening of this section was announced in *Voprosy truda*, 1925, nos. 5–6, p. 263.
25. Besides Moscow, institutes were established in Leningrad, Khar'kov, Gorkii, Sverdlovsk, Tbilisi and Tashkent. For more detail see A. I. Pakhomychev, 'Nekotorye cherty razvitiya gigienu truda v SSSR za 40 let sushchestvovaniya sovetskoi vlasti', *Gigiena i sanitariya*, 1957, no. 10, pp. 43–51.
26. GARF, f. 5515, o. 4, d. 8, l. 197: circular of Narkomtrud, 'o regulyarnikh soveshchaniyakh pri mestnykh organakh NKT po voprosam uluchsheniya i izucheniya zhenskogo truda', dated 3 July 1924.
27. *Ibid.*, l. 198. Tsyrlina was later involved in the work of the People's Commissariat of Education.
28. *Vestnik truda*, 1924, no. 10, p. 291.
29. GARF, f. 5515, o. 4, d. 8, l. 198.
30. The work of the commission is outlined briefly in B. Marsheva, 'O komissiyakh po izucheniyu i uluchsheniyu zhenskogo truda', *Rabotnitsa*, 1927, no. 5, p. 18.
31. GARF, f. 5515, o. 4, d. 8, l. 199: 'Rasporyazhenie po NKT'.
32. *Ibid.*, ll. 202–3.
33. *Ibid.*, ll. 200–1. The report on 'Unemployment and its Character' was given by Isaev from the Labour Market Department (*otdel rynka truda*).
34. *Ibid.*, l. 202. E. Tsyrlina drew on these data in her article, 'Blizhaishie zadachi v oblasti izucheniya i uluchsheniya zhenskogo truda', *Voprosy truda*, 1924, no. 9, pp. 21–5.
35. GARF, f. 5515, o. 13, d. 6, l. 16ob. Price, *op. cit.*, p. 86, estimated that female labour inspectors constituted 5.8 per cent of the total number working in 1926. S. M. Kingsbury and M. Fairchild, *Factory, Family and Woman in the Soviet Union* (New York, 1935), p. 108, cite the figure of

5.7 per cent for the proportion of female labour inspectors employed in 1930.

36. The archives of the 'komissiya uluchsheniya truda i byta zhenshchin (pri prezidiume VTsIK)' are located at GARF, f. 6983, o. 1, d. 5. For details of the initial meeting and functions of the commission see ll. 1–3. Significant discussions on reorganising the composition and work of the commission were held in October 1929, see ll. 26–31.

37. '*Polozhenie o Komissii Prezidiuma TsIK SSSR po uluchsheniyu truda i byta zhenshchin kul'turno-otstalykh narodnostei*', decree of TsIK, *SZ*, 1928, Article 321. See also *Izvestiya NKT*, 1928, no. 32, pp. 481–2.

38. See, for example, the report in *Izvestiya*, 28 February 1930, 'ob itogakh 2-go vsesoyuznogo soveshchaniya komissii po uluchsheniyu truda i byta zhenshchin'.

39. '*Polozhenie o glavnom inspektore po zhenskomu trudu pri NKT SSSR*', decree of Narkomtrud, *Izvestiya NKT*, 1928, no. 34–35, p. 515.

40. '*Primernoe Polozhenie o starshikh inspektorakh po zhenskomu trudu pri NKT soyuznykh respublik i ob inspektorakh po zhenskomu trudu pri mestnykh organakh NKT soyuznykh respublik*', decree of Narkomtrud, *Izvestiya NKT*, 1928, nos. 34–5, pp. 515–16.

41. '*O reorganizatsii raboty po izucheniyu i uluchsheniyu zhenskogo truda v proizvodstve*', circular of Narkomtrud, 18 July 1928, *ibid.*, p. 515.

42. '*O rabote inspektsii po zhenskomu trudu*', circular of Narkomtrud, *Izvestiya NKT*, 1929, nos. 22–3, pp. 348–50.

43. '*O rabote inspektsii po okhrane zhenskogo truda*', circular of Narkomtrud RSFSR, *Izvestiya NKT*, 1929, no. 24, pp. 381–2.

44. See, for example, 'ob izuchenii primeneniya zhenskogo truda v metallopromyshlennosti', GARF, f. 5451, o. 11, d. 384, ll. 10–11, dated 5 April 1927, and 'okhrana truda shakhterok plokho okhranyaet', GARF, f. 5451, o. 11, d. 384, ll. 12–13.

45. VTsSPS, *Shestoi s"ezd professional'nykh soyuzov* (Moscow, 1925), pp. 182–5, 221–3, 620–1, 638–9. See also A. Artyukhina, 'Chto skazal 6-i S"ezd Profsoyuzov o rabotnitse', *Rabotnitsa*, 1924, no. 24 (36), pp. 3–4, O. Chernysheva, 'Rabotnitsa v resheniyakh VI s"ezda profsoyuzov', *Vestnik truda*, 1925, no. 1, pp. 67–71, and M. Dewar, *Labour Policy in the USSR, 1917–1928* (New York, 1956), p. 115.

46. GARF, f. 5451, o. 14, d. 417, ll. 35–6. The file contains details of the meeting of the social-cultural sector held on 13 August 1930.

47. For example, 'Rabota profsoyuzov sredi zhenshchin', *Trud*, 19 August 1928, notes the discussion on aims to provide extended child care facilities in institutions transferring to a seven-hour day and three-shift system, where working mothers would be employed on night shifts.

48. See, for example, the report by Tolstopyatov, 'Ratsionalizatsiya proizvodstva, provedenie 7-chasovogo rabochego dnya i uchastiya v ekonom rabote soyuzov', GARF, f. 5451, o. 12, d. 168, ll. 17–19.

49. Short reports on the proceedings of the conference are to be found in *Izvestiya*, 2–5 February, 1931.

50. The reports of the conference are held at GARF, f. 5451, o. 15, dd. 357, 358. Serina spoke on 2 February 1931 and her comments

on labour protection are to be found at GARF, f. 5451, o. 15, d. 357, ll. 16–19.

51. See, for example, the speeches by Okuneva, from the Moscow Institute for the Protection of Labour, and Antselovich, GARF, f. 5451, o. 15, d. 358, ll. 72–7, 278–97.
52. '*Ob obshchestvennykh inspektorakh po okhrane truda*', decree of Sovnarkom, *SZ*, 1931, Article 289.
53. 'Ob obshchestvennom inspektore po okhrane truda', *Trud*, 22 December 1934.
54. N. Yakovleva-Bulina, 'Rabotnitsa-mat' i profsoyuzy', *Voprosy prof-dvizheniya*, July 1936, no. 7 (73), p. 5.
55. *Trud*, 22 December 1934.
56. '*Ob ob"edinenii NKT SSSR s VTsSPS*', decree of TsIK, Sovnarkom and VTsSPS, *SZ*, 1933, Article, 238, and '*O poryadke sliyaniya NKT SSSR i VTsSPS*', decree of Sovnarkom and VTsSPS, 10 September 1933, *ibid.*, 1933, Article 333. The decrees were published also in *Izvestiya*, 24 June 1933, and 11 September 1933.
57. The transfer of functions from Narkomtrud to the trade unions is outlined in N. Shvernik, 'O zadachakh VTsSPS i professional'nykh soyuzov v svyazi s peredachei im funktsii Narkomtruda', *Voprosy profdvizheniya*, August 1933, no. 9, pp. 3–19, and S. Kaplun, 'Okhrana truda i prof-soyuzy', *Voprosy profdvizheniya*, January 1934, no. 1, pp. 65–74.
58. *Sovetskoe trudovoe pravo: kratkii uchebnik* (Moscow, 1938), p. 59.
59. J. J. Rossman, 'The Teikovo Cotton Workers' Strike of April 1932: Class, Gender and Identity Politics in Stalin's Russia', *Russian Review*, January 1997, vol. 56, p. 66.
60. See, for example, 'Nakanune 8 marta', *Trud*, 5 March 1936.
61. See, for example, '*ob obsledovanii Nauchno-issledovatel'skogo instituta okhrany truda VTsSPS v Rostov na Donu v svyazi so statei v gazete "Pravda" ot 20 yanvarya 1936 g.*', decree of the secretariat of VTsSPS, 26 March 1936, and '*o rabote Tashkentskogo instituta okhrany truda*', decree of the secretariat of VTsSPS, 23 June 1936, *Byulleten' VTsSPS*, 1936, no. 8, pp. 15–16. The *Pravda* article by A. Kozlov and Dm. Kotlyarskii, 'Profsoyuznye bezdel'niki', was critical of the many changes undergone by the Rostov-on-Don research institute during its seven-year existence and of its lack of a concrete plan of work.
62. '*O rabote laboratorii po okhrane truda*', decree of the secretariat of VTsSPS, 28 August 1936, *Byulleten' VTsSPS*, 1936, no. 16, p. 4, and '*o rabote laboratorii po okhrane truda*', decree of the secretariat of VTsSPS, 2 September 1936, *ibid.*, 1936, no. 18, pp. 5–6.
63. See, for example, '*o rabote Kazanskogo instituta okhrany truda*', decree of the secretariat of VTsSPS, 13 December 1936, *Byulleten' VTsSPS*, 1937, no. 1, pp. 17–18, and '*o rabote nauchno-issledovatel'skikh institutov okhrany truda VTsSPS*', decree of the secretariat of VTsSPS, 21 October 1937, *ibid.*, 1937, no. 12, p. 6.
64. See, for example, *Sovetskoe trudovoe pravo*, p. 60.
65. B. A. Ruble, *Soviet Trade Unions* (Cambridge, 1981), pp. 14–15.

5 MATERNITY

1. R. W. Davies, M. Harrison and S. G. Wheatcroft, *The Economic Transformation of the Soviet Union, 1913–45* (Cambridge, 1994), pp. 90, 276. See also *Women and Children in the USSR: Brief Statistical Returns* (Moscow, 1963), pp. 45–6.
2. The reduction in maternal mortality can be attributed partly to the legalisation of abortion in 1920 and the more extensive use of antibiotics. See B. Ts. Urlanis, *Istoriya odnogo pokoleniya* (Moscow, 1968), pp. 224–6, which provides data for Leningrad (1923–27), Volgograd (1923–28) and Ivanov (1927–31). See also I. Loudon, *Death in Childbirth: An International Study of Maternal Care and Maternal Mortality, 1800–1950* (Oxford 1992), p. 120.
3. G. N. Serebrennikov, *The Position of Women in the USSR* (London, 1937), p. 21.
4. 'Ocherednye zadachi po okhrane materinstva i mladenchestva', *Kommunistka*, July 1929, no. 13, p. 17.
5. '*Kodeks zakonov o trude*', decree of VTsIK, *SU*, 1918, Article 905.
6. *Soviet Russia: An Investigation by British Women Trade Unionists – April to July, 1925* (London, 1925), p. 28.
7. '*O sotsial'nom obespechenii trudyashchikhsya*', decree of Sovnarkom, *SU*, 1918, Article 906.
8. *Soviet Russia*, p. 29.
9. N. T. Dodge, *Women in the Soviet Economy* (Baltimore, 1966), p. 58.
10. '*Spisok professii, koi naravne s fizicheskim trudom dayut pravo na otpusk v techenie vos'mi nedel' do i vos'mi nedel' posle rodov*', decree of Narkomtrud RSFSR, *Izvestiya*, 16 November 1920. The decree is noted in the archives, GARF, f. 5515, o. 4, d. 312, l. 11.
	A full list of the white-collar and service occupations granted extended maternity leave is also provided in S. I. Kaplun, *Zhenskii trud i okhrana ego v sovetskoi Rossii* (Moscow, 1921), pp. 23–4, and in V. Lebedeva, *Okhrana materinstva i mladenchestva v sovetskoi trudovoi respublike* (Moscow, 1921), p. 55 (and in English in A. W. Field, *Protection of Women and Children in Soviet Russia* (London, 1932), pp. 65–6).
11. '*Ob otpuskakh po beremennosti zhenshchinam-farmatsevtam*', decree of Narkomtrud RSFSR, dated 4 January 1921, *Byulleten' trudogo fronta*, 1921, no. 1, p. 11; '*Ob otpuskakh po beremennosti sortirovshchitsam pochty pochtovo-telegrafnykh kontor*', decree of Narkomtrud RSFSR, dated 10 March 1921, *Byulleten' trudogo fronta*, 1921, no. 11, p. 1; '*Ob otpuskakh po beremennosti mashinistkam*', decree of VTsSPS, dated 9 September 1921, *Byulleten' VTsSPS*, 1921, no. 24.
12. See V. V. Sokolov, *Prava zhenshchin po sovetskim zakonam* (Moscow, 1928), p. 23.
13. Decree of Narkomtrud RSFSR and Narkomzdrav, cited in Lebedeva, *op. cit.*, p. 57.
14. 'Okhrana materinstva', *Pravda*, 5 September 1920.
15. '*Ob osvobozhdenii ot rabot posle vykidysha*', decree of Narkomtrud RSFSR, *SU*, 1920, Article 462. See also M. Bukhov, *Kak okhranyaetsya trud*

rabotnits po sovetskim zakonam (Moscow, 1925), pp. 18–19, and *Izvestiya*, 9 November 1920.

16. '*O merakh okhrany truda i zdorov'ya materei, kormyashchikh grud'yu*', decree of Narkomtrud RSFSR and Narkomzdrav, *SU*, 1920, Article 456.

17. '*Ob okhrane truda beremennykh i kormyashchikh grud'yu zhenshchin*', decree of Narkomtrud RSFSR and VTsSPS, *SU*, 1920. See also '*O perevode i komandirovkakh zhenshchin, podrostkov i maloletnikh*', decree of Narkomtrud RSFSR and VTsSPS, *ibid.*, 1921, Article 218.

18. '*O vospreshchenii nochnykh rabot beremennym i kormyashchim grud'yu zhenshchinam*', decree of Narkomtrud RSFSR and VTsSPS, *SU*, 1920, Article 478.

19. '*Kodeks zakonov o trude*', decree of VTsIK, *SU*, 1922, Article 903.

    Details of the 1922 Labour Code provisions for women workers are also to be found in a number of contemporary published sources, including P. D. Kaminskaya, *Sovetskoe trudovoe pravo* (Kharkov, 1925), pp. 214–18, and E. I. Snezhkov, *Prakticheskii komentarii k kodeksu zakonov o trude* (Moscow, 1928), pp. 213–26.

20. '*O dopol'nitel'nykh posobiyakh rozhdenitsam*', decree of Sovnarkom, *SU*, 1921, Article 668. See also *Izvestiya*, 1 January 1922. See also A. S. Kalygina, *Prava rabotnits i krest'yanok v SSSR* (Moscow-Leningrad, 1925), pp. 28–30.

21. '*O vyplate dopolnitel'nogo posobiya na kormlenie rebenka*', dated 15 February 1923, *Rabotnitsa*, 1923, no. 4, p. 38.

22. *Soviet Russia*, p. 29.

23. S. Schwarz, *Labor in the Soviet Union* (New York, 1952), p. 319, citing N. A. Vigdorchik, *Social Insurance: A Popular Exposition* (Moscow, 1927), p. 183. This appears to have been part of a general trend to restrict the levels of health insurance payments.

24. '*O poryadke uvol'neniya beremennykh zhenshchin*', decree of Narkomtrud RSFSR and VTsSPS, *Izvestiya NKT*, no. 5/14, 1922, p. 27.

25. GARF, f. A-390, o. 3, d. 1032, ll. 1–11.

26. '*Ob usloviyakh i poryadke uvol'neniya ot raboty zhenshchin v svyazi s sokrashcheniem shtatov*', decree of Narkomtrud RSFSR, Narkomsobes, VTsSPS and VSNKh, *SU*, 1922, Article 203.

    The decree is reprinted in full in M. S. Bukhov, *Trudovoe zakonodatel'stvo: polnoe sobranie deistvuyushchikh zakonov o trude v alfavitno-predmetnom poryadke* (Moscow, 1924), p. 302.

27. '*O trude zhenshchin na zheleznykh dorogakh*', circular of Narkomtrud and railway workers' trade union, *Izvestiya NKT*, 1924, no. 23, pp. 20–1. See also *Vestnik truda*, 1924, no. 8, pp. 231–2.

28. '*O poryadke uvol'neniya ot raboty odinokikh zhenshchin, imeyushchikh detei do odnogo goda*', decree of Narkomtrud RSFSR, *Izvestiya NKT*, 1925, no. 33, p. 16.

    The decree is also listed in the archives at GARF, f. 5515, o. 13, d. 12, l. 54. M. Bukhov, *Okhrana zhenskogo truda* (Moscow, 1926), cites in addition *Trud*, 9 October 1925.

29. See *Izvestiya NKT*, 1929, nos. 15–16, p. 250, citing *Sudebnaya Praktika RSFSR*, no. 3, 15 February 1929.

30. Kaplun, *Zhenskii trud* (Moscow, 1921), pp. 41–2.

31. S. I. Kaplun, *Okhrana truda v Soyuze SSR v tsifrakh* (Moscow, 1928), p. 16–17.
32. S. I. Kaplun, *Sovremennye problemy zhenskogo truda i byta* (Moscow, 1925), p. 92.
33. GARF, f. A-390, o. 3, d. 1032, ll. 2–5.
34. The dilemmas facing pregnant military personnel are portrayed in the film *Komissar*, which traces the story of a female Red Army officer during the civil war.
35. GARF, f. 5515, o. 4, d. 298, ll. 10–11.
36. *Ibid.*, ll. 33–4.
37. *Ibid.*, l. 32.
38. '*Ob udilenii otpuskov po beremennosti i materinstvu dlya nekotorykh kategorii zhenshchin, rabotayushchikh v lechebnom dele*', decree of Narkomtrud, *Izvestiya NKT*, 1924, no 29, p. 6. See also *Vestnik truda*, 1924, no. 10, p. 300.
39. '*Ob otpuskakh po materinstvu dlya telefonistok*', decree of Narkomtrud, *Izvestiya NKT*, 1925, no. 1, p. 13. The decree granted extended maternity leave to telephonists at urban, suburban and inter-city telephone exchanges and to telephonists in enterprises and establishments continually employed on switchboards with at least 100 telephone extensions.
40. GARF, f. 5515, o. 4, d. 298, ll. 23–8. Despite this decision, the response to a letter to *Trud* several years later, on 15 July 1934, notes that women statisticians working with adding machines were entitled to maternity leave of only 42 days before plus 42 days after the birth.
41. '*O rabochem vremeni i otpuskakh dlya stenografov, zanyatykh na postoyannoi rabote v uchrezhdeniyakh i predpriyatiyakh*', decree of Narkomtrud, *Izvestiya NKT*, 1925, nos. 37–8, pp. 8–9; '*ob okhrane truda rabotnikov v rentgenovskikh kabinetakh*', decree of Narkomtrud, *ibid.*, p. 16. See also *Trud*, 9 October 1925.
42. '*O dopolnenii i izmenenii "spiska professii, koi naravne s fizicheskim trudom dayut pravo na otpusk v techenie 8 nedel' do i 8 nedel' posle rodov"*', decree of Narkomtrud, *Izvestiya NKT*, 1927, no. 52, p. 796.
43. GARF, f. 5515, o. 4, d. 311, ll. 50–4, 67.
44. GARF, f. 5515, o. 4, d. 312, ll. 5–6, 18–20.
45. *Ibid.*, ll. 7–11.
46. '*Ob utverzhdenii Spiska professii, dayushchikh, naravne s professiyami fizicheskogo truda, pravo na otpusk v techenie vos'mi nedel' do rodov i vos'mi nedel' posle rodov*', decree of Narkomtrud, *Izvestiya NKT*, 1929, nos. 1–2, pp. 13–14, which made provision in the following categories: administration (3); office personnel (2); engineering-technical workers and agronomists (1); trade (2); transport and communications (4); medicine (13); teaching (5); artistic workers (1); and others (2 – librarians and peripatetics).
47. See the various reports contained at GARF, f. 5515, o. 4, d. 346, and GARF, f. A-390, o. 3, d. 1267. On dental assistants see also GARF, f. A-390, o. 3, d. 1264, ll. 2–6.
48. GARF, f. A-390, o. 3, d. 1032, ll. 6–11.
49. On women workers in the glass industry see *ibid.*, ll. 19–29.
50. '*O dopolnenii spiska professii dayushikh naravne s professiyami fizicheskogo truda pravo na 8 nedel'nyi otpusk do i posle rodov*', decree of Narkomtrud, *Izvestiya NKT*, 1929, no. 30, p. 474.

51. '*Ob utverzhdenii v novoi redaktsii spiska professii, dayushchikh naravne s pro-fessiyami fizicheskogo truda pravo na otpusk v techenie 56 dnei do i 56 dnei posle rodov*', decree of Narkomtrud, *Izvestiya NKT*, 1930, no. 23–4, pp. 533–5. The nine main groups were: administration (3); office personnel (4); engineering-technical workers and agronomists (1); trade (3); transport and communications (14); medicine (22); culture and publishing (8); artistic workers (8); and 'others' (4).

52. '*O predostavlenii zhenshchinam-pis'monostsam i zhenshchinam-parikhmakheram otpuska po beremennosti i rodam naravne s rabotnitsami fizicheskogo truda*', decree of the Secretariat of VTsSPS, *Byulleten' VTsSPS*, 1935, no. 8, p. 2.

53. GARF, f. 5515, o. 13, d. 15b, l. 13, dated 11 June 1929.

54. See for example the arguments discussed in C. Ward, *Russian Cotton Workers and the New Economic Policy* (Cambridge, 1985), pp. 225–7.

55. E. Strogova, 'Womenfolk: Factory Sketches', quoted directly from the translation in C. Kelly (ed.), *An Anthology of Russian Women's Writing, 1777-1992* (Oxford, 1994), p. 281.

56. A detailed account of changes in the criteria of eligibility for receipt of maternity benefit is provided by Schwarz, *op. cit.* and Dodge, *op. cit.*

57. '*Ob izmenenii Pravil o naznachenii i vydache dopolnitel'nykh posobii po sotsial'nomu strakhovaniyu*', *Izvestiya NKT*, 1927, no. 23, pp. 346–7.

58. See Schwarz, *op. cit.*, p. 318.

59. '*O rasshirenii kruga rabochikh i sluzhashchikh, imeyushchikh pravo na posobiya na predmety ukhoda za rebenkom i na kormlenie rebenka*', decree of Narkomtrud, *Izvestiya NKT*, 1931, no. 25, p. 508.

60. GARF, f. 5515, o. 20, d. 83, ll. 93–4, '*ob uvelichenii razmerov posobiya novorozhdennym*'. The factories with whom the agreement was made included 'AMO', 'Serp i Molot', 'Trekhgorka', 'Manometr' and 'Molotov'.

61. Schwarz, *op. cit.*, p. 319.

62. *Ibid.*, pp. 289–90.

63. *British Documents on Foreign Affairs*, 21 August 1935 [N 4368/472/38].

64. *Trud*, 29 July 1934.

65. 'Bezdushnoe otnoshenie k zhenshchine-materi', *Rabotnitsa*, 1937, no. 9, p. 16.

66. '*O kormyashchikh materyakh*', *Trud*, 21 November 1934.

67. *Trud*, 12 March 1936.

68. '*Komnati dlya kormleniya detei*', *Trud*, 4 April 1936.

69. '*Dosadnaya neuvyazka*', *Trud*, 5 March 1936.

70. '*Interesy materi ili udobstva bukhgaltera*', *Trud*, 21 October 1936.

71. I. Sheingauz, 'Zabota zavkoma o mnogodetnoi materi', *Voprosy profdvizheniya*, no. 8 (74), August 1936, pp. 89–91, implies that it was only the income of the father that should be taken into account.

72. V. Mironov, 'O nekotorykh voprosakh strakhovogo zakonodatel'stva', *Voprosy profdvizheniya*, 1937, no. 4, pp. 32–4.

73. '*Ob otmene ogranicheniya posobii po beremennosti i rodam dlya zhenshchin-sluzhashchikh maksimumom v 300 rub.*', decree of the Presidium of VTsSPS, *Byulleten' VTsSPS*, 1937, no. 4, pp. 8–9.

74. These developments are noted in Serebrennikov, *op. cit.*, p. 20.

75. These policies are discussed in detail in J. Evans, 'The CPSU and the "Women's Question": the Case of the 1936 Decree "In Defence of Mother and Child"', *Journal of Contemporary History*, 1981, no. 16, pp. 757–75, and more recently in W. Z. Goldman, *Women, the State and Revolution* (Cambridge, 1993).

76. '*O zapreshchenii abortov, uvelichenii material'noi pomoshchi rozhnitsam, ustanovlenii gosudarstvennoi pomoshchi mnogosemeinym, rasshirenii seti rodil'nykh domov, detskikh yaslei i detskikh sadov, usilenii ugolovnogo nakazaniya za neplatazh alimentov i o nekotorykh izmeneniyakh v zakonodatel'stve o razvodakh*', decree of TsIK and Sovnarkom SSSR, *SZ*, 1936, Article 309.

77. For other aspects of the 27 June 1936 decree see also N. Yakovleva-Bulina, 'Rabotnitsa-mat' i profsoyuzy', *Voprosy profdvizheniya*, no. 7 (73), July 1936, pp. 3–10.

78. '*Ob ugolovnoi otvetstvennosti za otkaz v prieme zhenshchin na rabotu i za snizhenie im zarabotnoi platy po motivam beremennosti*', decree of TsIK and Sovnarkom SSSR, *SZ*, 1936, Article 419. The decree was amended slightly a few months later: see '*O primenenii postanovleniya ob ugolovnoi otvetstvennosti za otkaz v prieme zhenshchin na rabotu po motivam beremennosti*', decree of TsIK and Sovnarkom SSSR, *ibid.*, 1937, Article 99. See also *Byulleten' VTsSPS*, 1936, no. 19, p. 2, and *ibid.*, 1937, no. 4, p. 20. See also *Trud*, 8 October 1936 and 10 April 1937.

79. '*O meropriyatiyakh po uporyadocheniyu trudovoi distsipliny, uluchsheniya praktiki gosudarstvennogo sotsial'nogo strakhovaniya i bor'be s zloupotrebleniyami v etom dele*', decree of Sovnarkom SSSR, Central Committee of the CPSU and VTsSPS, *SZ*, 1939, Article 1.

80. '*O primenenii truda beremennykh i kormyashchikh zhenshchin na predpriyatiyakh khlopchatobumazhnoi, trikotazhnoi i tabachnoi promyshlennosti*', decree of the Secretariat of VTsSPS, *Byuletten' VTsSPS*, 1938, no. 1, pp. 13–16. See also *Okhrana truda*, 1938, no. 1, p. 62.

81. The 1938 decree cites '*o meropriyatiyakh po bor'be s narusheniyami zakonodatel'stva o trude*', decree of TsIK and Sovnarkom SSSR, dated 2 January 1929, *SZ*, 1929, Article 31.

82. Schwarz, *op. cit.*, p. 289, citing *Trud*, 23 February 1937.

83. Yakovleva-Bulina, *op. cit.*, p. 6.

84. K. Bykova, 'Strogo soblyudat' zakony ob okhrane materinstva', *Rabotnitsa*, 1938, no. 13, pp. 14–15.

6 HOURS OF WORK

1. '*O vos'mychasovom rabochem dne, prodolzhitel'nosti i raspredelenii rabochego vremeni*', decree of Sovnarkom RSFSR, *SU*, 1917, Article 7.

2. '*Kodeks zakonov o trude*', decree of Narkomtrud RSFSR, *SU*, 1918, Article 905.

3. Z. A. Astapovich, *Pervye meropriyatiya sovetskoi vlasti v oblasti truda* (Moscow, 1958), pp. 54–5.

4. '*O nochnoi rabote zhenshchin*', decree of Narkomtrud RSFSR, *SU*, 1919, Article 470.
5. See, for example, the circular (no. 59) issued by Narkomtrud in 1919, '*o sutochnykh dezhurstvakh*', section ii, '*o nochnoi rabote zhenshchin*', *Byulleten' NKT*, 1919, nos. 11–12, pp. 77–8. Men were to be recruited first to night work, followed by adult women. The prohibition remained in force for young workers under the age of 18 years.
6. '*O nochnom rabote v tabachnom proizvodstve*', decree of Narkomtrud RSFSR, *Byulleten' NKT*, 1919, nos. 11–12, p. 80.
7. S. I. Kaplun, *Zhenskii trud i okhrana ego v sovetskoi Rossii* (Moscow, 1921), p. 20.
8. Z. Tettenborn, *Sovetskoe zakonodatel'stvo o trude: lektsii, prochitannye na kursakh dlya Inspektorov Truda* (Moscow, 1920), p. 95.
9. '*O vremenoi razreshennii sverkhurochnykh rabot zhenshchin v sovetskikh uchrezhdeniyakh*', decree of Narkomtrud RSFSR, *SU*, 1919, Article 587. See also *Byulleten' NKT*, 1919, nos. 11–12, p. 80.
10. '*Ob okhrane truda beremennykh i kormyashchikh grud'yu zhenshchin*', decree of Narkomtrud RSFSR and VTsSPS, *SU*, 1920, Article 477; and '*o vospreshchenii nochnykh rabot beremennym i kormyashchim grud'yu zhenshchinami*', decree of Narkomtrud and VTsSPS, *ibid.*, 1920, Article 478.
11. S. I. Kaplun, *Sovremennye problemy zhenskogo truda i byta* (Moscow, 1925; 2nd edn.), pp. 91–2.
12. *Ibid.*, pp. 94–5.
13. M. Bukhov, *Kak okhranyaetsya trud rabotnits po sovetskim zakonam* (Moscow, 1925), p. 5.
14. '*Kodeks zakonov o trude*', decree of VTsIK, *SU*, 1922, Article 903.
15. '*O nochnykh rabotakh v khlebopekarnyakh*', decree of Narkomtrud, *Izvestiya NKT*, 1923, no. 7, p. 8.
16. '*O nochnoi rabote zhenshchin na telegrafe i telefone*', decree of Narkomtrud, *Izvestiya NKT*, 1923, no. 6, p. 14. The decree is also to be found in the trade union archives: see GARF, f. 5451, o. 6, d. 365, l. 7 (dated 28 April 1923).
17. See, for example, A. Pasternak, *Chto dolzhna znat' rabotnitsa ob okhrane zhenskogo truda: s prilozheniem deistvuyushchego zakonodatel'stva v oblasti okrany zhenskogo truda i okhrany materinstva* (Kharkov, 1923), p. 11, and M. Bukhov, *Kak okhranyaetsya trud rabotnits po sovetskim zakonam* (Moscow, 1925), p. 6.
18. '*O nochnoi rabote zhenshchin na transporte*', decree of Narkomtrud, *Izvestiya NKT*, 1923, no. 12/36, p. 8. See also *Trud*, 2 December 1923.
19. '*O nochnoi rabote zhenshchin na zheleznodorozhnom transporte*', decree of Narkomtrud, *Izvestiya NKT*, 1924, no. 14, p. 12. See also *Trud*, 13 April 1924.
20. '*Ob usloviyakh truda na sezonnykh rabotakh*', decree of TsIK and Sovnarkom, *SZ*, 1926, Article 29. See also *Izvestiya*, 15 June 1926.
21. For example, see V. V. Sokolov, *Prava zhenshchiny po sovetskim zakonam* (Moscow, 1928), p. 20.
22. Lavrova, 'Za proizvoditel'nost' truda (Vyksunskii zavod)', *Rabotnitsa*, 1925, no. 6, p. 7.

23. D. Koenker, 'Men against Women on the Shop Floor in Early Soviet Russia: Gender and Class in the Socialist Workplace', *American Historical Review*, 1995, vol. 100, no. 5, p. 1454.
24. *'O nochnykh rabotakh zhenshchin'*, circular no. 23/907, *Izvestiya NKT*, 1924, no. 9, pp. 12–13. The circular is also to be found in the trade union archives: GARF, f. 5451, o. 8, d. 90, l. 134.
25. GARF, f. 5515, o. 4, d. 8, l. 202. Minutes of a meeting of the Commission on 19 June 1924 with a report by Vinnikov, of the Labour Protection Department, 'Measures in the area of protection of female labour'.
26. VTsSPS, *Shestoi s"ezd professional'nykh soyuzov SSSR* (11–18 November 1924) (Moscow, 1925), pp. 184–5.
27. *Ibid.*, pp. 222–4.
28. *Ibid.*, pp. 638–9, meeting of the tariff-economic sub-committee. See also A. Artyukhina, 'Chto skazal 6-i s"ezd profsoyuzov o rabotnitse', *Rabotnitsa*, 1924, no. 24 (36), pp. 3–4.
29. E. Waters, 'From the Old Family to the New: Work, Marriage and Motherhood in Urban Soviet Russia, 1917–1931', unpublished PhD thesis (CREES, University of Birmingham, 1985), p. 100. See also E. H. Carr, *Socialism in One Country*, vol. I (London, 1958), pp. 368–9, and *The Bolshevik Revolution, 1917–23*, vol. II (London, 1952), p. 70.
30. *'O nochnykh rabotakh zhenshchin'*, circular no. 109/346, *Izvestiya NKT*, 1925, no. 20, p. 11.
31. *Soviet Russia: An Investigation by British Women Trade Unionist: April–July, 1925* (London, 1925), pp. 26–7. The report cites the examples of the relaxation of night shift regulations for workers in transportation and the postal and telegraph services, which were covered by specific decrees.
32. S. I. Kaplun, *Sovremennye problemy zhenskogo truda i byta* (Moscow, 1925; 2nd edn.), p. 93.
33. GARF, f. A–390, o. 3, d. 1032, l. 85.
34. P. D. Kaminskaya, *Sovetskoe trudovoe pravo* (Khar'kov, 1925), p. 216.
35. *'Ob usloviyakh truda rabotnikov po naimu, vypolnyayushchikh na domu u nanimatelya (domashnie rabotniki) raboty po lichnomu obsluzhivaniyu nanimatelya i ego sem'i'*, decree of VTsIK and Sovnarkom RSFSR, *Izvestiya NKT*, 1926, no. 8, pp. 21–4. See also *Izvestiya*, 14 February 1926.
36. *'O semichasovom rabochem dne'*, decree of TsIK and Sovnarkom, *SZ*, 1929, Article 30.
37. *'Ob izmenenii st. 8 postanovleniya TsIK i SNK soyuza SSR ot 2 yanvarya 1929g. o semichasovom rabochem dne'*, decree of TsIK and Sovnarkom, *SZ*, 1929, Article 133.
38. *'Ob izmenenii statei 75, 94, 96 i 131 kodeksa zakonov o trude i o dopol'nenii etogo kodeksa statei 97'*, decree of VTsIK and Sovnarkom RSFSR, *SU*, 1929, Article 414.
39. GARF, f. 5515, o. 4, d. 312, ll. 29–30.
40. *Ibid.*, l. 14.
41. 'Proizvoditel'nost' truda i byudzhet vremeni tkachei', GARF, f. 5515, o. 13, d. 6, l. 4.
42. L. Kagan, *Ratsionalizatsiya i rabotnitsa* (Moscow, 1928).

43. N. E. Akim, 'K voprosu o vyrabotke ratsional'nogo rezhima dlya tek-stil'nykh fabrik s semichasovym rabochim dnem', *Gigiena, bezopasnost' i patalogiya truda*, 1929, no. 9, p. 46.
44. *Ibid.*, pp. 46–8.
45. D. Granick, *Soviet Metal Fabricating and Economic Development* (London, 1967), pp. 99–103.
46. Z. Prishchepchik, 'O semichasovom rabochem dne', *Kommunistka*, 1928, no. 1, pp. 28–9. See also B. Svetlanov, '7 chasovoi rabochii den'', *Delegatka*, February 1928, no. 3, pp. 1–2.
47. Prishchepchik, 'O semichasovom', p. 28.
48. A-na [A. Artyukhina], 'Itogi promyshlennogo soveshchaniya', *Kommunistka*, 1928, no. 2, p. 23.
49. Tolstopyatov, 'Ratsionalizatsiya proizvodstva provedenie 7 chasovogo rabochego dnya i uchastiya v ekonomrabote soyuzov', GARF, f. 5451, o. 12, d. 168, ll. 17–19. The convention was held 25–30 June 1928.
50. I. Reznikov, 'Semichasovoi rabochii den'', *Trud*, 3 January 1928.
51. The problems experienced by this group of workers in Shuya are discussed in N. Alekseeva, 'Na khoroshie mashiny – v dnevnuyu smenu', *Rabotnitsa*, 1928, no. 48, p. 6. The dangers of night-time employment for pregnant women and nursing mother are outlined also in I. S., 'Beremennym i kormyashchim grud'yu nel'zya rabotat' noch'yu', *ibid.*, 1928, no. 48, p. 18.
52. See for example the discussion in Z. Prishchepchik, 'Semichasovoi rabochii den' i nashi zadachi', *Kommunistka*, 1928, no. 3, p. 30.
53. A-na, 'Itogi ...', p. 25, and Prishchepchik, 'Semichasovoi rabochii den'...', p. 30.
54. Prishchepchik, 'O semichasovom ...', p. 29.
55. 'Usloviya truda pri 7-chasovom rabochem dne', *Trud*, 12 January 1928.
56. N. T. Dodge, *Women in the Soviet Economy* (Baltimore, 1966), p. 62.
57. C. Ward, *Russian Cotton Workers and the New Economic Policy* (Cambridge, 1988). See particularly pp. 214–27 for the debates on the issues which follow.
58. See, for example, the articles by Prishchepchik, 'O semichasovom ...', p. 29, and 'Semichasovoi rabochii den'...', p. 30.
59. See Prishchepchik, 'Semichasovoi rabochii den'...', p. 30, and the example provided by N. Gurvich, 'Opyt perekhoda na semichasovoi rabochii den'', *Kommunistka*, 1928, no. 3, p. 37.
60. See, for example, the account given by Borisova, 'Trudnosti perekhoda', *Kommunistka*, 1928, no. 5, p. 48.
61. A. Vinnikov, 'Semichasovoi rabochii den'', *Kommunistka*, 1928, no. 12, p. 38. See also Il'ina, 'Gotovy li k perekhodu na semichasovoi rabochii den'', *Rabotnitsa*, 1928, no. 48, pp. 3–4.
62. A-na, 'Itogi ...', p. 24.
63. N. A., 'Pereshli na semichasovoi', *Kommunistka*, 1928, no. 2, p. 64.
64. Pishchepchik, 'Semichasovoi rabochii den'...', p. 29.
65. 'Usloviya truda pri 7-chasovom rabochem dne', *Trud*, 12 January 1928.
66. N. A., 'Pereshli ...', p. 66.
67. B. Kaplun, 'Kogda nachinat' rabotu?', *Trud*, 12 January 1928. Kaplun was acting as special correspondent at the Sobolevo-Shchelkovskoi

textile factory, which needed to recruit 400 new workers on transferring to the three-shift system of operation.

68. Prishchepchik, 'Semichasovoi rabochii den'...', p. 29.
69. N. E. Akim, 'Voprosy okhrany truda na tekstil'nykh fabrikakh Moskovskoi gub. s semichasovym rabochim dnem', *Gigiena truda*, 1928, no. 8, p. 93.
70. For a report on ten Leningrad textile factories which had transferred to the seven-hour day in 1928 see, 'O vyvode beremennykh i kormyashchikh iz nochnykh smen po tekstil'noi promyshlennosti', GARF, f. A-390, o. 3, d. 1267, l. 29. For a further discussion on the Leningrad textile industry on 26 August 1929 see GARF, f. A-390, o. 3, d. 1267, l. 122, and the various notes on related issues, ll. 116–21.
71. S. I. Kaplun, *Nauka na sluzhbe okhrany truda*: kak rabotaet gosudarstvennyi nauchnyi institut okhrany truda (Moscow, 1930), p. 19.
72. S. Kaplun, 'Okhrana truda i profsoyuzy', *Voprosy profdvizheniya*, January 1934, no. 1, p. 71.
73. 'Izmeneniya v trudovom zakonodatel'stve RSFSR', *Za industrializatsiyu*, 20 September 1931.
74. L. Korber, *Life in a Soviet Factory* (London, 1933), *passim*.
75. Dodge, *op. cit.*, p. 64.
76. See, for example, the evidence which came to light under Gorbachev in A. Levina, 'Tysyacha i odna noch', *Rabotnitsa*, 1988, no. 4, pp. 12–15, and 'Zhenshchiny v SSSR', *Vestnik statistiki*, 1990, no. 1, p. 42. These and other protective labour law violations are discussed in M. Ilič, '"Generals without Armies, Commanders without Troops": Gorbachev's "Protection" of Female Workers', in R. Marsh (ed.), *Women in Russia and Ukraine* (Cambridge, 1995), pp. 228–40.

7 PROVISION FOR 'MENSTRUAL LEAVE'

1. Issues of 'equality' and 'difference' with regard to protective labour legislation in both historical debates and contemporary controversies are discussed in C. L. Bacchi, *Same Difference*: Feminism and Sexual Difference (London, 1990). In discussing a more recent Australian debate, Bacchi, p. 150, quotes 'menstruation does not normally incapacitate a woman, and that work will not normally make menstruation more painful or uncomfortable provided work is organised with women's comfort in mind', citing J. Matthews, *Health and Safety at Work* (Sydney, 1985), p. 424.
2. A. W. Field, *Protection of Women and Children in Soviet Russia* (London, 1932), pp. 11, 60–1.
3. See for example S. I. Kaplun, *Zhenskii trud i okhrana ego v sovetskoi Rossii* (Moscow, 1921).
4. See for example W. Z. Goldman, *Women, the State and Revolution*: Soviet Family Policy and Social Life, 1917–1936 (Cambridge, 1993), pp. 331–6, and J. Evans, 'The CPSU and the "Woman Question": the Case of the 1936 Decree "In Defence of Mother and Child"', *Journal of Contemporary History*, vol. 16, 1981, pp. 757–75.

5. Ts. Pik, 'Novye meropriyatiya po okhrane zhenskogo truda. (K voprosu ob osvobozhdenii zhenshchini ot raboty vo vremya menstruatsii)', *Vestnik truda*, 1922, no. 2 (17), pp. 73–7.
6. An outline of the conditions of work in the garment industry, including comments on noise, temperature, fatigue and ventilation as well as ill-health, is provided by Dr A. Sokolov, 'Chem vreden trud tkachikhi', *Rabotnitsa*, 1928, no. 42, p. 22.
7. Pik, *op. cit.*, p. 76.
8. '*Ob osvobozhdenii ot raboty na vremya menstruatsii mashinistok i gladil'shchits, rabotayushchikh na nozhnykh mashinakh bez mekhanicheskikh privodov v shveinoi promyshlennosti*', decree of VTsSPS, *Byulleten' VTsSPS*, 1922, no. 4.
   The decree is printed in full in M. Bukhov (ed.), *Trudovoe zakonodatel'stvo: polnoe sobranie deistvuyushchikh zakonov o trude v alfavitno-predmetnom poryadke* (Moscow, 1924), p. 291. Reference to the decree is also made in M. Bukhov, *Kak okhranyaetsya trud rabotnits po sovetskim zakonam* (Moscow, 1925), p. 10, and in a list of supplementary legislation in M. Bukhov, *Okhrana zhenskogo truda* (Moscow, 1926). E. I. Snezhkov, *Prakticheskii kommentarii k kodeksu zakonov o trude: postateinye raz'yasneniya, dopolneniya, sudebnaya i konsul'tatsionnaya praktika (po 1 sentyabrya 1927 goda)* (Moscow, 1928), p. 225, notes the decree as clause 5 of Article 132 of the 1922 Labour Code, which sets out provisions for maternity leave. The decree allowing two days leave for women workers on cutting machines and clothes presses is also noted in the archives. See GARF, f. 5515, o. 4, d. 8, l. 202.
9. E. Waters, 'From the Old Family to the New: Work, Marriage and Motherhood in Urban Soviet Russia, 1917–31', unpublished PhD thesis (CREES, University of Birmingham, 1985), p. 101. Her research on this particular issue, however, does not appear to have been extensive.
10. J. Smith, *Woman in Soviet Russia* (New York, 1928), p. 23.
11. *Soviet Russia: An Investigation by British Women Trade Unionists – April to July, 1925* (London, 1925), p. 27.
12. GARF, f. 5515, o. 4, d. 8, l. 103.
13. *Ibid.*, l. 112, dated 19 February, 1924.
14. GARF, f. 5515, o. 13, d. 15b, l. 12, letter dated 11 June 1929.
15. See, for example, GARF, f. 5515, o. 4, d. 33, ll. 28–31.
16. Z. Izrael'son and V. Petikov, 'Zhenskii trud v Orlovskoi gubernii', *Voprosy truda*, 1926, nos. 8–9, p. 229.
17. B. A. Engel, *Between the Fields and the City: Women, Work and Family in Russia, 1861–1914* (Cambridge, 1994), p. 46.
18. Gol'denberg, 'Zhenskie bolezni', *Rabotnitsa*, 1925, no. 2, p. 31. See also 'Okhrana zdorov'ya: zhenskie bolezni i ikh priznaki', *ibid.*, 1928, no. 28, p. 17, and A. A. Bogdanova, 'Gigiena zhenshchiny', *ibid.*, 1936, no. 14, pp. 18–19.
19. For more details on these campaigns see E. Waters, 'Teaching Mothercraft in Post-Revolutionary Russia', *Australian Journal of Slavonic and East European Studies*, 1987, vol. 1, no. 2, pp. 29–56, and 'The Modernisation of Russian Motherhood, 1917–1937', *Soviet Studies*, 1992, vol. 44, no. 1, pp. 123–35.

20. B. A. Libov, 'Vliyanie promyshlennogo truda na polovuyu sferu zhen-shchiny', *Leningradskii meditsinskii zhurnal*, 1926, no. 7, pp. 78–82.
21. *Ibid.*, p. 79.
22. Gofmekler, 'Voprosy zdorov'ya: o menstruatsiyakh', *Rabotnitsa*, 1926, no. 11, pp. 20–1.
23. Bol'shakov, 'O chem govoryat: mozhet li byt' zhenshchina slesarem', *Rabotnitsa*, 1926, no. 8, p. 20, and the responses: 1926, no. 11, p. 17; and 1926, no. 13, p. 14.
24. *Soviet Russia*, p. 28.
25. See the various notes on this topic at GARF, f. A-390, o. 3, d. 1032, ll. 77–8.
26. GARF, f. 5515, o. 4, d. 311, l. 1–2.
27. GARF, f. A-390, o. 3, d. 1264, ll. 7–11.
28. A. G. Pap, B. I. Shkol'nik and Ya. P. Sol'skii, *Gigiena zhenshchiny* (Kiev, 1964), p. 41, notes that in cases where menstruation results in illness or significantly undermines the physical constitution women workers can be released from work temporarily on the confirmation of a doctor.
29. M. Gordon, *Workers Before and After Lenin* (New York, 1941), pp. 274–5, citing *Obzor sotsial'nogo strakhovaniya, 1928-29* (1930), p. 54.
30. GARF, f. 5515, o. 13, d. 9, ll. 6–8.
31. *Ibid.*, l. 6.
32. *Ibid.*, l. 7ob.
33. *Ibid.*, l. 8.
34. Ya. Srulevich, 'Trud i zdorov'ye konduktorshi', *Rabotnitsa i krest'yanka*, January 1928, no. 2, p. 24.
35. The impact of vibrations, and of constantly standing or sitting whilst at work, on the menstrual cycle and pregnancy is discussed briefly also in V. K. Navrotskii, *Gigiena truda* (Moscow, 1967), pp. 259–60.
36. See the various reports contained in GARF, f. 5515, o. 13, d. 15a and especially ll. 2–3.
37. N. Serov, 'Tramvaishchitsy', *Rabotnitsa*, 1928, no. 35, pp. 13–14.
38. See for example, I. I. Okuneva and Ye. Ye. Shteinbakh, 'O primenenii zhenskogo truda na traktorakh', *Gigiena, bezopasnost' i patologii truda*, 1931, no. 7, pp. 3–15.
39. 'Ob usloviyakh truda zhenshchin-traktoristok i shoferov na gruzovykh avtomashinakh', decree of Narkomtrud SSSR, *Izvestiya NKT*, 1931, nos. 14–15, p. 277.

     The decree is also cited in *Sbornik normativnykh aktov o trude*, chast' 2 (Moscow, 1985), p. 536. V. N. Tolkunova, *Pravo zhenshchin na trud i ego garantii* (Moscow, 1967), pp. 127–8, notes the decree as amongst the number of occupations in which women could be employed only if pre-determined conditions of work, as set out in the decrees, were observed. In this example, amongst other requirements, a preliminary monthly medical examination was necessary. This statute was retained when the Labour Code was reviewed in 1978.

     Revisions to the protective labour laws which were introduced in the early 1990s effectively invalidated the terms of these provisions. S. Bridger, 'The Heirs of Pasha: The Rise and Fall of the Soviet Woman Tractor Driver', unpublished conference paper presented to the

Conference on Gender and Perceptions of Sexual Difference in Russian
Culture and History, University of Birmingham, 3–5 July 1996, p. 13,
notes that 'from 1 January 1991 women could no longer be trained to
drive tractors; from 1 January 1992, it would be illegal to recruit women
to drive either tractors or lorries'. She cites as reference V. Demin,
'Pomoshch' prekrasnomu polu', *Chelovek i zakon*, 1992, no. 3, p. 9.

40. V. E. Bonnell, 'The Peasant Woman in Stalinist Political Art of the
1930s', *American Historical Review*, 1993, vol. 98, no. 1, p. 69, citing
E. K. Kravchenko, *Krest'yanka pri sovetskoi vlasti* (Moscow, 1932), p. 46.

41. P. M. Chirkov, *Reshenie zhenskogo voprosa v SSSR (1917–1937 gg.)*
(Moscow, 1978), p. 144. Women were also employed as drivers on
other mechanised equipment. V. Bil'shai, *Reshenie zhenskogo voprosa v
SSSR* (Moscow, 1956), p. 143, offers the more conservative figure of
7000 female tractor drivers on the collective farms by the end of 1933.

42. GARF, f. 5515, o. 13, d. 22, ll. 6–8.

43. GARF, f. 5451, o. 19, d. 277, ll. 12–13.

44. Lili Korber, *Life in a Soviet Factory* (London, 1933), pp. 161–2; first
published in German as *Eine Frau erlebt den Roten Alltag*, translated by
C. W. Sykes.

45. GARF, f. 5515, o. 13, d. 22, ll. 9–18.

46. L. P. Kuzovkova-Aryanova, 'Vliyanie fizkul'tpauzy na techenie menstrual'nogo perioda i rabotosposobnost', *Gigiena truda i tekhnika bezopasnosti*, 1936, no. 4, pp. 84–5.

47. A report in *Rabotnitsa* in the following year suggested that physical exercise during menstruation was not only desirable but was also necessary
for women's well-being. See M. Nikitin, 'Gigiena vo vremya menstruatsii', *Rabotnitsa*, 1937, no. 20, p. 18. This suggestion was contradicted
somewhat in a subsequent article in the same magazine. See V. G. Dik,
'Chto neobkhodimo znat' zhenshchine', *ibid.*, 1940, no. 9, p. 19.

48. See, for example, B. Harrison, *Not Only the 'Dangerous Trades': Women's
Work and Health in Britain, 1880–1914* (London, 1996), pp. 88–92.

49. More recent examples which have followed the Soviet Union's initiative
are Argentina and China. K. Dalton, *Once a Month* (London, 1991),
p. 122, notes that 'in Argentina, by constitution, women are allowed to
take the necessary days off for their menstrual miseries'! According to
the *Law of the People's Republic of China on the Protection of Rights and
Interests of Women* (Order of the President of the People's Republic of
China, no. 58), with effect from 1 October 1992 and with regard to
'Rights and Interests Relating to Work' (Chapter 4, Article 25) 'women
shall be under special protection during menstrual period, pregnancy,
obstetrical period and nursing period'.

8 WEIGHTS OF LOADS

1. R. Glickman, *Russian Factory Women: Workplace and Society, 1880–1914*
(London, 1984) provides a detailed study of legislative enactments
concerning working women in tsarist Russia. She mentions no state

regulations on this issue but does note that local bureaux 'had the power to pass so-called "obligatory regulations" intended to have the force of law. Regulations... ranged from forbidding pregnant women to carry weights to the more generous provision of periodic visits by a midwife to factories...'. See p. 124.

2. '*O primenenii truda maloletnykh i podrostkov na torfyanykh razrabotakh*', decree of Narkomtrud RSFSR, *SU*, 1920, Article 200, allowed young women to be employed in the drying out and stacking of peat, as store workers and in the carrying of peat in baskets.

3. '*O primenenii zhenskogo truda pri zagotovke topliva v poryadke trudpovinnosti*', decree of Narkomtrud RSFSR, *Ekonomicheskaya zhizn'*, 1921, no. 60. The established norms for women were not to exceed one-half of those established for men. This decree and the peat work regulations are also listed in M. Bukhov, *Chto dolzhna znat' delegatka o trudovykh pravakh rabonits* (Moscow, 1925), p. 10.

4. S. M. Kingsbury and M. Fairchild, *Factory, Family and Women in the Soviet Union* (New York, 1935), p. 114.

5. A. Letavet, 'K voprosu o zakonodatel'nom ogranichenii perenoski tyazhestei podrostkami i zhenshchinami', *Vestnik truda*, 1921, no. 6 (9), pp. 30–5.

6. A. F. Nikitin, 'Ocherk sanitarno-ekonomicheskogo polozheniya gruzhchikov na Volge', cited in *ibid.*, p. 30.

7. Cited here as set out in M. Bukhov, *Okhrana zhenskogo truda* (Moscow, 1926), pp. 107–11. Note that the weights are listed in a variety of measures as cited in the original legislation. R. E. F. Smith, *A Russian–English Social Science Dictionary* (Birmingham, 2nd edn, n.d.), p. 590, appendix 6, 'Conversions Co-Efficients', gives the following conversions:

   1 *pud* = 16.3805 kg or 36.1128 lb
   1 *funt* = 0.4095 kg or 0.9028 lb
   [1 kg = 2.2046 lb]

8. I. I. Okuneva et al., 'Opyt izucheniya vliyaniya pod"ema i perenoski tyazhestei na organizm zhenshchini', *Gigiena truda*, 1927, no. 8, p. 12.

9. S. I. Kaplun, *Nauka na sluzhbe okhrany truda: kak rabotaet gosudarstvennyi nauchnyi institut okhrany truda* (Moscow, 1930), p. 52.

10. '*O predel'nykh normakh perenoski i perdvizheniya tyazhestei podrostkami i zhenshchinami*', decree of Narkomtrud and VSNKh SSSR, *Izvestiya NKT*, 1923, no. 11/35. It is also cited in the terms of the subsequent 1932 revisions.

11. '*O predel'noi norme dlya gruzchikov-zhenshchin*', tsirkulyar VTsSPS, no. 425, 15 January 1922, GARF, f. 5451, o. 5, d. 536, l. 16 (and duplicated at f. 5451, o. 6, d. 365, l. 6, dated 15 December 1921, as a copy to local transport organisations).

12. '*Kodeks zakonov o trude*', decree of VTsIK, *SU*, 1922, Article 903.

13. '*Ob usloviyakh truda na splavnykh rabotakh*', decree of Narkomtrud, *Izvestiya NKT*, 1923, no. 14, p. 6. The decree is cited also in M. Bukhov, *Kak okhranyaetsya trud rabotnits po sovetskim zakonam* (Moscow, 1925), p. 19.

14. '*Ob ustroistve i soderzhenii khlebopekaren'*', decree of Narkomtrud, *Izvestiya NKT*, 1924, no. 12, p. 22, and '*o sanitarnykh pravilakh raboty na kholodnykh*

ruchnykh moikakh shersti', decree of Narkomtrud, *Izvestiya NKT*, 1924, no. 23, p. 10.

15. '*Ob okhrane truda gruzchikov pogruzochno-razgruzochnykh i perevalochnykh rabot na transporte*', decree of Narkomtrud, *Izvestiya NKT*, 1924, no. 6–7, pp. 20–1. It is also noted in the archives at GARF, f. 5515, o. 4, d. 8. l. 76.

16. GARF, f. 5515, o. 4, d. 311, l. 71.

17. GARF, f. 5515, o. 4, d. 298, l. 7.

18. GARF, f. 5515, o. 4, d. 8, l. 202.

19. GARF, f. 5515, o. 4, d. 311, ll. 3–19.

20. *Ibid.*, l. 72.

21. The research is briefly outlined and illustrated with photographs in Kaplun, *op. cit.*, pp. 51–4.

22. I. I. Okuneva, Ye. Ye. Shteinbakh and L. N. Shcheglova, 'Opyt izucheniya vliyaniya pod"ema i perenoski tyazhestei na organizm zhen-shchiny', *Gigiena truda*, 1927, no. 8, pp. 12–19, and part 2, 'Issledovanie dykhaniya u zhenshchin v svyazi s vnutribryushnym davleniem vo vre-mya pod"ema tyazhestei', *ibid.*, 1927, no. 11, pp. 30–40. A different and much shorter version of the research findings is to be found in the archives (reprinted from an unnamed journal): I. I. Okuneva, 'Izuchenie voprosa o dopustimykh normakh perenoski tyazhestei zhen-shchinami', GARF, f. 5515, o. 13, d. 13, ll. 4–5. This paper constituted a report to the Labour Protection Department in their discussions of the revision of the norms.

23. The findings of this survey are to be found in the first part of the *Gigiena truda* article. See also GARF, f. 5515, o. 13, d. 6, ll. 45–6.

24. Z. Ostrovskii, 'U torfyanits', *Rabotnitsa*, 1924, no. 7, p. 22, which provides illustrations of the tasks involved in peat production.

25. 'Yelena', 'U torfushek', *Rabotnitsa*, 1927, no. 21, p. 14, and Ye. Chernysheva, 'Na torfyanykh bolotakh', *Delegatka*, June 1928, no. 12, pp. 8–9.

26. Lavrova, 'Za proizvoditel'nost' truda (Vyksunskii zavod)', *Rabotnitsa*, 1925, no. 6, p. 7. The survey also included the 'Serp i Molot' factory in Moscow: see GARF, f. 5515, o. 13, d. 6, ll. 45–6.

27. This work is illustrated in the following articles: 'Na Donbasse', *Rabotnitsa*, 1924, no. 3 (15), pp. 21–2, and 'Na shakhte', *Rabotnitsa*, 1925, no. 9, pp. 10–11.

28. The findings of the laboratory tests are to be found in the second part of the *Gigiena truda* article and in the reports in the archives.

29. See Kaplun, *op. cit.*, p. 53.

30. Okuneva et al., *Gigiena truda*, 1927, no. 11, p. 40.

31. GARF, f. 5515, o. 13, d. 13, ll. 1–3. See also 'Po voprosu ob izuchenii vliyaniya perenoski i pod"ema tyazhestei na organizm zhenshchiny', GARF, f. 5515, o. 13, d. 15b. l. 73, dated 12 June 1929.

32. GARF, f. 5515, o. 13, d. 15b, l. 93, dated 19 December 1929.

33. GARF, f. 5451, o. 15, d. 357, l. 108. Okuneva was speaking on the third day of the meeting.

34. '*Pravila ob usloviyakh truda gruznikov na pogruzochno-razgruzochnykh rabo-takh*', decree of Narkomtrud (see in particular Articles 3 and 10),

Izvestiya NKT, 1931, no. 30, pp. 587–9. It is noted also in Ya. L. Kiselev and S. Ye. Malkin (eds.), *Sbornik vazhneishikh postanovlenii po trudu* (Moscow, 1936), pp. 231–3, and in I. Drobnikov et al., *Trudovoe zakonodatel'stvo: spravochnaya kniga dlya profaktiva* (Moscow, 1971), p. 385, which notes the conditions for female labour, citing *Okhrana truda* (1963), p. 112. The maximum norms applied also to young male workers between the ages of 16 and 18 years.

35. GARF, f. 5451, o. 16, d. 590, l. 4.
36. This method of lifting and transportation is illustrated in picture 6 of Kaplun, *op. cit.*, p. 24.
37. These requirements are set out in V. N. Tolkunova, *Pravo zhenshchin na trud i ego garantii* (Moscow, 1967), p. 135.
38. 'O primenenie truda podrostkov', decree of Narkomtrud, *Izvestiya NKT*, 1932, nos. 28–29, pp. 362–3. The prohibition was included as part of the general restrictions on the employment of young workers, under the age of 18 years, in especially heavy jobs and occupations which were injurious to their health.
39. *Trudovoe zakonodatel'stvo SSSR* (Moscow, 1941), p. 219. See also V. Yadin, 'Znatnye lesoruby', *Rabotnitsa*, 1939, no. 7, p. 13.
40. M. Jordan, *Women in Soviet Society* (London, 1944), p. 11.
41. *Ibid.*, p. 11.
42. A. McAuley, *Women's Work and Wages in the Soviet Union* (London, 1981), p. 165.

9 RESTRICTED OCCUPATIONS

1. 'Kodeks zakonov o trude', decree of VTsIK, *SU*, 1918, Article 905.
2. *Izvestiya*, 8 October 1919.
3. 'Kodeks zakonov o trude', decree of VTsIK, *SU*, 1922, Article 903. Article 129 of the Labour Code applied also to young workers of both sexes under the age of 18 years and included the prohibition on the employment of women in underground work.
4. 'O trude zhenshchin na zheleznykh dorogakh', circular of the Narkomtrud Department of Labour Protection and the central committee of the railway workers' trade union, *Izvestiya NKT*, 1924, no. 23, pp. 20–1. See also *Vestnik truda*, 1924, no. 8, pp. 231–2.
5. 'O zhenskom trude v poligraficheskom proizvodstve', GARF, f. 5515, o. 4, d. 8, l. 53.
6. 'Obyazatel'noe postanovlenie o merakh sanitarnoe okhrany truda v neftyanoi promyshlennosti', GARF, f. 5515, o. 4, d. 8, l. 173.
7. GARF, f. 5515, o. 4, d. 8, l. 202.
8. 'O zapreshchenii zhenskogo truda na osobo-vrednykh i tyazhelykh rabotakh', decree of Narkomtrud, *Izvestiya NKT*, 1925, no. 45, pp. 8–10, which details tasks in the following sectors: chemicals (5); metallurgy and metal working (9); mining (4); printing (2); textiles (3); municipal services (2); writing paper (1); rail transport (2); and wood processing and floating (2).

9. *Soviet Russia: An Investigation by British Women Trade Unionists, April–July 1925* (London, 1925), p. 27.
10. *Women in Russia* (London, 1928), p. 9.
11. *Ibid.*, p. 14.
12. J. Smith, *Woman in Soviet Russia* (New York, 1928), pp. 14–15.
13. *Ibid.*, p. 16.
14. *Ibid.*, p. 16. The 1925 delegation also recorded similar impressions of the textile industry.
15. On the dangers of working with nicotine-based substances see 'Professional'nye zabolevaniya rabotnits tabachnoi promyshlennosti i mery preduprezhdeniya ikh', *Rabotnitsa*, 1929, no. 46, p. 20.
16. On work in the rubber shoe industry see I. S., 'O trude kaloshnits', *Rabotnitsa*, 1929, no. 15, p. 16, where women were entreated to take an active part in improving their own conditions of work.
17. 'Na farforovom zavode', *Delegatka*, February 1928, no. 3, p. 12.
18. D. P. Koenker, 'Men Against Women on the Shop Floor in Early Soviet Russia: Gender and Class in the Socialist Workplace', *American Historical Review*, 1995, vol. 100, no. 5, p. 1454.
19. A. Pasternak, *Chto dolzhna znat' rabotnitsa ob okhrane zhenskogo truda: s prilozheniem deistvuyushchego zakonodatel'stva v oblasti okhrany zhenskogo truda i okhrany materinstva* (Khar'kov, 1923), pp. 5–6.
20. M. Bukhov, *Kak okhranyaetsya trud rabotnits po sovetskim zakonam* (Moscow, 1925), pp. 11–12.
21. *Ibid.*
22. L. Korber, *Life in a Soviet Factory* (London, 1933), p. 53.
23. 'Vrednosti tabachnogo proizvodstva', GARF, f. 5515, o. 13, d. 6, ll. 10–12.
24. *Ibid.*, l. 15ob.
25. See, for example, 'Otchet: o prodelannoi nauchnoi rabote po izucheniyu zhenskogo truda', GARF, f. 5515, o. 13, d. 6, l. 45, dated October 1925, noting that the research by the Institute of Labour Protection was still at an experimental stage.
26. S. V. Vol'ter, 'Ob opredelenii nikotina v moloke rabotnits tabachnykh fabrik', *Gigiena truda*, 1927, no. 1, pp. 31–7.
27. *Ibid.*, p. 32.
28. 'Ob obsledovanie tabachnykh fabrik goroda Moskvy', GARF, f. 5515, o. 13, d. 15b, ll. 106–9 (n.d. [1929]). The three tobacco factories were 'Yava', 'Dukat' and 'Krasnaya Zvezda'.
29. Report by Romanov, 'Ob izuchenii primeneniya zhenskogo truda v metallopromyshlennosti', to a meeting of the central committee of the All-union Council of the Metallurgical Industry, 5 April 1927, GARF, f. 5451, o. 11, d. 384, ll. 10–11.
30. The studies involved the following enterprises: 'AMO', 'Duks', 'Kolomenskoe', 'Ikar' and 'Manometr'.
31. A. I. Pakhomychev, 'Nekotorye cherty razvitiya gigienu truda v SSSR za 40 let sushchestvovaniya sovetskoi vlasti', *Gigiena i sanitariya*, 1957, no. 10, pp. 43–51, outlines some of the research developments in the 1920s.
32. V. E. Bonnell, 'The Peasant Woman in Stalinist Political Art of the 1930s', *American Historical Review*, 1993, vol. 98, no. 1, pp. 55–82.

216 *Notes*

Bonnell points out, p. 64, that 'the tractor becomes a key signifier for collective farms in visual propaganda and a symbol of progress more generally. Many political posters featured tractors, and men often sat in the driver's seat. But in collectivisation posters, women also make an appearance as tractor drivers. Out of 106 political posters relating to agriculture between 1930 and 1934 that include images of women, 37 (35 per cent) depict women behind the wheel of a tractor.'
33. I. I. Okuneva and Ye. Ye. Shteinbakh, 'O primenenii zhenskogo truda na traktorakh', *Gigiena, bezopasnost' i patologiya truda*, 1931, no. 7, pp. 3–15.
34. *Ibid.*, p. 12.
35. GARF, f. 5451, o. 15, d. 358, ll. 74–5.
36. *Ibid.*, p. 75.
37. '*Ob usloviyakh truda zhenshchin-traktoristok i shoferov na gruzovykh avtomashinakh*', decree of Narkomtrud, *Izvestiya NKT*, 1931, nos. 14–15, p. 277. The decree is reproduced in abbreviated form in English in *Soviet Legislation on Women's Rights: Collection of Normative Acts* (Moscow, 1978), pp. 98–9.
38. The draft decree, '*o trude zhenshchin-traktoristok*', is to be found in the trade union archives at GARF, f. 5451, o. 19, d. 277, ll. 12–13.
39. See for example 'o rasshirenie kruga professii po rechnomu i morskomu transportu, dopuskayushchikh primenenie zhenskogo truda', GARF, f. 5451, o. 19, d. 277, ll. 2–3 (dated 8 March 1935), 15, 142.
40. '*O zapreshchenii zhenskogo truda na osobo tyazhelykh i vrednykh rabotakh i professiyakh*', decree of Narkomtrud, *Izvestiya NKT*, 1930, no. 16, pp. 561–3, which lists seventy-nine tasks in ten separate industrial sectors: mining (4); metallurgy (9), chemicals (9); textiles (3); paper (1); printing (1); construction (1); municipal services (2), transport – railways (24), river (14), sea (9); wood processing and floating work (2).
41. '*Ob ispol'zovanii zhenskogo truda na proizvodstve i v gosudarstvennom i kooperativnom apparata*', decree of Sovnarkom RSFSR, *Izvestiya NKT*, 1931, no. 5–6, p. 108.
42. '*Ob utverzhdenii spisok professii po otdel'nym otraslyam promyshlennosti, a takzhe spisok dolzhnostei gosudarstvennogo i kooperativnogo apparata, v kotorykh dolzhen primenyavsya isklyuchitel'no libo preimyshchestvenno zhenskii trud*', decree of Narkomtrud RSFSR, *Izvestiya NKT*, 1931, no. 5–6, pp. 108–11. The list of jobs which offered preferential employment for women included: mining (25), mica (11); metallurgy (26); power stations (6); chemicals – resin (15), glass and porcelain (15), matches (20), lacquer and dye (7); leather shoes (17); paper (48). The list of jobs reserved exclusively for women included: metallurgy (18); chemicals (14); textiles (15); garment workers (13); office workers (28); old and young shop assistants (16); young non-productive service personnel (33).
43. '*Ob utverzhdenii spisok professii i dolzhnostei, na kotorykh primeneniya zhenskogo truda dolzhno byt' znachitel'no rasshireno*', decree of Narkomtrud SSSR, *Izvestiya NKT*, 1931, no. 14–15, pp. 268–71. The list included: mining (exclusively in surface work) (26); metallurgy (60); chemicals (55); leather shoes (4); paper (10); printing (28); food processing (80); transport (26); communications (13); construction (12); social and cultural institutions (30); trading enterprises (5).

44. '*Dopolnitel'nyi spisok professii i dolzhnostei, na kotorykh primenenie zhenskogo truda dolzhno byt' znachitel'no rasshireno*', decree of Narkomtrud, *Izvestiya NKT*, 1932, no. 22–3, pp. 295–6, adding to the list: oil (21); chemicals (25); leather and shoes (57); paper (5).

45. '*Ob utverzhdenii novogo spiska osobo tyazhelykh i vrednykh rabot i professii, k kotorym ne dopuskayutsya zhenshchiny*', decree of Narkomtrud and VTsSPS, *Izvestiya NKT*, 1932, no. 22–3, pp. 296–8. The decree listed seventy-two tasks in twelve different sectors of the economy: mining (4); metallurgy (6); chemicals (16); leather (1); textiles (2); paper (1); printing (3); meat preservation (1); transport – railways (11), river (5), sea (6), local (2); construction (7); municipal services (3); wood processing and floating work (4).

46. G. N. Serebrennikov, *The Position of Women in the USSR* (London, 1937), p. 15.

47. A. McAuley, *Women's Work and Wages in the Soviet Union* (London, 1981), pp. 166–7.

48. The research and findings are outlined in G. Serebrennikov, 'Itogi nauchno-issledovatel'skoi raboty po izucheniyu zhenskogo truda', *Voprosy truda*, 1933, nos. 2–3, pp. 63–7. The industrial sectors under review were: mining, metallurgy, machine-building, chemicals, timber, paper, leather and railway transport.

49. *Ibid.*, p. 65. A more detailed study of women's employment in the machine-building industry is provided by B. Marsheva, A. Isaev and E. Shteinbakh, *Zhenskii trud v mashinostroenii* (Moscow, 1933).

50. Serebrennikov, 'Itogi nauchno-issledovatel'skoi raboty', pp. 65–6.

51. See R. Kutlinskaya, 'Pervye zhenshchiny-buril'shchitsy', *Rabotnitsa*, 1939, no. 22, p. 9, and 'Ovladenie novymi professiyami', *Rabotnitsa*, 1939, no. 31, p. 9.

52. '*Ob izmenenii spiska osobo tyazhelykh i vrednykh rabot i professii, k kotorym ne dopuskayutsya zhenshchin*', decree of Sovnarkom, *SZ*, 1938, Article 282.

53. On the employment of women steam locomotive workers see also V. Shapovalova, 'Zhenshchina na parovoze', *Rabotnitsa*, 1939, no. 20. p. 5; Zhenya Yelmanova, 'Mechtaem vodit' tyazhelovesnye poezda', *Rabotnitsa*, 1939, no. 20, p. 7; Konev, 'Pomoshchniki parovoznykh mashinistov', *Rabotnitsa*, 1939, no. 20, pp. 8–9; Mariya Soroka, 'Na parovoze', *Rabotnitsa*, 1940, no. 21, p. 6; A. Zabolotskaya, 'Provodnitsy' and F. Annenkov, 'Boevye podrugi zheleznodorozhnikov', *Rabotnitsa*, 1940, no. 34, pp. 5–6.

54. J. N. Westwood, *Soviet Locomotive Technology During Industrialisation, 1928–1952* (London, 1982), p. 167, citing various articles in *Gudok*.

55. '*O primenenii truda zhenshchin na rabotakh v sisteme khozyaistva rechnogo flota*', decree of the secretariat of VTsSPS, *Byulleten' VTsSPS*, 1940, no. 6, p. 3.

10 UNDERGROUND WORK

1. The pioneering study of British women mine workers was published by Angela John, *By the Sweat of Their Brow* (London, 1984). For a critical

account of the protection of female mine workers in Britain see J. Humphries, 'Protective Legislation, the Capitalist State and Working Class Men: the Case of the 1842 Mines Regulation Act', *Feminist Review*, 1981, no. 7, pp. 1–33.

2. T. H. Friedgut, *Iuzovka and Revolution: Life and Work in the Donbass, 1869–1924* (New Jersey, 1989).
3. A. Meyer states that 'as early as 1915 women began working in mining operations underground, as did juveniles of 12 years or older'. See 'The Impact of World War I on Russian Women's Lives' in B. E. Clements et al., *Russia's Women: Accommodation, Resistance, Transformation* (Berkeley, 1991), pp. 213–14.
4. A painting by N. A. Kasatkin entitled 'Shakhterka' (1894) depicts a female mine worker, and a painting by Kozlova, 'Smena shakterok' (originally 'Smena motoristok'), reproduced in *Rabotnitsa*, 1938, nos. 5–6, p. 21, depicts a group of women mine workers on their way to a shift underground.
5. G. A. Beilikhis, 'Iz istorii bor'by za okhranu zdorov'ya rabochikh v 1917 g.', *Gigiena i sanitariya*, 1957, no. 11, p. 48.
6. '*Kodeks zakonov o trude*', decree of VTsIK, *SU*, 1918, Article 905.
7. '*Kodeks zakonov o trude*', decree of VTsIK, *SU*, 1922, Article 903.
8. See, for example, GARF, f. 5515, o. 4, d. 298, ll. 9, 14.
9. B. Markus, 'Okhrana truda v gornoi promyshlennosti v 1924–1925 gg.', *Voprosy truda*, 1926, no. 1, pp. 34–42. On p. 36 the article also notes that the survey included 762 young workers between the ages of 16 and 18 years and 38 workers under the age of 16 years.
10. *Ibid.*, p. 36. On the predominance of women in unskilled work, and the impact of this in situations of redundancy on levels of female unemployment, see also V. Ch., 'Kvalifikatsiya gornyachki (Donbass, Gorlovka)', *Rabotnitsa*, 1925, no. 22, p. 13.
11. Markus, *op. cit.*, p. 37.
12. *Ibid.*, p. 34.
13. '*O zapreshchenii zhenskogo truda na osobo-vrednykh i tyazhelykh rabotakh*', decree of Narkomtrud, *Izvestiya NKT*, 1925 no. 45, pp. 8–10.
14. GARF, f. 5515, o. 4, d. 298, l. 38.
15. GARF, f. 5515, o. 13, d. 6, ll. 77–9 (23 December 1927).
16. 'Zaklyuchenie po voprosu o prigodnosti zhenshchin k trudu mashinista v shakhtakh', GARF, f. 5515, o. 13, d. 6, l. 80.
17. GARF, f. 5515, o. 4, d. 33, l. 70.
18. GARF, f. 5515, o. 4, d. 34, ll. 26–7.
19. J. Smith, *Woman in Soviet Russia* (New York, 1928), pp. 23–4.
20. See, for example, H. Browning, *Women Under Fascism and Communism* (London, n.d.), p. 34.
21. M. Jordan, *Woman in Soviet Society* (A Russia Today Publication) (London, 1944), p. 11.
22. GARF, f. 5515, o. 13, d. 6, l. 31.
23. See, for example, GARF, f. 5515, o. 13, d. 15b, ll. 27–8, dated June 1929.
24. The proportion of women employed in the extraction and processing of minerals over this period was significantly higher, ranging from

22.5 per cent to 23.4 per cent. In comparing data on the employment of women in the German mining industry the report cites the slightly higher figure of 8.7 per cent for the Soviet Union in 1928, compared to 7.1 per cent in Germany in 1927. GARF, f. 5515, o. 13, d. 6, l. 31.

25. 'Okhrana truda shakhterok plokho okhranyaet (po shakhtem Donbassa)', GARF, f. 5451, o. 11, d. 384, ll. 12–13.
26. On the shortage of protective clothing see also, for example, Shakter Eremeev, 'Na shakhte (Donbass)', *Rabotnitsa*, 1925, no. 9, p. 10.
27. Unfortunately, the archival reports offer no more detail of such incidences than is noted here.
28. N. Afanas'ev, 'Sostoyanie okhrany truda v gornoi promyshlennosti Shakhtinskogo okruga', *Voprosy truda*, 1929, no. 2, pp. 102–8.
29. *Ibid.*, p. 104.
30. *Ibid.*, p. 103.
31. For an illustrated report see L. Girla-Badaeva, 'Na Donbasse (Shakta 'Proletarskaya diktatura')', *Rabotnitsa*, 1924, no. 3 (15), pp. 21–2.
32. *Women in Russia* (London, 1928), p. 19. The pamphlet includes a photograph with Soviet women mine workers 'after being down a pit in the Donetz coalfield'.
33. *Russia as seen by Two Tilmanstone Miners. A Record of a Tour to the Donetz Basin in Aug.–Sept. 1929* (Dover, 1929). The separate reports of the two miners (one a 'Secretary of the local Labour Party' and the other 'a Communist') and the school teacher were edited and summarised in the pamphlet in order, it was claimed, to avoid any distortion in the local press.
34. *Ibid.*, pp. 12–13.
35. *Ibid.*, p. 13.
36. *Ibid.*, p. 20.
37. *Ibid.*, p. 14.
38. *Ibid.*, p. 19.
39. GARF, f. 5451, o. 13, d. 69, ll. 49–50, dated 28 March 1929.
40. 'O nedopushchenii zhenskogo truda v podzemnykh vyrabotkakh', GARF, f. A-390, o. 3, d. 1269, l. 145.
41. N. Popova, *Women in the Land of Socialism* (Moscow, 1949), p. 64.
42. GARF, f. 6983, o. 1, d. 159, l. 270.
43. *Ibid.*, l. 271.
44. GARF, f. 5451, o. 15, d. 361, l. 1ob, dated 20 April 1931.
45. See the Sovnarkom report, 'Zhenskii trud v pyatiletnoi plane narodnogo khozyaistva', GARF, f. 6983, o. 1, d. 159, ll. 73–6.
46. '*Ob utverzhdenii spiska professii i dolzhnostei, na kotorykh primenenie zhenskogo truda dolzhno byt' znachitel'no rasshireno*', decree of Narkomtrud, *Izvestiya NKT*, 1931, no. 14–15, pp. 268–71.
47. '*Ob utverzhdenii novogo spiska osobo tyazhelikh i vrednykh rabot i professii, k kotorym ne dopuskayutsya zhenshchiny*', decree of Narkomtrud, *Izvestiya NKT*, 1932, no. 22–3, pp. 296–8, which restates the provisions of the 1925 decree in respect to the mining industry. An earlier list had been issued on 17 May 1930: '*Spisok osobo-tyazhelykh i vrednykh rabot i professii, k kotorym ne dopuskayutsya zhenshchin*', decree of Narkomtrud, *Izvestiya NKT*, 1930, no. 16, pp. 561–3.

220 *Notes*

48. GARF, f. A-390, o. 3, d. 1824, ll. 1–12.
49. GARF, f. 5451, o. 16, d. 557, ll. 1–2.
50. '*Ob utverzhdenii spisok profesii po otdel'nym otraslyam promyshlennosti. a takzhe spisok dolzhnostei gosudarstvennogo i kooperativnogo apparata, v kotorykh dolzhen primenyavsya isklyuchitel'no libo preimushchestvenno zhenskii trud*', decree of Narkomtrud RSFSR, *Izvestiya NKT*, 1931, no. 5–6, pp. 108–11; and '*Ob utverzhdenii 'spisok professii i dolzhnostei, na kotorykh primeneniya zhenskogo truda dolzhno byt' znachitel'no rasshireno*', decree of Narkomtrud SSSR, *Izvestiya NKT*, 1931, no. 14–15, pp. 268–71.
51. GARF, f. 5515, o. 20. d. 83, ll. 197–8. 1932 file on the protection of labour in the mining industry. These pages are headed 'Vsesoyuznaya upravleniya otrasli kassa sotsstrakha ugol'noi promyshlennosti'.
52. GARF, f. 5451, o. 15, d. 357, l. 40.
53. GARF, f. 5451, o. 16, d. 557, l. 30.
54. *Ibid.*, ll. 30–1. GARF, f. 5451, o. 15, d. 360, l. 208 cites the figure of 5.6 per cent for the proportion of women employed in underground work on 1 May 1931 and notes that this figure increased to 9.4 per cent by July/August 1931.
55. 'Itogi vnedreniya zhenskogo truda v promyshlennost' (za 1-oe polugodie 1931)', report of the presidium of VTsIK, GARF, f. 6983, o. 1, d. 165, l. 18.
56. GARF, f. 5451, o. 15, d. 360, l. 210, although it is not clear to which specific regulations this is referring.
57. GARF, f. 5451, o. 16, d. 557, l. 31.
58. GARF, f. 5451, o. 15, d. 360, l. 211.
59. 'Sostoyanie massovoi raboty sredi rabotn. v svyazi o vovlechniem novykh sloev zhenshchin v shakhte "Il'icha" i "No. 22"', GARF, f. 5451, o. 15, d. 360, ll. 183–91. Details of this report are also to be found at GARF, f. 5451, o. 15, d. 364, ll. 261–3, and GARF, f., A-390, o. 3, d. 1657, ll. 10–11. For an earlier glimpse of work at the 'Il'ich' mine and progress in the mechanisation of surface tasks', see S. V., 'Gornyachka, vykhodi na sorevnovanie (Donbass, shakhta No. 1 "Il'ich")', *Rabotnitsa*, 1929, no. 9, p. 9.
60. GARF, f. 5451, o. 15, d. 360, l. 183.
61. GARF, f. A-390, o. 3, d. 1657, ll. 10–10ob.
62. On the inadequate provision of cultural facilities at this mine see the short comment by A. K-va, 'Dopustimo li takoe polozhenie?', *Rabotnitsa*, 1931, no. 2, p. 10.
63. 'Zhenskii trud v kamenougol'noi promyshlennosti Donbassa', GARF, f. A-390, o. 3, d. 1861, ll. 1–9. A preliminary report on Aushev's study of nine different mine shafts conducted in January 1932 is located at GARF, f. A-390, o. 3, d. 1653, ll. 98–100.
64. GARF, f. A-390, o. 3, d. 1861, ll. 9–17.
65. The research and findings are outlined in G. Serebrennikov, 'Itogi nauchno-issledovatel'skoi raboty po izucheniyu zhenskogo truda', *Voprosy truda*, 1933, nos. 2–3, pp. 63–7.
66. J. Grunfeld, 'Women's Work in Russia's Planned Economy', *Social Research*, no. 1, vol. 9, February, 1942, pp. 37–8.
67. GARF, f. A-390, o. 3, d. 1863, ll. 8ob–11.

68. S. M. Kingsbury and M. Fairchild, *Factory, Family and Women in the Soviet Union* (New York, 1935), p. 115.
69. This is illustrated by a number of photographs: see M. Jordan, *op. cit.*; and in other reports: 'My stroim luchshii v mire metro', *Rabotnitsa*, 1933, no. 28, pp. 6–8, E. F., 'Inzhener Metrostroya', *Rabotnitsa*, 1937, no. 2, p. 15, and *Industriya*, 4 September 1938.
70. 'More Women in Russian Pits', *Daily Telegraph*, 19 October 1954.
71. K. Legay, *Un mineur français chez les Russes* (Paris, 1937), pp. 56–60.
72. GARF, f. 5451, o. 19, d. 277, ll. 4–11, details the initial plans for the project, which also included the metallurgical and chemical industries. Except for a few odd pages, however, the reports of these two sectors are not included amongst the findings in the remainder of this particular file. The findings of the investigation into the mining industry are located in the file at ll. 47–141.
73. GARF, f. 5451, o. 19, d. 277, ll. 86–90.
74. This age breakdown totals 982, despite the recorded 984 in employment!
75. Again these figures add up to 39 instead of 36, although it is possible here that women were employed in more than one of the listed tasks.
76. See, for example, the reports of 'mine no. 18' of the Stalin Trust and 'mine no. 1' of the Krasnaya Zvesda Trust: GARF, f. 5451, o. 19, d. 277, ll. 84, 96.
77. 'Mine no. 17' of Stalinogorskugol', *ibid.*, l. 129.
78. See the report of 'mine no. 10' in the Don region, for example. *Ibid.*, l. 130.
79. 'Mine no. 8' of Stalinogorskugol' reported that there was not one single child care institution provided for the whole mine. *Ibid.*, l. 128.
80. *Ibid.*, l. 121.
81. V. A. Zubkova, 'Pomozhem nashim muzh'yam', *Rabotnitsa*, 1939, no. 16, p. 7.
82. See Guseva, 'Domokhozyaiki idut v shakhtu', *Rabotnitsa*, 1939, no. 22, p. 8, and V. Zubkova, 'Zhenshchiny prishli na shakhty', *Industriya*, 26 June 1939. See also M. Buckley, 'The Untold Story of *Obshchetvennitsa* in the 1930s', *Europe-Asia Studies*, 1996, no. 4, vol. 48, pp. 569–86.
83. 'O primenenii truda zhenshchin na podzemnykh rabotakh v gornodobyvayushchei promyshlennosti', decree of Sovnarkom, SZ, 1940, Article 730. See also A. Yarmal', 'Nachal'nik podzemnogo transporta', *Rabotnitsa*, 1941, no. 15, pp. 5–6.
84. N. Dodge, *Women in the Soviet Economy* (Baltimore, 1966), p. 59.

11 CONCLUSION

1. In the area of family policy see, for example, Ya. Brandenburgskii et al., *Sem'ya i novyi byt: sbornik* (Moscow-Leningrad, 1926).
2. B. Marsheva and I. Okuneva, 'Zhenskii trud v usloviyakh sotsialisticheskogo stroitel'stva', *Bol'shevik*, June 1932, no. 11–12, p. 113.

3. D. Koenker, 'Men Against Women on the Shop Floor in Early Soviet Russia: Gender and Class in the Socialist Workplace', *American Historical Review*, 1995, vol. 100, no. 5, p. 1446.

4. Citing the example of protective labour legislation in England in the first half of the nineteenth century, it has been argued that 'the Factory Acts played some part in excluding women from particular jobs, but generally this occurred in conjunction with other factors'. See R. Gray, 'Factory Legislation and the Gendering of Jobs in the North of England, 1830–1860', *Gender and History*, 1993, vol. 5, no. 1, p. 75.

5. On this point, it has subsequently been argued that 'on heavy and uncongenial jobs, it would seem that neither men nor women are adequately protected: that in terms of health and safety women are probably better off, but in terms of money, men are. Here men need more protection, which should, in itself, close the pay gap by removing the reasons for discrimination'. See B. Lockwood, 'Protective Legislation: Who Benefits – Men or Women?', *Journal of the Society for Occupational Medicine*, 1979, no. 29, p. 10.

6. J. Grunfeld, 'Women's Work in Russia's Planned Economy', *Social Research*, 1942, vol. 9, no. 1, p. 39.

7. G. W. Lapidus, *Women in Soviet Society: Equality, Development and Social Change* (London, 1978), pp. 95–6, in analysing the general trends in Soviet policy towards women, characterises these decades as moving from 'libertarianism' in the 1920s to 'instrumentalism' in the 1930s.

8. S. Reid, 'All Stalin's Women: Gender and Power in Soviet Art of the 1930s', *Slavic Review*, 1998, vol. 57, no. 1, p. 147.

9. See N. T. Dodge, *Women in the Soviet Economy* (Baltimore, 1966), pp. 70–5.

10. See, for example, A. McAuley, *Women's Work and Wages in the Soviet Union* (London, 1981), and N. T. Dodge, *op. cit.*

11. See D. Filtzer, 'Industrial Working Conditions and the Political Economy of Female Labour During Perestroika', in R. Marsh (ed.), *Women in Russia and Ukraine* (Cambridge, 1996), pp. 214–27, M. J. Ilič, '"Generals Without Armies, Commanders Without Troops": Gorbachev's "Protection" of Female Workers', in *ibid.*, pp. 228–40, and M. J. Ilič, '"Equal Rights with Restrictions": Women, Work and Protective Legislation in Russia', in S. Bridger (ed.), *Women in Post-Communist Russia* (Bradford, 1995), pp. 22–34.

    For two recent Russian assessments, see V. V. Koval, 'Women and Work in Russia', and Ye. B. Klinova, 'Women and Legal Rights in Russia', in V. Koval, *Women in Contemporary Russia* (Oxford, 1995), pp. 17–33, 47–59. Klinova, p. 58, argues that 'the success of legal reforms will largely depend on effective control over their implementation, and on how well the government reduces and finally abolishes the discrepancy between legislation and practice'.

Bibliography

ARCHIVAL AND UNPUBLISHED SOURCES

Archives

GARF:
- f. 5515: Narodnyi komissariat truda SSSR
  - o. 4: upravlenie okhrany truda i tekhnika bezopasnosti, 1923–33 gg.
  - o. 13: zhenskaya inspektsiya, 1924–29 gg.
  - o. 20: otdel trudogo zakonodatel'stva i trudovoi distsiplini, 1929–33 gg.
- f. 5451: Vsesoyuznyi tsentral'nyi sovet professional'nykh soyuzov
  - o. 1: (1917) to
  - o. 23: (1939)
- f. 6983: o. 1: Komissiya po uluchsheniyu truda i byta zhenshchin (pri prezidiume VTsIK), 1926–30 gg.
  - Komitet po uluchsheniyu truda i byta rabotnits i krest'yanok (pri prezidiume VTsIK), 1930–2 gg.
- f. A-390: Narodnyi komissariat truda RSFSR
  - o. 3: otdel okhrany truda, 1918–33 gg.
  - o. 21: komissiya po izucheniyu i uluchsheniyu zhenskogo truda, 1923–8 gg.

Dissertations

Blagg, H., 'The Development of Soviet Social Insurance from 1917 to the Eve of the First Five-Year Plan', unpublished M.Soc.Sci. thesis (CREES, University of Birmingham, 1981)

Coleman, H. J., 'Mobilizing Urban Women for the First Five-Year Plan: the Zhenotdel and the Rapid Industrialisation of the USSR, 1928–1932', unpublished MA thesis (Queen's University, Kingston, Ontario, 1992)

Evans, J., 'Women and Family Policy in the USSR, 1936-1941', unpublished PhD thesis (CREES, University of Birmingham, 1987)

Redding, A. D., 'Nonagricultural Employment in the USSR, 1928–55', unpublished PhD thesis (University of Columbia, 1958)

Waters, E., 'From the Old Family to the New: Work, Marriage and Motherhood in Urban Soviet Russia, 1917–31', unpublished PhD thesis (CREES, University of Birmingham, 1985)

Unpublished Discussion and Conference Papers

L. Attwood, 'Rationality versus Romanticism: Representations of Women in the Stalinist Press', paper presented to Conference on Gender and Perceptions of Sexual Difference in Russian Culture and History, University of Birmingham, 3–5 July 1996

J. Barber, 'The Composition of the Soviet Working Class, 1928–1941', unpublished *Discussion Papers*, SIPS no. 16 (CREES, University of Birmingham, 1978)

S. Bridger, 'The Heirs of Pasha: the Rise and Fall of the Soviet Woman Tractor Driver', paper presented to Conference on Gender and Perceptions of Sexual Difference in Russian Culture and History, University of Birmingham, 3–5 July 1996

M. Buckley, '"Realities" of "New" Women in the 1930s: Assertive, Superior, Belittled and Beaten', paper presented to Conference on Gender and Perceptions of Sexual Difference in Russian Culture and History, University of Birmingham, 3–5 July 1996

JOURNALS/NEWSPAPERS/SERIALS

Byulleten' Narkomtruda
Byulleten' trudogo fronta
Byulleten' VTsSPS
Delegatka
Ekonomicheskaya zhizn'
Gigiena, bezopasnost' i patologiya truda
Gigiena i sanitariya
Gigiena truda
Gigiena truda i tekhnika bezopasnosti
Industriya
Izvestiya
Izvestiya Narkomtruda
Izvestiya VTsSPS
Kommunistka
Okhrana truda
Pravda
Rabotnitsa
Rabotnitsa i krest'yanka
Sobranie uzakonenii i rasporyazhenii RSFSR
Sobranie zakonov i rasporyazhenii SSSR
Trud
Trud v SSSR
Vestnik truda
Voprosy profdvizheniya
Voprosy truda
Za industrializatsiyu
Zhenshchiny v SSSR

RUSSIAN LANGUAGE SOURCES

Abramova, A., *Okhrana truda zhenshchin: spravochnik po trudovomu zakonodatel'stvu* (Moscow, 1967)

Astapovich, Z. A., *Pervye meropriyatiya sovetskoi vlasti v oblasti truda (1917–1918 gg.)* (Moscow, 1958)

Bil'shai, V., *Reshenie zhenskogo voprosa v SSSR* (Moscow, 1956)

Bineman, Ya. M. (ed.), *Trud v SSSR: spravochnik 1926–1930* (Moscow, 1930)

Brandenburgskii, Ya., et al., *Sem'ya i novyi byt* (Moscow-Leningrad, 1926)

Bukhov, M., *Trudovoe zakonodatel'stvo: polnoe sobranie deistvuyushchikh zakonov o trude v alfavitno-predmetnom poryadke* (Moscow, 1924)

Bukhov, M., *Chto dolzhna znat' delegatka o trudovykh pravakh rabotnits* (Moscow, 1925)

Bukhov, M., *Kak okhranyaetsa trud rabotnits po sovetskim zakonam* (Moscow, 1925)

Bukhov, M., *Okhrana zhenskogo truda* (Moscow, 1926)

Chirkov, P. M., *Reshenie zhenskogo voprosa v SSSR (1917–1937 gg.)* (Mosocw, 1978)

Datsuk, G., 'Zhenskii trud – v proizvodstvo', *Puti industrializatsii*, no. 2, 1931, pp. 37–46

Drobnikov, I., Livshits, R. and Rumyantseva, M., *Trudovoe zakonodatel'stvo: spravochnaya kniga dlya profaktiva* (Moscow, 1971)

Gosplan SSSR, *Proekt vtorogo pyatiletnego plana razvitiya narodnogo khozyaistva SSSR (1933–1937 gg.)*, tom 1 (Moscow, 1934)

Gosplan SSSR, *Pyatiletnii plan narodno-khozyaistvennogo stroitel'stva SSSR*, tom 1 (Moscow, 1930)

Gosplan SSSR, *Pyatiletnii plan narodno-khozyaistvennogo stroitel'stva SSSR*, tom 2, chast' 2 (Moscow, 1930)

Gosplan SSSR, *Trud v SSSR: spravochnik 1926–1930* (Moscow, 1930)

Gosplan SSSR, *Vtoroi pyatiletnii plan razvitiya narodnogo khozyaistva SSSR (1933–1937 gg.)*, tom 1 (Moscow, 1934)

Griffin, P. O. and Mogilevskii, M. I., *Trud zhenshchiny po deistvuyushchemu zakonodatel'stvu* (Leningrad, 1924)

Gruzdeva, Ye. B. and Chertikhina, E. S., *Trud i byt sovetskikh zhenshchin* (Moscow, 1983)

Kagan, L., *Ratsionalizatsiya i rabotnitsa* (Moscow, 1928)

Kalygina, A. S., *Prava rabotnits i krest'yanok v SSSR* (Moscow-Leningrad, 1925)

Kaminskaya, P. D., *Sovetskoe trudovoe pravo: obzor deistvuyushchego zakonodatel'stva s prakticheskim kommentariem* (Kharkov, 1925)

Kaminskaya, P. D., *Zhenskii trud* (Moscow, 1927)

Kaplun, S. I., *Nauka na sluzhbe okhrany truda: kak rabotaet gosudarstvennyi nauchnyi institut okhrany truda* (Moscow, 1930)

Kaplun, S. I., *Okhrana truda v SSSR v tsifrakh* (Moscow, 1928)

Kaplun, S. I., *Okhrana truda za 2 goda proletarskoi revolyutsii, 1917–1919 gg.* (Moscow, 1920)

Kaplun, S. I., *Okhranyaete zhenskii trud!* (Moscow, 1926)

Kaplun, S. I., *Pyatiletnii plan raboty gosudarstvennogo nauchnogo instituta okhrany truda. NarkomTrud, NarkomZdrav i VSNKh SSSR* (Moscow, 1930)

Kaplun, S. I., *Sovremmenye problemy zhenskogo truda i byta* (Moscow, 1925; 2nd edn)

Kaplun, S. I., *Zhenskii trud i okhrana ego v sovetskoi Rossii* (Moscow, 1921)

Kiselev, Ya. L., *Osnovy trudogo zakonodatel'stva SSSR* (Moscow, 1964)

Kiselev, Ya. L. and Malkin, S. Ye. (eds.), *Sbornik vazhneishikh postanovlenii po trudu* (Moscow, 1936)

Kodeks zakonov o trude (Moscow, 1938)

Kraval', I. A., *Zhenshchina v SSSR* (Moscow, 1937)

Lebedeva, V., *Okhrana materinstva i mladenchestva v sovetskoi trudovoi respublike* (Moscow, 1921)

Libov, B. A., 'Vliyanie promyshlennogo truda na polovuyu sferu zhenshchiny', *Leningradskii meditsinskii zhurnal*, no. 7, 1926, pp. 78–82

Marsheva, B., Isaev, A. and Shteinbakh, *Zhenskii trud v mashinostroenii* (Moscow, 1933)

Mints, L. Ye., 'Ocherki razvitiya statistiki chislennosti i sostava promyshlennogo proletariata v Rossii', *Ocherki po istorii statistiki SSSR*, tom 2 (Moscow, 1957), pp. 171–267

Navrotskii, V. K., *Gigiena truda* (Moscow, 1967)

Nefedov, M. G., *Zhenskii trud v Moskovskoi gubernii* (Moscow, 1926)

Opyt KPSS v reshenii zhenskogo voprosa (Moscow, 1981)

Orlikova, Ye., 'Sovetskaya zhenshchina v obshchestvennom proizvodstve', *Problemy ekonomiki*, no. 7, July 1940

Pap, A. G., Shkol'nik, B. I., and Sol'skii, Ya. P., *Gigiena zhenshchiny* (Kiev, 1964)

Pasternak, A., *Chto dolzhna znat' rabotnitsa ob okhrane zhenskogo truda: s prilozheniem deistvuyushchego zakonodatel'stva v oblasti okhrany zhenskogo truda i okhrany materinstva* (Kharkov, 1923)

Pergament, A. I. and Stavtseva, A. I., *Sovetskoe zakonodatel'stvo po pravakh zhenshchin* (Moscow, 1962)

Polyakov, V. I., *Trud zhenshchin* (Tashkent, 1937)

Popov, P., *Okhrana truda v Sovetskom Soyuze* (Moscow, 1946)

Rashin, A. G., *Zhenskii trud v SSSR* (Moscow, 1928)

Rezolyutsii IV Vsesoyuznogo soveshchaniya po okhrane truda, 29 sentyabrya–3 oktyabrya 1926 g. (Moscow, 1927)

Rezolyutsii V Vsesoyuznogo soveshchaniya po okhrane truda, 6–11 fevralya 1928 g. (Moscow, 1928)

Ryazanova, A. L., *Zhenskii trud* (Moscow-Leningrad, 1926)

Sbornik normativnykh aktov o trude, chast' 2 (Moscow, 1985)

Sbornik vazhneishikh zakonov i postanovlenii o trude (Moscow, 1959)

Snezhkov, E. I., *Prakticheskii komentarii k kodeksu zakonov o trude: postateinye raz'yasneniya, dopolneniya, sudebnaya i konsul'tatsionaya praktika (po 1 sentyabrya 1927 goda)* (Moscow, 1928)

Sokolov, V. V., *Prava zhenshchiny po sovetskim zakonam* (Moscow, 1928)

Sovetskaya vlast' i raskreposhchenie zhenshchiny: sbornik dekretov i postanovlenii RSFSR (Moscow, 1921)

Sovetskoe trudovoe pravo: kratkii uchebnik (Moscow, 1938)

Sovetskoe trudovoe pravo (Moscow, 1946)

Sovetskoe trudovoe pravo (Moscow, 1949)

Tettenborn, Z., *Sovetskoe zakonodatel'stvo o trude: lektsii, prochitannye na kursakh dlya Inspektorov Truda* (Moscow, 1920)

Tolkunova, V. N., *Pravo zhenshchin na trud i ego garantii* (Moscow, 1967)
Trud v SSSR: kratkii statisticheskii sbornik (Moscow, 1988)
Trud v SSSR: statisticheskii spravochnik (Moscow, 1936)
Trudovoe zakonodatel'stvo SSSR (Moscow, 1941)
TsSU SSSR, *Zhenshchiny v SSSR: statisticheskii sbornik* (Moscow, 1975)
TsUNKhU, *Trud v SSSR: ekonomiko-statisticheskii spravochnik* (Moscow, 1932)
Urlanis, B. Ts., *Istoriya odnogo pokoleniya* (Moscow, 1968)
Voitinskii, I. S., *Trudovoe pravo SSSR* (Moscow, 1925)
Voitinskii, I. S., *Azbuka sovetskogo trudogo prava* (Moscow, 1929)
Voprosy bor'by s zhenskoi bezrabotitsei (Moscow, 1922)
VTsSPS, *Shestoi s"ezd professional'nykh soyuzov SSSR (11–18 noyabrya 1924 g.): plenumy i sektsii* (Moscow, 1925)
VTsSPS, *Sostav fabrichno-zavodskogo proletariata SSSR v diagrammakh i tablitsakh: itogi perepisi metallistov, gornorabochikh i tekstil'shchikov 1929 goda* (Mosocw, 1930)
VTsSPS, *Trud v SSSR 1926–1928 gg.: Diagramy* (Moscow, 1928)
Yankovskii, V. and Nikitin, V., *Vazhneishie zakonodatel'nye i vedomstvennye postanovleniya po trudu i zarabotnoi plate* (Moscow, 1940)
Zakonodatel'stvo po okhrane truda: sbornik ofitsial'nykh dokumentov (Moscow, 1966)
Zhenshchiny strany sovetov: kratkii istoricheskii ocherk (Moscow, 1977)

ENGLISH (AND NON-RUSSIAN) LANGUAGE SOURCES

Andrle, V., *A Social History of Twentieth-Century Russia* (London, 1994)
Attwood, L., *People Made From a Specal Mould: Representations of the 'New Woman' in Soviet Women's Magazines* (forthcoming)
Bacchi, C. L., *Same Difference: Feminism and Sexual Difference* (London, 1990)
Baxandall, R. F., *Words on Fire: the Life and Writing of Elizabeth Gurley Flynn* (London, 1987)
Bebel, A., *Woman in the Past, Present and Future* (London, n.d. [orig. 1883])
Bilshai, V., *The Status of Women in the Soviet Union* (Moscow, 1957)
Bonnell, V. E., *The Russian Worker: Life and Labour Under the Tsarist Regime* (Berkeley, California, 1983)
Bonnell, V. E., 'The Peasant Woman in Stalinist Political Art of the 1930s', *American Historical Review*, 1993, vol. 98, no. 1, pp. 55–82
Bridger, S. (ed.), *Women in Post-Communist Russia* (Bradford, 1995)
British Documents on Foreign Affairs: Reports and Papers from the Foreign Office, part 2: *From the First to the Second World War*, series A: *The Soviet Union* (1935)
Browning, H., *Women Under Fascism and Communism* (London, n.d.)
Bryson, V., *Feminist Political Theory: An Introduction* (London, 1992)
Buckley, M., *Women and Ideology in the Soviet Union* (London, 1989)
Buckley, M., 'The Untold Story of *Obshchestvennitsa* in the 1930s', *Europe-Asia Studies*, 1996, vol. 48, no. 4, pp. 569–86
Carr, E. H., *The Bolshevik Revolution, 1917–1923* (vol. II) (London, 1952)
Carr, E. H., *Socialism in One Country* (vol. I) (London, 1958)

Carr, E. H. and Davies, R. W., *Foundations of a Planned Economy* (vol. I, part ii) (London, 1969)

Chase, W. J., *Workers, Society, and the Soviet State: Labor and Life in Moscow, 1918–1929* (Urbana, 1990)

Clements, B. E., *Bolshevik Women* (Cambridge, 1997)

Clements, B. E. et al., *Russia's Women: Accommodation, Resistance, Transformation* (Berkeley, 1991)

Conquest, R. (ed.), *Industrial Workers in the USSR* (London, 1967)

Cook, B. W. (ed.), *Crystal Eastman: On Women and Revolution* (London, 1978)

Cott, N. F., *The Grounding of Modern Feminism* (London, 1987)

Cott, N. F., 'Historical Perspectives: the Equal Rights Amendment Conflict in the 1920s', in M. Hirsch and E. F. Keller, *Conflicts in Feminism* (London, 1990)

Crisp, O., 'Labour and Industrialisation in Russia', *Cambridge Economic History of Europe*, vol. VII, part ii (Cambridge, 1978)

Dalton, K., *Once a Month* (London, 1991)

Davies, R. W., *The Development of the Soviet Budgetary System* (Cambridge, 1958)

Davies, R. W., *The Soviet Economy in Turmoil, 1929–1930* (London, 1989)

Davies, R. W., *Crisis and Progress in the Soviet Economy, 1931–1933* (London, 1996)

Davies, R. W. (ed.), *From Tsarism to the New Economic Policy: Continuity and Change in the Economy of the USSR* (London, 1990)

Davies, R. W., Harrison, M. and Wheatcroft, S. G., *The Economic Transformation of the Soviet Union, 1913–1945* (Cambridge, 1994)

Davies, S., *Popular Opinion in Stalin's Russia: Terror, Propaganda and Dissent, 1934–41* (Cambridge, 1997)

Dewar, M., *Labour Policy in the USSR, 1917–1928* (New York, 1956)

Dobb, M., *Soviet Economic Development since 1917* (London, 1946)

Dodge, N. T., *Women in the Soviet Economy: Their Role in Economic, Scientific and Technical Development* (Baltimore, 1966)

Edmondson, L. H., *Feminism in Russia, 1900–1917* (London, 1984)

Edmondson, L. H. (ed.), *Gender in Russian History and Culture, 1800–1990* (forthcoming)

Engel, B. A., *Between the Fields and the City: Women, Work and Family in Russia, 1861–1914* (Cambridge, 1994)

Engel, B. A., 'Women in Russia and the Soviet Union', *Signs*, 1987, vol. 12, no. 4, pp. 781–96

Engel, B. A., 'Engendering Russia's History: Women in Post-Emancipation Russia and the Soviet Union', *Slavic Review*, 1992, vol. 51, no. 2, pp. 309–21

Erickson, N. S., 'Historical Background of Protective Labor Legislation: Muller v. Oregon', in D. K. Weisberg (ed.), *Women and the Law: A Social Historical Perspective*, vol. II, *Property, Family and the Legal Profession* (Cambridge, Mass., 1982)

Evans, J., 'The CPSU and the "Woman Question": the Case of the 1936 Decree "In Defence of Mother and Child"', *Journal of Contemporary History*, 1981, vol. 16, pp. 757–75

Farnsworth, B. and Viola, L., *Russian Peasant Women* (Oxford, 1992)

Feurer, R., 'The Meaning of "Sisterhood": the British Women's Movement and Protective Labor Legislation, 1870–1900', *Victorian Studies*, 1988, vol. 31, no. 2, pp. 233–60

Field, A. W., *Protection of Women and Children in Soviet Russia* (London, 1932)

Filtzer, D., *Soviet Workers and Stalinist Industrialisation* (London, 1986)

Fitzpatrick, S. and Viola, L., *A Researcher's Guide to Sources on Soviet Social History in the 1930s* (London, 1990)

Friedgut, T. H., *Iuzovka and Revolution: Life and Work in Russia's Donbass, 1869–1924* (New Jersey, 1989)

German Miners in the Donbass (London, 1931)

Giffin, F. C., 'The Prohibition of Night Work for Women and Young Persons: the Russian Factory Law of June 3, 1885', *Canadian Slavonic Papers*, 1968, vol. 2, no. 2, pp. 208–18

Glickman, R. L., *Russian Factory Women: Workplace and Society, 1880–1914* (London, 1984)

Goldman, W. Z., *Women, the State and Revolution: Soviet Family Policy and Social Life, 1917–1936* (Cambridge, 1993)

Goldman, W. Z., 'Industrial Politics, Peasant Rebellion and the Death of the Proletarian Women's Movement in the USSR', *Slavic Review*, 1996, vol. 55, no. 1, pp. 46–77

Gordon, M., *Workers Before and After Lenin* (New York, 1941)

Granick, D., *Soviet Metal-Fabricating and Economic Development: Practice versus Policy* (London, 1967)

Gray, R., 'Factory Legislation and the Gendering of Jobs in the North of England, 1830–1860', *Gender and History*, 1993, vol. 5, no. 1, pp. 56–80

Grunfeld, J., 'Women's Work in Russia's Planned Economy', *Social Research*, February 1942, vol. 9, no. 1, pp. 22–45

Gullickson, G. L., 'Womanhood and Motherhood: the Rouen Manufacturing Community, Women Workers and the French Factory Acts', in R. L. Rudolph (ed.), *The European Peasant Family and Society: Historical Studies* (Liverpool, 1995)

Halle, F., *Woman in Soviet Russia* (London, 1935)

Harrison, B., *Not only the 'Dangerous Trades': Women's Work and Health in Britain, 1880–1914* (London, 1996)

Harrison, B., 'Some of Them gets Lead Poisoned: Occupational Lead Exposure in Women, 1880–1914', *Social History of Medicine*, 1989, vol. 2, no. 2, pp. 171–95

Hilden, P., *Working Women and Socialist Politics in France, 1880–1914: A Regional Study* (Oxford, 1986)

Hollis, P., *Women in Public: the Women's Movement, 1850–1900* (London, 1981)

Humphries, J., 'Protective Legislation, the Capitalist State and Working Class Men: the Case of the 1842 Mines Regulation Act', *Feminist Review*, 1981, no. 7, pp. 1–33

John, A., *By the Sweat of Their Brow* (London, 1984)

Jordan, M., *Woman in Soviet Society* (London, 1944)

Kaplun, S. I., *The Protection of Labour in Soviet Russia* (Moscow, 1920)

Kelly, C., 'A Stick with Two Ends, or, Misogyny in Popular Culture: A Case Study of the Puppet Text "Petrushka"', in J. Costlow et al. (eds.), *Sexuality and the Body in Russian Culture* (Cambridge, 1993)

Kingsbury, S. M. and Fairchild, M., *Factory, Family and Woman in the Soviet Union* (New York, 1935)

Koenker, D. P., 'Men Against Women on the Shop Floor in Early Soviet Russia: Gender and Class in the Socialist Workplace', *American Historical Review*, 1995, vol. 100, no. 5, pp. 1438–64

Korber, L., *Life in a Soviet Factory* (London, 1933); first published in German as *Eine Frau erlebt den Roten Alltag*, translated by C. W. Sykes

Koval, V. (ed.), *Women in Contemporary Russia* (Oxford, 1995)

Kulski, W. W., *The Soviet Regime: Communism in Practice* (New York, 1954)

Lapidus, G. W., *Women in Soviet Society: Equality, Development and Social Change* (London, 1978)

Law of the People's Republic of China on the Protection of Rights and Interests of Women (1992)

Legay, K., *Un mineur français chez les Russes* (Paris, 1937)

Liljestrom, M., et al., *Gender Restructuring in Russian Studies* (Tampere, 1993)

Lockwood, B., 'Protective Legislation: Who Benefits – Men or Women?', *Journal of the Society for Occupational Medicine*, 1979, no. 29, pp. 3–11

Loudon, I., *Death in Childbirth: An International Study of Maternal Care and Maternal Mortality, 1800–1950* (Oxford, 1992)

Mallet, C., 'Dangerous Trades for Women' [orig. 1893], reprinted in M. M. Roberts and T. Mizuta (eds.), *The Exploited: Women and Work* (Sources of British Feminism) (London, 1993)

Marsh, R. (ed.), *Women in Russia and Ukraine* (Cambridge, 1995)

McAuley, A., *Women's Work and Wages in the Soviet Union* (London, 1981)

McDaniel, T., *Autocracy, Capitalism and Revolution in Russia* (London, 1988)

McFeely, M. D., *Lady Inspectors: the Campaign for a Better Workplace, 1893–1921* (Oxford, 1988)

McKean, R. B., 'Social Insurance in Tsarist Russia: St. Petersburg, 1907–17', *Revolutionary Russia*, 1990, vol. 3, no. 1, pp. 55–89

McKean, R. B. (ed.), *New Perspectives on Modern Russian History* (London, 1992)

Meyer, A., *Selected Writings on Feminism and Socialism: Lily Braun* (Indiana, 1987)

Mezentseva, Ye., 'Equal Opportunities or Protectionist Measures? The Choice Facing Women', in A. Posadskaya (ed.), *Women in Russia: A New Era in Russian Feminism* (London, 1994)

Moeller, R. G., 'Protecting Mother's Work: From Production to Reproduction in Postwar West Germany', *Journal of Social History*, Spring 1989, pp. 413–37

'More Women in Russian Pits', *Daily Telegraph*, 19 October 1954

Nove, A., *An Economic History of the USSR* (London, 1969)

Nurina, F. E., *Women in the Soviet Union: The Role of Women in Socialist Construction* (United States, International Publishers Co. Inc., 1934)

O'Donovan, K., *Sexual Divisions in Law* (London, 1985)

Perrie, M., *Alexander II: Emancipation and Reform in Russia, 1855–1881* (London, 1989)

Popova, N., *Women in the Land of Socialism* (Moscow, 1949)

Pospielovsky, D., *Russian Police Trade Unionism: Experiment or Provocation?* (London, 1971)

Price, G. M., *Labor Protection in Soviet Russia* (London, 1928)

Razumova, A., *Russian Women in the Building of Socialism* (London, n.d. [1930])

Reid, S., 'All Stalin's Women: Gender and Power in Soviet Art of the 1930s', *Slavic Review*, 1998, vol. 57, no. 1, pp. 133–73.

Rossman, J. J., 'The Teikovo Cooton Workers' Strike of April 1932: Class, Gender and Identity Politics in Stalin's Russia', *Russian Review*, January 1997, vol. 56, pp. 44–69

Rowbotham, S., *Women, Resistance and Revolution* (London, 1972)

Ruble, B. A., *Soviet Trade Unions: their Development in the 1970s* (Cambridge, 1981)

Russia as seen by Two Tilmanstone Miners. A Record of a Tour to the Donetz Basin in Aug.–Sept., 1929 (Dover, 1929)

Rust, T., *Where Women Enjoy Freedom! A Graphic Account of the Rights and Freedom Enjoyed by Women in Soviet Russia* (Russia Today Society; London, n.d.)

Ruthchild, R., 'Engendering History: Women in Russia and the Soviet Union', *European History Quarterly*, 1994, vol. 24, pp. 555–62

Schwarz, S., *Labor in the Soviet Union* (New York, 1952)

Scott, J. W., 'Deconstructing Equality-versus-Difference: Or, the Uses of Poststructuralist Theory for Feminism', in M. Hirsch and E. F. Keller, *Conflicts in Feminism* (London, 1990)

A Selection of Documents Relative to the Labour Legislation in force in the Union of Soviet Socialist Republics (London, 1931)

Serebrennikov, G., *The Position of Women in the USSR* (London, 1937)

Serebrennikov, T., *Woman in the Soviet Union* (Moscow, 1943)

Seton-Watson, H., *The Russian Empire, 1801–1917* (Oxford, 1967)

Shanley, M. L., 'Suffrage, Protective Labor Legislation, and Married Women's Property Laws in England', *Signs*, 1986, vol. 12, no. 1, pp. 62–77

Sheptulina, N. N., 'The Protection of Female Labour', in G. W. Lapidus, *Women, Work and Family in the Soviet Union* (London, 1982)

Sibiriak V., *The Working Woman in the Soviet Union* (Moscow, 1932)

Siegelbaum, L. H., 'Okhrana Truda: Industrial Hygiene, Psychotechnics and Industrialisation in the USSR', in S. Solomon (ed.), *Health and Society in Revolutionary Russia* (Bloomington, Indiana, 1990)

Smith, J., *Woman in Soviet Russia* (New York, 1928)

Soviet Legislation on Women's Rights: Collection of Normative Acts (Moscow, 1978)

Soviet Russia: An Investigation by British Women Trade Unionists, April to July, 1925 (London, 1925)

Stewart, M. L., *Women, Work and the French State: Labour Protection and Social Patriarchy, 1879–1919* (London, 1989)

Stites, R., *The Women's Liberation Movement in Russia: Feminism, Nihilism and Bolshevism, 1860–1930* (Princeton, 1978)

Strogova, E., 'The Womenfolk: Factory Sketches', in C. Kelly (ed.), *An Anthology of Russian Women's Writing, 1777–1992* (Oxford, 1994)

Valverde, M., '"Giving the Female a Domestic Turn": the Social, Legal and Moral Regulation of Women's Work in British Cotton Mills, 1820–1850', *Journal of Social History*, 1988, vol. 21, no. 4, pp. 619–34

Vogel, L., *Marxism and the Oppression of Women: Toward a Unitary Theory* (New Jersey, 1989)

Vyshinskii, A. Ya., *The Law of the Soviet State* (New York, 1948)

Walsh, W. B., *Readings in Russian History: From Ancient Times to the Post-Stalin Era*. Vol. III, *The Revolutionary Era and the Soviet Period* (New York, 1963)

Ward, C., *Russian Cotton Workers and the New Economic Policy* (Cambridge, 1988)

Waters, E., 'Teaching Mothercraft in Post-Revolutionary Russia', *Australian Journal of Slavonic and East European Studies*, 1987, vol. 1, no. 2, pp. 29–56

Waters, E., 'The Modernisation of Russian Motherhood, 1917–1937', *Soviet Studies*, 1992, vol. 44, no. 1, pp. 123–35

Westwood, J., *Soviet Locomotive Technology During Industrialisation, 1928–1952* (London, 1982)

White, J. D., *The Russian Revolution, 1917–1921* (London, 1994)

Winter, E., *Red Virtue: Human Relations in the New Russia* (London, 1933)

Witte, E. E., 'The Effects of Special Labor Legislation for Women', *Quarterly Journal of Economics*, 1927, vol. 42, pp. 153–64

Women and Children in the USSR: Brief Statistical Returns (Moscow, 1963)

Women and Communism: Selections from the Writings of Marx, Engels, Lenin and Stalin (London, 1950)

Women in Russia (London, 1928)

Women in the Soviet Union: With Impressions by G. G. L. Alexander and F. Niurina (London, 1929)

Work Among Women (CPGB, London, 1924)

Index

abortion, 59, 63, 67, 70, 75, 92, 102, 200 n2
absenteeism, 38, 160, 163
ACCTU, 9, 45, 52–4, 55, 98, 100, 109
  VI Congress (November 1924), 53, 83–4
  Conference on Work amongst Women (February 1931), 38, 54, 125, 141, 160
agriculture, 10, 25, 171
Akim, N. E., 87–8
Alexander II, 14
All-Russian Conference of Labour Research Institutes (January 1933), 164
All-Russian Congress of Women, First (1908), 22
All-Russian Congress of Women (1927), 154
All-Union Central Council of Trade Unions, see ACCTU
All-Union Congress on the Protection of Maternity and Childhood, 57
All-Union Meeting of Work amongst Women, Second (June 1928), 53, 89
amenorrhoea, 122
America, 1, 60, 114, 186 nn1, 3, 190 n25
AMO factory, 203 n60, 215 n30
Amosova, 156
anaemia, 97, 107, 135
apprenticeships, 38
archives, 9, 87, 100, 152, 156, 166
Argentina, 211 n49
arsenic, 130
art, 149, 174
artisans, 10, 20, 25
Artyukhina, A., 57
asbestos production, 42
Astapovich, Z. A., 78
Astrakhan, 124

Aushev, 163
Australia, 208 n1

bakeries, 80, 117
ballet dancers, 67
Bebel, A., 2
Belorussian Institute of Sanitation and Organisation of Labour, 110
benzene, 130
blue-collar workers, see workers
Bolshevik party, see Communist Party
Bolsheviks, 7, 11, 43, 44
Bonnell, V., 20, 109, 139
breast feeding, 22, 62–3, 86, 137, 167, see also nursing mothers
Britain, 6, 186 nn2, 3, 189 n22, 190 n11, 217–18 n1, 222 n4
Bukhov, M., 80, 99
Bunge, N. K., 17
business trips, 59, 60

Carr, E. H., 44
cashiers, 64, 65
catering, 30, 33, 39
Central Executive Committee, see TsIK
Central Industrial Region, 16, 17
Central Museum for the Protection of Labour, 48
Central Statistical Administration, see TsSU
chemical industry, 25, 41, 136, 143, 144
Chief Inspector of Women's Labour, 51–2
child care, 22, 53, 76, 90, 143, 156, 160, 162, 167
China, 211 n49
china industry, 32
Chirkov, P. M., 109
civil war, 7, 79, 130, 202 n34
clerical staff, 20

233